Francis Samuel Drake

Tea Leaves

Being a Collection of Letters, and Documents Relating to the Shipment ....

Francis Samuel Drake

Tea Leaves
Being a Collection of Letters, and Documents Relating to the Shipment ....

ISBN/EAN: 9783337015176

Printed in Europe, USA, Canada, Australia, Japan

Cover: Foto ©ninafisch / pixelio.de

More available books at **www.hansebooks.com**

TEA LEAVES:

BEING A COLLECTION OF LETTERS AND DOCUMENTS

RELATING TO THE SHIPMENT OF

TEA

TO THE AMERICAN COLONIES IN THE YEAR 1773, BY THE

East India Tea Company.

NOW FIRST PRINTED FROM THE ORIGINAL MANUSCRIPT.

WITH AN INTRODUCTION, NOTES, AND
BIOGRAPHICAL NOTICES OF THE BOSTON TEA PARTY,

BY

FRANCIS S. DRAKE.

BOSTON:
A. O. CRANE.
1884.

PREFATORY NOTE.

The collection of letters and documents which has occasioned the preparation of the present volume, though it has been so long buried in obscurity, appears to have been originally made with a view to publication. It was for many years, and until his decease, in the possession of Mr. Abel Bowen, a well-known engraver and publisher, of Boston, sixty years ago, and was obtained by him from a person who procured it in Halifax, N.S., whither many valuable papers, both public and private, relating to New England, were carried, when in March, 1776, the British and Tories evacuated Boston. It contains interesting information relative to the tea troubles that preceded the American Revolution, much of it new to students of that eventful period.

To the kindness of Mrs. Benjamin Phipps and Mrs. Charles G. Butts, of Chelsea, daughters of Mr. Bowen, the publisher is indebted for permission to make public this valuable contribution to American history.

PUBLISHER'S PREFACE.

When contemplating the publication of "Tea Leaves," we issued a circular, stating our intention, and that, judging from the material then in our possession, the book would contain about two hundred and fifty pages, with six illustrations, three of them portraits.

We are happy to announce on the completion of the work, not only fulfillment of our promises, but much that is additional thereto. Included in its four hundred pages are twenty portraits, taken from family paintings, (one-half never before published,) eight other illustrations, fifty autographs, one hundred and twelve names of members of the Tea Party, (fifty-eight more than have been heretofore publicly known), and ninety-six biographies of the same.

Our circular called for a subscription book. All our paper-covered copies have been subscribed for. The balance of the edition is nicely bound in cloth, with embellished covers. Price, (as before), five dollars.

The publisher will welcome all new matter relating to the Tea question, and will be especially grateful for any hitherto unpublished portraits. Such material is desired for possible publication in a companion work to "Tea Leaves."

All who desire the Portraits and Illustrations separate from this volume, to be used in works on American history, can obtain them from the Publisher.

In conclusion, we thank our friends who have kindly assisted us, and if we have not given all credit by name, the neglect has been unintentional.

A. O. CRANE,
2169 WASHINGTON ST.,
BOSTON, MASS.

INTRODUCTION.

Among the causes which led to the American Revolution, the one most prominent in the popular judgment is the "tax on tea," imposed by Great Britain on her American colonies. The destruction, in Boston harbor, in December, 1773, of the cargoes of tea sent to that port by the East India Company, was undoubtedly the proximate cause of that memorable event, and in view of this fact, the occurrence, — "by far the most momentous in the annals of the town," says the historian Bancroft, — merits a more thorough and particular consideration than it has yet received.

The silence necessarily preserved by the actors in this daring exploit, respecting their connection with it, has rendered this part of the task one of no little difficulty. Their secret was remarkably well kept; and but for the family traditions which survive, we should know very little of the men who composed the famous Boston tea party.

Nevertheless, the attempt to gather up the scattered fragments of personal reminiscence and biography, in order to give a little more completeness to this interesting chapter of our revolutionary history, is here made. The fortunate recovery, by the publisher of this volume, of the letters of the

INTRODUCTION.

American consignees to the East India Company, and other papers shedding light upon the transaction, affords material aid in the accomplishment of our purpose.

When King Charles II. had finished that first cup of tea ever brewed in England,— the gift of the newly-created East India Company,— no sibyl was at hand to peer into the monarch's cup and foretell from its dregs, the dire disaster to his realm, hidden among those insignificant particles. Could a vision of those battered tea chests, floating in Boston harbor, with *tu doces*, in the legible handwriting of history, inscribed upon them, have been disclosed to him, even that careless, pleasure-loving prince would have been sobered by the lesson. It was left for his successor, George III., who failed to read the handwriting on the wall,— visible to all but the willfully blind,— to realize its meaning in the dismemberment of an empire.

A survey of the progress of the revolution up to the beginning of the year 1773, will help us to understand the political situation. Ten years of constant agitation had educated the people of the colonies to a clear perception of their rights, and also to a knowledge that it was the fixed purpose of the home government to deprive them of the one they most valued, namely, that of being taxed with their own consent, through their local assemblies, as had always been the custom, and not at the arbitrary will of the British parliament— a body in which they were not and could not be represented— three thousand miles away. The strange thing about this is, that the people of Great Britain should not have seen in the light of their own past history— what they have since seen clearly enough — that the Americans were only contending for principles for which their own ancestors had often fought, and which they had more than once succeeded in wresting from the grasp of arbitrary and tyrannical sovereigns.

Their difficulty seems to have been that they looked upon the Americans, not as equals, but as inferiors, as their subjects, and as having no rights that an Englishman was bound to respect. Even the celebrated moralist, Dr. Johnson, could say of the Americans, " They are a race of convicts, and ought to be thankful for anything we allow them short of hanging." King George III., that obstinate but well-meaning monarch, and his ministers, no doubt honestly believed that the republican tendencies of the colonists endangered British supremacy. Perhaps they were right in this, for it was the kind and degree of supremacy that was really in question. But in entertaining the belief that these tendencies could be eradicated at a blow, they were, as the event proved, grievously mistaken.

Another moving cause for the new policy toward the colonies was the heavy taxation at home, — a result of the late war. Some of this burden they hoped to transfer from their own shoulders to those of their transatlantic brethren.

The stamp act of 1765, repealed in the year following, was in .1767, succeeded by Charles Townshend's revenue acts, imposing duties on paper, painters' colors, glass and tea. The Americans opposed this measure with the only weapon at their command — the policy of non-importation. This policy, while causing much inconvenience to themselves, yet helped them materially in two ways. In the first place it stimulated home manufactures, and accustomed the people to do without luxuries, and in the second place by distressing British merchants and manufacturers, it brought the united influence of these two powerful bodies to bear upon parliament for a change in its policy.

The people of the colonies everywhere seconded the non-importation movement, entering at once upon a course of rigid self-denial, and their legislatures commended the scheme. An agreement, presented in the Virginia House of Burgesses, by Washington, was signed by every member. For more than a year, this powerful engine of retaliation waged war upon British commerce, in a constitutional way, before ministers would listen to petitions and remonstrances; and it was not until virtual rebellion in the British capital, born of commercial distress, menaced the ministry, that the expostulations of the Americans were noticed, except with sneers. Early in the year 1770, the obnoxious act was repealed, except as regarded tea. This item was retained in order that the right of parliamentary taxation of the colonies might be upheld. The liberal leaders of parliament did their best to prevent this exception, and the subject was fully and ably discussed, but they were overruled.

Besides these acts, which had aroused in the colonies a sentiment of union, and embodied an intelligent public opinion, there were others which had contributed to the same result. Such were the royal instructions by which, among other things, accused persons were to be sent to England, for trial. Still another, was the publication of a collection of letters from Governor Hutchinson, and other prominent colonial officials, revealing their agency in instigating the obnoxious measures. These and other aggravating causes had at

INTRODUCTION.

length brought about that, without which, no revolution can succeed, — organization. Committees of correspondence, local and general, had been created, and were now in full operation.

One thing more was essential to the success of the colonists, — union. Instead of pulling different ways, as from a variety of causes they had hitherto done, the different colonies must bring their combined efforts to bear in order to effect the desired result. This was brought about by the destruction of the tea in Boston harbor, and by the Boston port bill, and other coercive measures, its immediate consequence.

The impolitic reservation of the duty on tea produced an association not to drink it, and caused all the merchants, except a few in Boston, to refuse its importation.

Three hundred women of Boston, heads of families, among them many of the highest standing, had, as early as February, 1770, signed an agreement not to drink any tea until the impost clause of the revenue acts was repealed. The daughters of liberty, both north and south, did the same. The young women of Boston followed the example of their mothers, and subscribed to the following pledge:

"We, the daughters of those patriots who have, and do now appear for the public interest, and in that principally regard their posterity, as such do with pleasure engage with them in denying ourselves the drinking of foreign tea, in hopes to frustrate a plan that tends to deprive a whole community of all that is valuable in life."

From this time forth tea was a proscribed beverage throughout the colonies. "Balsamic hyperion," made from the dried leaves of the raspberry plant; thyme, extensively used by the women of Connecticut; and various other substitutes came into general use. The newspapers of the day abound with details of social gatherings, in which foreign tea was totally discarded.

They also voiced the public abhorrence for it, or what it represented, by applying to it all the objurgatory and abusive epithets they could muster—and their vocabulary was by no means limited—such as "detestable," "cruel," "villainous," "pernicious," "fatal," "devilish," "fiendish," etc.

Of course there were those who would not deny themselves the use of tea,—drinking it clandestinely in garrets, or preparing it in coffee-pots to deceive the eye, resorting to any subterfuge in order to indulge in the use of their favorite beverage. These people, when found out, did not fail to receive the condemnation of the patriotic men and women, who, from principle, abstained. There was still a considerable consumption of tea in America, as the article could be obtained more cheaply from Holland than from the English East India Company, and on arrival here could easily be smuggled ashore. It was supposed that of the three millions of inhabitants of the colonies, one-third drank tea twice a day, Bohea being the kind preferred; and it was estimated that the annual consumption, in Massachusetts alone, was two thousand four hundred chests, some eight hundred thousand pounds.

Tea continued to arrive in Boston, but as no one would risk its sale, it was stored. The "Boston Gazette," in April, 1770, said: "There is not above one seller of tea in town who has not signed an agreement not to dispose of any tea until the late revenue acts are repealed."

John Hancock offered one of his vessels, free of charge, to re-ship the tea then stored in Boston. His offer was accepted, and a cargo despatched to London. So strict was the watch kept upon the traders, that many of those suspected of illicit dealings in tea, among whom was Hancock himself, found it convenient to publish cards declaring their innocence. Governor Hutchinson wrote at this time (April, 1770,) to Lord Hillsborough, the English secretary, "That the importers pleaded that they should be utterly ruined by this combination, but the Boston zealots had no bowels, and gave for answer, 'that if a ship was to bring us the plague, nobody would doubt what was necessary to be done with her;' but the present case is much worse than that." Theophilus Lillie, who was selling tea contrary to the agreement, found, one morning, a post planted before his door, upon which was a carved head, with the names of some tea importers on it, and underneath, a hand pointing towards his shop. One of his neighbors, an informer, named Richardson, asked a countryman to break the post down with his cart. A crowd gathered, and boys threw stones and chased Richardson to his house. He fired into them with a shotgun, and killed a German lad of eleven years, named Snider. At his funeral, five hundred children walked in front of the bier; six of his school-fellows held the pall, and a large procession moved from liberty tree to the townhouse, and thence to the burying-place. This exciting affair, preceded by a few days only, the memorable "Boston massacre" of March 5, 1770.

The application of the East India Company to the British government for relief from pecuniary embarrassment, occasioned by the great falling off in its American tea trade, afforded the ministry just the opportunity it desired to fasten taxation upon the American colonies. The company asked permission to export tea to British America, free of duty, offering to allow government to retain sixpence per pound, as an exportation tariff, if they would take off the three per cent. duty, in America. This gave an opportunity for conciliating the colonies in an honorable way, and also to procure double the amount of revenue. But no! under the existing coercive policy, this request was of course inadmissible. At this time the company had in its warehouses upwards of seventeen millions of pounds, in addition to which the importations of the current year were expected to be larger than usual. To such a strait was it reduced, that it could neither pay its dividends nor its debts.

By an act of parliament, passed on May 10, 1773, "with little debate and no opposition," the company, on exportation of its teas to America, was allowed a drawback of the full amount of English duties, binding itself only to pay the threepence duty, on its being landed in the English colonies.

In accordance with this act, the lords-commissioners of the treasury gave the company a license (August 20, 1773,) for the exportation of six hundred thousand pounds, which were to be sent to Boston, New York, Philadelphia and Charleston, S.C., the principal American ports. As soon as this became known, applications were made to the directors by a number of merchants in the colonial trade, soliciting a share of what promised to be a very profitable business. The establishment of a branch East India house, in a central part of America, whence the tea could be distributed to other points, was suggested. The plan finally adopted was to bestow the agency on merchants, in good repute, in the colonies, who were friendly to the administration, and who could give satisfactory security, or obtain the guaranty of London houses.

The company and its agents viewed this matter solely in a commercial light. No one supposed that the Americans would oppose the measure on the ground of abstract

INTRODUCTION. xiii

principle. The only doubt was as to whether the company could, merely with the threepenny duty, compete successfully with the smugglers, who brought tea from Holland. It was hoped they might, and that the difference would not compensate for the risk in smuggling. But the Americans at once saw through the scheme, and that its success would be fatal to their liberties.

The new tea act, by again raising the question of general taxation, diverted attention from local issues, and concentrated it upon one which had been already fully discussed, and on which the popular verdict had been definitely made up. Right and justice were clearly on their side. It was not that they were poor and unable to pay, but because they would not submit to wrong. The amount of the tax was paltry, and had never been in question. Their case was not — as in most revolutions — that of a people who rose against real and palpable oppression. It was an abstract principle alone for which they contended. They were prosperous and happy. It was upon a community, at the very height of its prosperity, that this insidious scheme suddenly fell, and it immediately aroused a more general opposition than had been created by the stamp act. "The measure," says the judicious English historian, Massey, "was beneficial to the colonies; but when was a people engaged in a generous struggle for freedom, deviated by an insidious attempt to practice on their selfish interests?"

"The ministry believe," wrote Franklin, "that threepence on a pound of tea, of which one does not perhaps drink ten pounds a year, is sufficient to overcome all the patriotism of an American." The measure gave universal offence, not only as the enforcement of taxation, but as an odious monopoly of

INTRODUCTION.

trade. To the warning of Americans that their adventure would end in loss, and to the scruples of the company, Lord North answered peremptorily, "It is to no purpose making objections, the king will have it so. The king means to try the question with America." How absurd was this assertion of prerogative, and how weak the government, was seen when on the first forcible resistance to his plans, the king was compelled to apply to the petty German states for soldiers. Lord North believed that no difficulty could arise, as America, under the new regulation, would be able to buy tea[1] from the company at a lower price than from any other European nation, and that buyers would always go to the cheapest market.

Before receiving intelligence of the passage of the new act, in the summer of 1773, political agitation in the colonies had in great measure subsided. The ministry had abandoned its design of transporting Americans to England for trial; the people were prosperous; loyal to the king; considered themselves as fellow subjects with Britons, and indignantly repelled the idea of severing their political connection. The king, however, was obstinately bent upon maintaining the supreme authority of parliament to make laws binding on the colonies "in all cases whatsoever." He was unfortunate in having for his chief adviser, Lord North, who sought to please the king even against his own better judgment. He was still more unfortunate in North's colleagues,—Mansfield,

---

[1] Dr. Holmes, the annalist, says, that tea began to be used in New England in 1720. Small quantities, must, however, have been made many years before, as small copper tea-kettles were in use in Plymouth, in 1702. The first cast-iron tea-kettles were made in Plympton, (now Carver,) Mass., between 1760 and 1765. When ladies went to visiting parties, each one carried her tea-cup, saucer, and spoon. The cups were of the best china, very small, containing about as much as a common wine-glass.

INTRODUCTION. xv

Sandwich, Germaine, Wedderburne and Thurlow,—violent or corrupt men, wholly unfit for the grave responsibilities they had assumed.

Governor Hutchinson[1] asserts that "when the intelligence first came to Boston it caused no alarm. The threepenny duty had been paid the last two years without any stir, and some of the great friends to liberty had been importers of tea. The body of the people were pleased with the prospect of drinking tea at less expense than ever. The only apparent discontent was among the importers of tea, as well those who had been legal importers from England, as others who had illegally imported from Holland, and the complaint was against the East India Company for monopolizing a branch of commerce which had been beneficial to a great number of merchants."

The circular-letter of the Massachusetts Committee of Correspondence of October 21, 1773, — by which time the public sentiment against the new regulation had been thoroughly aroused, — said of it: "It is easy to see how aptly this scheme will serve both to destroy the trade of the colonies and increase the revenue. How necessary then it is that each colony should take effectual methods to prevent this measure from having its designed effects."

One of the Boston consignees writing to London, says, under date of 18th October: "But what difficulties may arise from the disaffection of the merchants and importers of tea to this measure of the East India Company, I am not yet able to say. It seems at present to be a matter of much speculation, and if one is to credit the prints, no small opposition will be made thereto. . . . My friends seem to think it will

[1] Hist. of Mass., iii. 422.

subside; others are of a contrary opinion." Another, under date of October 30th, gives it as his opinion that the uneasiness is fomented, if not originated, by persons concerned in the Holland trade, a trade which, he is informed, is much more practiced in the Southern governments than here.

In a letter dated New York, November 5th, Abraham Lott, one of the New York consignees, says, that if the tea arrives subject to duty, "there will be no such thing as selling it, as the people would rather buy so much poison, as they say it is calculated to enslave them and their posterity, and are therefore determined not to take what they call the nauseous draught." The tenor of these letters and of the American newspapers, must have given the British public an inkling of what was to come.

It was thought by all the colonies that this was the precise point of time when it was absolutely necessary to make a stand, and that all opposition to parliamentary taxation must be for ever given up, if this critical moment was neglected. The only practical way open to defeat the measure seemed to be through popular demonstrations.

The press now became more active than ever in its political discussions. As to the mode of payment of the tea duty, it said: "We know that on a certificate of its being landed here, the tribute is, by agreement, to be paid in London. The landing, therefore, is the point in view, and every nerve will be strained to obtain it." It was asked in New York, "are the Americans such blockheads as to care whether it be a hot red poker, or a red hot poker which they are to swallow, provided Lord North forces them to swallow one of the two?"

"All America is in a flame on account of the tea exportation," wrote a British officer at New York to a friend in London. "The New Yorkers, as well as the Bostonians and Philadelphians, it seems, are determined that no tea shall be landed. They have published a paper in numbers called the 'Alarm.' It begins, 'Dear countrymen,' and goes on exhorting them to open their eyes, and then, like sons of liberty, throw off all connection with the tyrant — the mother country.' They have on this occasion raised a company of artillery, and every day almost, are practicing at a target. Their independent companies are out, and exercise every day. The minds of the townspeople are influenced by the example of some of their principals. They swear that they will burn every tea-ship that comes in; but I believe that our six and twelve pounders, with the Royal Welch Fusileers, will prevent anything of that kind."

Philadelphia, the largest town in the colonies, led off in the work of opposing the plans of the home government. In a handbill signed "Scævola," circulated there, with the heading, "By uniting we stand, by dividing we fall," the factors appointed, by the East India Company were characterized as "political bombardiers to demolish the fair structure of liberty;" and it was said that all eyes were fixed on them, and they were urged to refuse to act.

At a large meeting held at the State House on October 18, resolutions were passed declaring that the duty on tea was a tax imposed on the colonists without their consent, and tended to render assemblies useless; that the shipment by the East India Company was an attempt to enforce the tax, and that every one who should be concerned in the unloading, receiving or vending the tea, was an enemy to his country. In accordance with one of the resolutions of the meeting, a committee was appointed to wait on the consignees in that city, to request them, from regard to their own characters and the public peace, and good order of the city and Province, immediately to resign their appointment. The Messrs. Wharton gave a satisfactory answer, which was received with shouts of applause. Groans and hisses greeted the refusal of another firm to commit themselves, until the tea arrived. So general and so commanding was the movement, however, that in a few days they also resigned. "Be assured," wrote Thomas Wharton, one of the consignees, "this was as respectable a body of inhabitants as has been together on any occasion, many of the first rank. Their proceedings were conducted with the greatest decency and firmness, and without one dissentient voice."

A few days after the action of Philadelphia, a meeting was held at the city hall, New York, (October 26,) when the tea consignees were denounced, and the attempted monopoly of trade was stigmatized as a "public robbery." The press was active, and handbills were circulated freely among the people. A series of these called the "Alarm," has been already mentioned. "If you touch one grain of the accursed tea you are undone," was the sentiment it conveyed. "America is threatened with worse than Egyptian slavery. . . . The language of the revenue act is, that you have no property you can call your own, that you are the vassals, the live stock, of Great Britain." Such were the bold utterances of the New Yorkers. Within three weeks the New York agents withdrew from the field. It was thereupon announced that government would take charge of the tea upon its arrival.

The New York Sons of Liberty at once reorganized; owners and occupants of stores were warned against harboring the

INTRODUCTION.

tea, and all who bought, sold or handled it, were threatened as enemies to the country. Handbills were issued, notifying the "Mohawks" to hold themselves in readiness for active work. At the very moment when the tea was being destroyed in Boston, handbills were circulating in New York calling a meeting of "all friends to the liberties and trade of America," for one o'clock the next day, at the city hall, "on business of the utmost importance."

John Lamb, one of the most active of the Sons of Liberty of New York, afterwards a colonel of artillery in the Revolutionary army, was the speaker at the meeting, and the large assembly unanimously voted that the tea should not be landed. The governor sent a message to the people by the mayor, engaging upon his honor that the tea should not be sold, but should remain in the barracks until the council advised to the delivery of it, or orders were received from England how to dispose of it, and that it should be delivered in an open manner at noon-day. The mayor having asked if the proposals were satisfactory, there was a general cry of "no! no!" The people were at length quieted with the assurance that the ship should be sent back.

It was at Boston, the ringleader in rebellion, that the issue was to be tried. It was then the most flourishing commercial town on the continent, and contained a population of about sixteen thousand, almost exclusively of English origin. Though there were no sidewalks in the town, and, except when driven aside by carts or carriages, every one walked in the middle of the street, "where the pavement was the smoothest," an English visitor had twenty years before pronounced it to be, "as large and better built than

Bristol, or any other city in England except London." The only land communication between Boston and the surrounding towns at that period, was by way of the narrow neck at its southern extremity. Her inhabitants were industrious, frugal and enterprising, and were equally distinguished for their pertinacity and independence. They were nearly all of the same church, and were strict in the observance of Sunday. Though many had acquired a competence, few were very rich or very poor, and their style of living had little diversity. In her free schools all were taught to read and write. A score of enterprising booksellers, among them Henry Knox, imported into the colony all the standard books on law, politics, history and theology, while a free press and town meetings instructed her citizens in political affairs. Her mechanics, many of whom were ship-builders, were active in all town meetings. Ever jealous of her rights, she had grown up in their habitual exercise, and was early and strenuous in her opposition to the claims of parliamentary supremacy. Even her divines, many of whom were distinguished by their learning and eloquence, gave the sanction of religion to the cause of freedom. For these reasons Boston was the fittest theatre for the decisive settlement of the grave question at issue.

Two men of very different metal were especially prominent in Boston at this time, — Thomas Hutchinson, the royal governor, and Samuel Adams, the man of the people. Both were natives of the town, and graduates of Harvard College. Hutchinson, during a public life of over thirty years, had held the offices of representative, councillor, chief justice and lieutenant-governor. No man was so experienced in the affairs of the colony, no one so familiar with its history, usages and laws. As a legislator and as a judge he had manifested ability and impartiality.

Unfortunately for his peace of mind, and for his reputation, he set himself squarely against the popular movement. He advised altering the charters of the New England provinces; the dismemberment of Massachusetts; the establishment of a citadel in Boston; the stationing of a fleet in its harbor; the experiment of martial law; the transportation of "incendiaries" to England, and the prohibition of the New England fisheries, at the same time entreating of his correspondents in England to keep his opinions secret.

For these errors of judgment he paid dearly in the obloquy heaped upon him by his countrymen, and his exile from his native land, in which he earnestly desired that his bones might be laid. The recent publication of his diary and letters shows that he not only acted honestly and conscientiously in opposing the popular current, but that he, at the same time, used his influence to mitigate the severe measures of government. He counselled them against the stamp act; against closing the port of Boston, and against some features of the regulating act, as too harsh and impolitic. It was his sincere wish that his countrymen would admit the supremacy of parliament, and he believed that such a result could be attained without bloodshed. He was courteously received in England,—where his course was very generally approved,—and offered a baronetcy, which, however, he declined on the score of the insufficiency of his estate. His judgment in American affairs, though often sought by the ministry, seems to have been seldom followed. Candor requires that in the light of his letters and diary, in which his real sentiments appear, the harsh judgment usually passed upon Hutchinson, should be materially modified.

His opponent, Samuel Adams, the great agitator, possessed precisely those qualities that the times required. His political creed was, that the colonies and England had a common king, but separate and independent legislatures, and as early as the year 1769, he had been a zealous advocate of independence. He was the organizer of the Revolution, through the committees of correspondence, which he initiated, and was one of those who matured the plan of a general congress. A genuine lover of liberty, he believed in the capacity of the Americans for self-government. It was Samuel Adams who, the day after the "massacre" of March 5, 1770, was chosen chairman of the committee, to demand of the governor the immediate removal of the troops from the town of Boston. The stern and inflexible patriot clearly exposed the fallacy of Hutchinson's reply to the demand, and compelled the governor to yield. No flattery could lull his vigilance, no sophistry deceive his penetration. Difficulties did not discourage, nor danger appall him. Though poor, he possessed a lofty and incorruptible spirit, and though grave and austere in manner, was warm in his feelings. His affable and persuasive address, reconciled conflicting interests, and promoted harmonious action. As a speaker he was pure, concise, logical and impressive, and the energy of his diction was not inferior to the depth of his mind. As a political writer he was clear and convincing, and was the author of able state papers. No man had equal influence over the popular mind with Samuel Adams, who has been aptly styled, "the last of the Puritans."

At Boston, where the feeling against receiving the tea

was strongest, the consignees were, "by a singular infelicity," either relatives of the hated governor, or in sympathy with the odious administration. Two of them were his sons. Richard Clarke was his nephew. One of Clarke's daughters married Copley, the painter, and became the mother of Lord Lyndhurst, the future lord-chancellor of England. Benjamin Faneuil and Joshua Winslow were respectable merchants. All but Faneuil were connected by marriage. They were well aware of the temper of the people, and of the proceedings in Philadelphia and New York; and would doubtless have yielded to the popular demands, but for Hutchinson. Public sentiment was stimulated against them by representing them as crown officers, whereas they were only factors. They were thus put upon the footing of the obnoxious stamp officers.

The North End Caucus,[1] composed mostly of mechanics, met frequently to consider what should be done, and voted (October 23d,) that they would oppose with their lives and fortunes, the vending of any tea that might be sent to the town for sale by the East India Company. "We were so careful," says Paul Revere, "that our meetings should be kept secret, that every time we met, every person swore upon the Bible not to discover any of our transactions, but

[1] This body, which originally consisted of sixty-one members, with Dr. Thomas Young for its president, was organized by Dr. Joseph Warren, who, with one other person, drew up its regulations. Its usual place of meeting was at William Campbell's house, near the North Battery, though its sessions were sometimes held at the Green Dragon tavern. Here the committees of public service were formed, and measures of defence, and resolves for the destruction of the tea, discussed. It was here, when the best mode of expelling the regulars from Boston was under consideration, that John Hancock exclaimed, "Burn Boston, and make John Hancock a beggar, if the public good requires it."

to Hancock, Warren or Church, and one or two more leaders."

The Caucus and the Long-Room Club were local organizations, and were all included in the larger and more important one, known as "The Sons of Liberty." This association pervaded nearly all the colonies. It was first known in Boston as the "Union Club," and gained its later name from the phrase employed in the British parliament by Col. Barré, in his famous speech. It was formed in 1765, soon after the passage of the stamp act, and had among its members most of the leading patriots of the day. Their organization was secret, with private pass-words, to protect them from Tory spies. On public occasions, each member wore, suspended from his neck, a medal, on one side of which was the figure of a stalwart arm, grasping in its hand a pole, surmounted with a cap of liberty, and surrounded by the words, "Sons of Liberty." On the reverse was a representation of Liberty Tree. It was under this tree, in the open space known as "Liberty Hall,"—at the junction of Newbury, Orange and Essex Streets,—that their public meetings in Boston were held.

The Sons of Liberty issued warrants for the arrest of suspected persons; arranged in secret caucus the preliminaries of elections, and the programme for public celebrations; and in fact were the mainspring, under the guidance of the popular leaders, of every public demonstration against the government. In Boston they probably numbered about three hundred. The 14th of August,— the anniversary of the repeal of the stamp act,— was celebrated by them for several years, with grand display and festivity.

Under date of January 15, 1766, John Adams says, in his

INTRODUCTION. xxv

diary: "I spent the evening with the Sons of Liberty, at their own apartment, in Hanover Square, near the Tree of Liberty. It is a counting-room, in Chase & Speakman's distillery; a very small room it is. There were present, John Avery, a distiller, of liberal education; John Smith, the brazier; Thomas Crafts,[1] the painter; Benjamin Edes,[2] the printer; Stephen Cleverly, brazier; Thomas Chase, distiller; Joseph Fields, master of a vessel; Henry Bass; George Trott, jeweller; and Henry Welles. I was very cordially and respectfully treated by all present. We had punch, wine, pipes and tobacco, biscuit and cheese, etc. They chose a committee to make preparations for grand rejoicings upon the arrival of the news of a repeal of the stamp act." The counting-room of which Adams speaks, could, from its small size, have been the committee-room of the body only.

Governor Bernard wished to send some of the leading Sons of Liberty to England, for trial, but did not dare do so. New York was the centre of the organization, to which all

---

[1] Thomas Crafts was, in 1789, a painter and japanner, opposite the site of the great tree (corner of Boylston and Washington Streets). He became a member of the Masonic Lodge of St. Andrew in 1762.

[2] Benjamin Edes, journalist, born in Charlestown, Mass., Oct. 14, 1732; died in Boston, December 11, 1803. In 1755, he began, with John Gill, the publication of the "Boston Gazette and Country Journal," a newspaper of deserved popularity, unsurpassed in its patriotic zeal for liberty, — the chosen mouth-piece of the Whigs. To its columns, Otis, the Adamses, Quincy and Warren, were constant contributors. Their printing-office, on the corner of Queen (now Court) Street and Dassett's Alley (now Franklin Avenue), was the place of meeting of a party of the "Mohawks," on the afternoon of December 16, 1773. During the siege of Boston, the "Gazette" was issued at Watertown. It was discontinued September 17, 1798. At the opening of the war, Mr. Edes possessed a handsome property, which was wholly lost by the depreciation of the currency. Edes was a member of the Ancient and Honorable Artillery Company in 1760, and a prominent "Son of Liberty."

communications from the other colonies were sent. A correspondent in London kept them informed of the proceedings and designs of the British ministry.

At one o'clock in the morning of the 2d of November, 1773, the consignees were aroused from their slumbers by a violent knocking at their doors, and a summons was left for them to appear at Liberty Tree on the following Wednesday, to resign their commissions; and not to fail at their peril. A handbill was, at the same time, posted about the town, notifying the people of Boston and the vicinity to be present at the same time and place, to witness their resignation.

On the appointed day, a large flag was hung out at Liberty Tree. The public crier announced the meeting, at the top of his voice, and the church bells, were rung for an hour. At noon, five hundred persons assembled. Samuel Adams, John Hancock and William Phillips, representatives of Boston, were present, with William Cooper, — the patriotic town clerk, — and the board of selectmen. The consignees failing to appear, a committee, consisting of William Molineux, William Dennie, Dr. Joseph Warren, Dr. Benjamin Church,[1] Henderson Inches, Edward Proctor, Nathaniel

---

[1] Dr. Benjamin Church, physician, orator and poet, grandson of the famous Indian fighter of the name; born in Newport, R. I., August 24, 1734; was lost at sea in May, 1776. He graduated at Harvard College in 1754; studied medicine in London, and after his return to Boston, became eminent as a surgeon. For several years previous to the Revolution, he was a conspicuous and leading Whig. He was a representative, a member of the Provincial Congress of 1774, and physician-general to the patriot army. Pecuniary embarrassment is supposed to

INTRODUCTION. xxvii

Barber, Gabriel Johonnot,[1] and Ezekiel Cheever, waited on them at Clarke's warehouse, at the foot of King (now State) Street, where they, together with a number of their friends, had assembled. As they passed the town house, still standing at the head of this street, Hutchinson, who saw the procession, says that "the committee were attended by a large body of the people, many of them not of the lowest rank."

Molineux was the spokesman. "From whom are you a committee?" asked Clarke. "From the whole people," was the reply. "Who are the committee?" "I am one," said Molineux, and he named the rest. "What is your request?" "That you give us your word to sell none of the teas in

---

have led to his defection from the cause of his country. In September, 1775, an intercepted letter of his, in characters, to Major Cain, in Boston, was deciphered; and October 3, 1775, he was convicted by a court martial, of which Washington was president, of "holding a criminal correspondence with the enemy." Confined in jail at Norwich, Conn., he was released in May, 1776, on account of failing health; sailed for the West Indies, and was never afterwards heard from.

[1] Gabriel Johonnot, born in Boston, 1748; died in Hamden, Me., October 9, 1820. Zacharie, his father, a Huguenot, was a distiller and merchant. His dwelling-house and store was on Orange Street, and his distillery on Harvard Street, directly opposite. At the bottom of the street was his wharf, wooden distillery, storehouses, etc. The mansion house and store were burned in the great fire, 20th April, 1787. Gabriel was a member of St. John's Lodge, Boston, 1780, and a charter member of Hancock Lodge, Castine, Me., 1794. He was chairman of a committee appointed by the company of Cadets, of Boston, August 15, 1774, to proceed to Salem, and return to Governor Gage, the standard presented to them; and was Lieutenant-Colonel of the 14th Regiment of the Massachusetts line, known as the Marblehead regiment, commanded by Colonel Glover. He removed to Castine, Me., soon after the Revolutionary war; took a prominent part in town affairs, and at one time represented the town of Penobscot in the Massachusetts Legislature.

your charge, but return them to London in the same bottoms in which they were shipped. Will you comply?" "I shall have nothing to do with you," was the rough and peremptory reply, in which the other consignees, who were present, concurred. Molineux then read the resolve, passed at Liberty Tree, declaring that those who should refuse to comply with the request of the people, were "enemies to their country," and should be dealt with accordingly.

When the committee reported the result to the crowd outside, the cry was raised, "Out with them! out with them!" Those within attempted to close the doors; but the people unhinged them, and carried them off. Justice Nathaniel Hatch, who, in the king's name, now commanded the peace, was hooted at and struck, when the people were persuaded to desist. The committee returned to Liberty Tree, where they reported to the meeting, which quietly dispersed. Of those composing this gathering, the consignees wrote to the East India Company, as follows: "They consisted chiefly of people of the lowest rank; very few respectable tradesmen, as we are informed, appeared amongst them. The selectmen say they were present to prevent disorder." There can be little doubt that the political assemblies of that day, as do those at the present time, fairly represented the body of the people. The mechanics of Boston, whatever their rank in the social scale, were the active patriots of the revolutionary period.

The Sons of Liberty having failed, and the Tories asserting that the meeting at Liberty Tree was irregular, petitioners for a town meeting declared that the people were alarmed at a report that the tea had been shipped to America, and feared that the tribute would be exacted, and that the liberties, for which they had so long contended, would be lost to them and their posterity. A meeting was therefore called by the selectmen for the next day, at ten o'clock in the forenoon.

That night a threatening letter was placed under the door of Mr. Faneuil, one of the consignees, warning them that a much longer delay in complying, would not fail to bring upon them "the just reward of their avarice and insolence."

The town meeting, held on the 5th of November, was fully attended, and was presided over by John Hancock. After due consideration, it adopted the resolves of the Philadelphians of October 18, declaring that freemen have an inherent right to dispose of their property; that the tea tax was a mode of levying contributions on them without their consent; that its purpose tended to render assemblies useless, and to introduce arbitrary government; that a steady opposition to this ministerial plan was a duty which every freeman owed to his country, to himself, and to his posterity; that the East India Company's importation was an open attempt to enforce this plan; and that whoever countenanced the unloading, vending or receiving the tea, was an enemy to his country. A committee, consisting of the moderator, Henderson Inches, Benjamin Austin, and the selectmen of the town, were chosen to wait on the consignees and request them, from a regard to their own characters, and the peace and good of the town and province, immediately to resign their appointment.

At this meeting, a Tory handbill, called the "Tradesmen's Protest," against the proceedings of the merchants on the subject of tea importation, was introduced. After the reading, without comment, the tradesmen present were desired to collect themselves at the south side of the hall, where the question was put whether they acknowledged the "Tradesmen's Protest," and the whole, amounting to at least four hundred, voted in the negative. The paper, its printer, and those who circulated it, were denounced as base, false and scandalous. This gave a finishing blow to the "Protest," of which nothing more was heard.

After voting that it was the just expectation of the town that no one of its merchants should, under any pretext whatever, import any tea liable to duty, the meeting adjourned until three o'clock.

At that hour there was again a full assembly. The committee reported that they had communicated the resolves of the town to the Messrs. Clarke and Mr. Faneuil, who informed them that they must consult Thomas and Elisha Hutchinson, the other consignees, who were at Milton, and could not give an answer until the following Monday. Samuel Adams, Joseph Warren, and Molineux were then desired to acquaint Messrs. Clarke and Faneuil, that the town expected an immediate answer from them. This was very soon received, and pronounced unsatisfactory, by a unanimous vote. John Hancock, John Pitts, Samuel Adams, Samuel Abbott, Joseph Warren, William Powell, and Nathaniel Appleton,[1] were chosen a committee to wait on the

---

[1] Nathaniel Appleton, Commissioner of Loans for the State of Massachusetts, a resident of Atkinson (now Congress) Street, son of Rev. Dr. Nathaniel Appleton, of Cambridge; died in June, 1789, aged 66.

INTRODUCTION.

Hutchinsons, and request an immediate resignation, and the meeting adjourned until the next day.

On Saturday, Faneuil Hall was again crowded. The committee reported that it could not find Elisha Hutchinson, either at Milton or Boston. Thomas Hutchinson, Jr., informed them, in a letter, that when he and his brother were appointed factors, and the tea arrived, they would be sufficiently informed to answer the request of the inhabitants.

This reply stirred up some of the hot blood in the assembly, and a cry of "to arms! to arms!" was received with applause and clapping of hands. Discretion, as usual, prevailed, and the meeting voted that the replies were "daringly affrontive" to the town, and then dissolved. The governor tried to collect evidence of the inflammatory speeches that had been made, but could find no person willing to give it.

A quiet week followed. The tea-ships were nearing the harbor, and the journals were filled with political essays generally, strong, well put, and elevating in tone. Locke, in the "Boston Gazette," said: "It will be considered by Americans whether the *dernier ressort*, and only asylum for their liberties, is not an American Commonwealth." It was evident to the leaders on both sides, that a crisis was at hand. Hutchinson foresaw that this "would prove a more difficult affair than any which had preceded it;" and in his letters admits that the mass of the people acted in the conviction that their rights were invaded. Believing the supremacy of parliament was in issue, he determined, though standing almost alone, and in opposition to the advice of his political friends, to make no concession. In a letter written at this period, to Lord Dartmouth, Secretary for the

xxxii   INTRODUCTION.

Colonies, he describes, with minuteness, the state of political affairs. He says:

> . . . "At present, the spirits of the people in the town of Boston are in a great ferment. Everything that has been in my power, without the Council, I have done, and continue to do, for the preservation of the peace and good order of the town. If I had the aid, which I think the Council might give, my endeavors would be more effective. They profess to disapprove of the tumultuous, violent proceedings of the people, but they wish to see the professed end of the people in such proceedings attained in the regular way; and, instead of joining with me in proper measures to discourage an opposition to the landing of the teas expected, one and another of the gentlemen, of the greatest influence, intimate that the best thing that can be done to quiet the people, would be the refusal of the gentlemen to whom the teas are consigned, to execute the trust; and they declare they would do it if it was their case, and would advise all their connexions to do it. Nor will they ever countenance a measure which shall tend to carry into execution an act of parliament which lays taxes upon the colonies, for the purpose of a revenue. The same principle prevails with by far the greater part of the merchants who, though in general they declare against mobs and violence, yet they as generally wish the tea may not be imported. The persons to whom the teas are consigned, declare that whilst they can be protected from violence to their persons, they will not give way to the unreasonable demands which have been made of them. I wish the vessels bound to New York may arrive before those designed to this Province. Governor Tryon I know to be well disposed to do his duty, and the people there are less disposed to any violent proceedings, as I have reason to think, than they are here, and an example of peace and good order there may have its influence here."

Samuel Adams, Hancock, Warren, Molineux and Young, the most prominent of the popular leaders, apprehended fully the responsibilities of the hour. They had a great principle to maintain, and the courage to uphold it. They knew that, though the people were with them, the failure to obtain the resignation of the consignees had inspired doubt in other quarters, as to whether Boston would meet the expectations of the patriots of other colonies. To such as questioned whether it was not premature to push matters to extremities, they replied, that if fidelity to the common

INTRODUCTION.   xxxiii

cause was likely to bring on a quarrel with Great Britain, this was the best time for it to come. "Our credit," they said, "is at stake; we must venture, and unless we do, we shall be discarded by the Sons of Liberty in the other colonies, whose assistance we may expect, upon emergencies, in case they find us steady, resolute and faithful." With men like these "to the fore," though independence was scarcely dreamed of, revolution was a foregone conclusion.

Thomas Mifflin, an active patriot of Philadelphia, subsequently a general, and governor of Pennsylvania, when in Boston, said to some of these men, "will you engage that the tea shall not be landed? if so, I will answer for Philadelphia." And they pledged their honor that its landing should be prevented.

On November 11, Hutchinson issued the following order:

"Massachusetts Bay.   By the Governor.

To Colonel John Hancock, Captain of the Governor's Company of Cadets, &c.

The Cadet company, under your command, having signalized itself heretofore upon a very necessary occasion, and the late tumultuous proceedings in the town of Boston requiring that more than usual caution should be taken at this time for the preservation of the peace, I think it proper that you should forthwith summon each person belonging to the company to be ready, and to appear in arms at such place of parade as you think fit, whensoever there may be a tumultuous assembly of the people, in violation of the laws, in order to their being aiding and assisting to the civil magistrate as occasion may require."

This company, which was immediately under the governor's orders, had been of service during the stamp act riots, and had often been complimented for its discipline. The evident intent of this order, to use military force to suppress public assemblages, and the stationing of companies of British troops in the neighboring towns, augmented the uneasiness already felt. There was now, besides the soldiers at the castle, a considerable naval force in the harbor, under Admiral John Montagu.

On the morning of November 17, a little party of family friends had assembled at the house of Richard Clarke, Esq., known as the "Cooke House," near the King's Chapel, on School Street, to welcome young Jonathan Clarke, who had just arrived from London. All at once the inmates of the dwelling were startled by a violent beating at the door, accompanied with shouts and the blowing of horns, creating considerable alarm. The ladies were hastily bestowed in places of safety, while the gentlemen secured the avenues of the lower story, as well as they were able. The yard and vicinity were soon filled with people. One of the inmates warned them, from an upper window, to disperse, but getting no other reply than a shower of stones, he discharged a pistol. Then came a shower of missiles, which broke in the lower windows, and damaged some of the furniture. Influential patriots had by this time arrived, and put a stop to the proceedings, and the mob quietly dispersed. The consignees now called on the governor and council for protection.

During the day, an arrival from London brought the news that three ships, having the East India Company's tea on board, had sailed for Boston, and that others had cleared for Philadelphia.

A petition for a town meeting was at once presented to the selectmen, representing that the teas were shortly expected, and that it was apprehended that the consignees might now be sufficiently informed on the terms of its consignment,

INTRODUCTION.   xxxv

to be able to give their promised answer to the town. A meeting was therefore appointed for the next day.

John Hancock was the moderator of the last town meeting, in which public sentiment was legally brought to bear upon the consignees. It was held on the 18th. The meeting was quiet and orderly, and its business was speedily transacted.

A committee was appointed to wait on the consignees for a final answer to the request of the town, that they resign their appointment. This was their reply:

"BOSTON, November 18, 1773.

Sir, — In answer to the message we have this day received from the town, we beg leave to say that we have not yet received any order from the East India Company respecting the expected teas, but we are now further acquainted that our friends in England have entered into general engagements in our behalf, merely of a commercial nature, which puts it out of our power to comply with the request of the town.

We are, sir, your most humble servants,

RICHARD CLARKE & SONS,
BENJ. FANEUIL, JR., for self and
JOSHUA WINSLOW, Esq.,
ELISHA HUTCHINSON, for my
Brother and self."

Immediately on receiving this answer, the meeting, without vote or comment, dissolved: " This sudden dissolution struck more terror into the consignees," says Hutchinson, "than the most minatory resolves;" and but for his efforts, they would have followed the example of those of Philadelphia, who had resigned six weeks before.

Next day (November 19), the consignees, in a petition to the governor and council, asked leave to resign themselves, and the property committed to their care, to his Excellency and their Honors, as guardians and protectors of the people, and that means might be devised for the landing and securing the teas, until the petitioners could safely dispose of them, or could receive directions from their constituents. Their action was the cause of much comment in the newspapers, and debate in the council. It was urged in opposition to the scheme, that it was no part of the legitimate functions of this body to act as trustees and storekeepers for certain factors of the East India Company.

In a letter to a friend, dated November 24, Hutchinson thus expresses his views of the situation. He says:

> "When I saw the inhabitants of the town of Boston, assembled under color of law, and heard of the open declaration that we are now in a state of nature, and that we have a right to take up arms; and when in a town meeting, as I am informed, a call to arms was received with clapping and general applause; when a tumultuous assembly of people can, from time to time, attack the persons and the property of the king's subjects; and when assemblies are tolerated from night to night, in the public town hall; to counsel and determine upon further unlawful measures, and dark proposals and resolutions are made and agreed to there; when the infection is industriously spreading and the neighboring towns not only join their committees with the committee of Boston, but are assembled in town meetings to approve of the doings of the town of Boston; and, above all, when upon repeated summoning of the Council, they put off any advice to me from time to time, and I am obliged to consent to it, because all the voices there, as far as they declare their minds, I have reason to fear, would rather confirm than discourage the people in their irregular proceedings,—under all these circumstances, I think it time to deliberate whether his majesty's service does not call me to retire to the castle, where I may, with safety to my person, more freely give my sense of the criminality of these proceedings than whilst I am in the hands of the people, some of whom, and those most active, don't scruple to declare their designs against me."

And he concludes this doleful story with the question, "What am I in duty bound to do?" His position was certainly a very uncomfortable one.

Frequent conferences with the consignees were held by the selectmen of Boston. "Though we labored night and day in the affair, all our efforts could not produce an agreement between them and the town." So wrote John Scollay,[1] chairman of the Board of Selectmen, who also informs us, in a letter written December 23, that there was a way by which the consignees might have avoided trouble. "Had they," writes he, "on the terms of first application to them, offered to have stored the tea, subject to the inspection of a committee of gentlemen, till they could write their principals, and until that time (agreed that) no duty should be paid, — which no doubt the customs officers would have consented to, — I am persuaded the town would have closed with them."

The selectmen told the consignees plainly that nothing less than sending the tea back to England would satisfy the people. Some of their Tory friends also urged them to arrange matters in this way, but they would only agree (Nov. 27) that nothing should be done in a clandestine way; that the vessels should come up to the wharves, and that when they received the orders that accompanied the teas, they would hand in proposals to the selectmen, to be laid before the town. They meant only to gain time. They were determined to make the issue with the popular leaders

---

[1] The Scollays were an old Scotch family. A John Scollay, the first mention of whom is found here, in 1692 leased the Winnisimmet ferry for one year. John, whose name is conspicuous in the early Revolutionary records of Boston, was a merchant, and was chairman of the Board of Selectmen, from 1774 to 1790. His portrait, by Copley, represents a portly, florid man, with a powdered wig, seated, his hand resting on a ledger. Thomas Melvill married one of Scollay's daughters. Col. William Scollay, apothecary and druggist, son of John, resided at first on or near the spot where the Museum stands, and his garden extended back to Court Square. He was associated with Charles Bulfinch and others, in the improvement of Franklin Place, now Franklin Street, where they erected the first block of buildings in Boston. Col. William was commander of the Independent Company of Cadets.

on this question. They were backed by the governor and the influential Tories, and no doubt believed that they could carry their point.

On Monday, the 22d, the committees of correspondence of Dorchester, Brookline, Roxbury and Cambridge, met the Boston committee at the selectmen's chamber, Faneuil Hall.

They resolved unanimously to use their joint influence to prevent the landing and sale of the teas; prepared a letter to be sent to the other towns, representing that they were reduced to the dilemma, either to sit down in quiet, under this and every burden that might be put upon them, or to rise up in resistance, as became freemen; to impress the absolute necessity of making immediate and effectual opposition to the detestable measure, and soliciting their advice and co-operation. Charlestown was "so zealous in the cause," that its committee was added to the others. This body continued to hold daily conferences, "like a little senate," says Hutchinson.

The "Gazette" of November 22, said: "Americans! defeat this last effort of a most pernicious, expiring faction, and you may sit under your own vines and fig trees, and none shall, hereafter, dare to make you afraid."

On the 26th, the men of Cambridge assembled, and after adopting the Philadelphia resolves, "very unanimously" voted, "That as Boston was struggling for the liberties of their country, they could no longer stand idle spectators, but were ready, on the shortest notice, to join with it, and other towns, in any measure that might be thought proper, to deliver themselves and posterity from slavery."

On Sunday, the 28th, the ship "Dartmouth," Captain Hall,

(From the original, in the possession of GEORGE H. ALLAN, Boston.)

Francis Rotch
1750 - 1822.
Bond, April 3d 1773.
£1000.

INTRODUCTION. XLI

owned by the Quaker, Francis Rotch,[1] arrived in Boston harbor, with one hundred and fourteen chests of tea, and anchored below the castle. As the news spread, there was great excitement. Despite the rigid New England observance of the Sabbath, the selectmen immediately met,

[1] Francis Rotch, a Quaker merchant, part owner of the "Dartmouth" and the "Beaver," was born in Nantucket, Mass., 30th September, 1750, and died in New Bedford, in May, 1822. Joseph, his father, the founder of a family of eminent merchants, was born in Salisbury, England, in 1704, and died in New Bedford, 24th November, 1784. In early life he settled in Nantucket, and rose from poverty to affluence by his industry, energy and enterprise, gaining, at the same time, universal esteem for his integrity. These characteristics he transmitted to his sons, William, Joseph and Francis, — especially to William, whose commercial transactions were of the most extensive character. All were largely concerned in the whale fisheries of Nantucket, of which they may almost be said to have been the founders. Francis was in England for a short time in 1773, but had returned home before his tea ships arrived. This affair was a very troublesome one for a young man of twenty-three to manage, as there was a tremendous pressure brought to bear upon him by Samuel Adams, and other influential patriots, to return the teas to England. He yielded temporarily to this pressure, promising the meeting of November 30th, that the tea should go back; but, probably after consultation with his counsel, Sampson Salter Blowers and John Adams, decided to withdraw his promise. Rotch pleaded that a compliance would ruin him, and as he could not obtain a pass for his ships, they would either have been sunk by the British batteries, or captured and confiscated under the revenue laws. He succeeded eventually in escaping loss in the affair, as the East India Company paid him the freight due on the cargoes of teas. His ship, the "Bedford," is, said to have been the first to display the American flag on the Thames, after the war. The family settled in New Bedford, in 1768. He married his cousin, Nancy Rotch, who, at the time of her death, 24th April, 1867, was nine-two years of age. The accompanying portrait is copied from a silhouette, by Miers, profile painter, 111 Strand, London, apparently about 1795. It is very delicately painted, on a hard plaster surface. The features are well marked, and the lace ruffle at the bosom, and the queue, are exceedingly well done. It is now in the possession of Mr. George H. Allan, who received it from his uncle, A. A. Rotch.

6

XLII   INTRODUCTION.

and remained in session until nine o'clock in the evening, in the expectation of receiving the promised proposal of the consignees. These gentlemen were not to be found, and on the next day, bidding a final adieu to Boston, they took up their quarters at the castle.

Hutchinson advised the consignees to order the vessels, when they arrived, to anchor below the castle, that if it should appear unsafe to land the tea, they might go to sea again, and when the first ship arrived she anchored there accordingly, but when the master came up to town, Mr. Adams and others, a committee of the town, ordered him at his peril to bring the ship up to land the other goods, but to suffer no tea to be taken out.

The committee of correspondence, who also held a session that day, seeing that time was precious, and that the tea once entered it would be out of the power of the consignees to send it back, obtained the promise of the owner not to enter his ship till Tuesday, and authorized Samuel Adams to summon the committees and townspeople of the vicinity to a mass meeting, in Boston, on the next morning. The invitation read as follows:

"A part of the tea shipped by the East India Company is now arrived in this harbor, and we look upon ourselves bound to give you the earliest intimation of it, and we desire that you favor us with your company at Faneuil Hall, at nine o'clock to-morrow forenoon, there to give us your advice what steps are to be immediately taken, in order effectually to prevent the impending evil, and we request you to urge your friends in the town, to which you belong, to be in readiness to exert themselves in the most resolute manner, to assist this town in its efforts for saving this oppressed country."

The journals of Monday announced that the "Dartmouth" had anchored off Long Wharf, and that other ships with the poisonous herb might soon be here. They also contained

INTRODUCTION.

a call for a public meeting, as announced in the following handbill, already printed and distributed throughout the town :

"Friends ! Brethren ! Countrymen ! That worst of plagues, the detested tea, shipped for this port by the East India Company, is now arrived in this harbor; the hour of destruction or manly opposition to the machinations of tyranny stares you in the face; every friend to his country, to himself, and posterity, is now called upon to meet at Faneuil Hall, at nine o'clock this day, (at which time the bells will ring,) to make a united and successful resistance to this last, worst and most destructive measure of administration.
Boston, November 29, 1773."

At nine o'clock the bells were rung, and the people, to the number of at least five thousand, thronged in and around Faneuil Hall. This edifice, then about half as large as now, was entirely inadequate to hold the concourse that had gathered there. Jonathan Williams,[1] a citizen of character and wealth, was chosen moderator. The selectmen were John Scollay, John Hancock, Timothy Newell, Thomas Newhall, Samuel Austin, Oliver Wendell,[2] and John Pitts. The patriotic and efficient town clerk, William Cooper,[3]

[1] Jonathan Williams, a distinguished merchant and patriot, captain of the Ancient and Honorable Artillery Company, in 1751; died March 27, 1788. Jonathan, his father, was a member of the Artillery Company in 1711.

[2] Judge Oliver Wendell, son of Hon. Jacob Wendell, was born in Boston 5th March, 1733; died, 15th January, 1818. Harvard College, 1753. His daughter, Sarah, married Rev. Abiel Holmes, the father of the poet, Oliver Wendell Holmes.

[3] William Cooper, son of Rev. William, and brother of Rev. Samuel, of the Brattle Street Church, and forty-nine years town •clerk of Boston ; died November 28, 1809; aged 89. The brothers were both active patriots of the Revolution.

was also present. Samuel Adams, Dr. Warren, Hancock, Dr. Young and Molineux took the lead in the debate. The resolution offered by Adams, "that the tea should not be landed; that it should be sent back in the same bottom to the place whence it came, at all events, and that no duty should be paid on it," was unanimously adopted. On hearing of this vote the consignees withdrew to Castle William. For the better accommodation of the people, the meeting then adjourned to the Old South Meeting House.

The speeches made at the Old South have not been preserved. Some were violent, others were calm, advising the people by all means to abstain from violence, but the men in whom they placed confidence were unanimous upon the question of sending back the tea. Dr. Young held that the only way to get rid of it was to throw it overboard. Here we find the first suggestion of its ultimate fate. Both Whigs and Tories united in the action of the meeting. To give the consignees time to make the expected proposals, the meeting adjourned till three o'clock.

Of this assembly Hutchinson says: "Although it consisted principally of the lower ranks of the people, and even journeymen tradesmen were brought to increase the number, and the rabble were not excluded, yet there were divers gentlemen of good fortune among them." With regard to the speeches he observes: "Nothing can be more inflammatory than those made on this occasion; Adams was never in greater glory." And of the consignees he says: "They apprehended they should be seized, and may be, tarred and feathered and carted,—an American torture,—in order to compel them to a compliance. The friends of old Mr. Clarke, whose constitution being hurt by the repeated attacks made upon him, retired into the country, pressed his sons and the other consignees to a full compliance."

A visitor from Rhode Island who attended the meeting, speaking of its regular and sensible conduct, said he should have thought himself rather in the British senate than in the promiscuous assembly of the people of a remote colony.

At the afternoon meeting in the Old South, it was resolved, upon the motion of Samuel Adams, "that the tea in Captain Hall's ship must go back in the same bottom." The owner and the captain were informed that the entry of the tea, or the landing of it, would be at their peril. The ship was ordered to be moored at Griffins' wharf, and a watch of twenty-five men was appointed for the security of vessel and cargo, with Captain Edward Proctor as captain that night. It was also voted that the governor's call on the justices to meet that afternoon, to suppress attempted riots, was a reflection on the people.

Upon Hancock's representation that the consignees desired further time to meet and consult, the meeting consented, "out of great tenderness to them," and adjourned until next day. This meeting also voted that six persons "who are used to horses be in readiness to give an alarm in the country towns, when necessary." They were William Rogers, Jeremiah Belknap, Stephen Hall, Nathaniel Cobbett, and Thomas Gooding, and Benjamin Wood, of Charlestown.

The guard for the tea ships, which consisted of from twenty-four to thirty-four men, was kept up until December 16. It was armed with muskets and bayonets, and proceeded with military regularity, — indeed it was composed in part of the military of the town, — and every half hour during the night regularly passed the word "all's well," like sentinels

INTRODUCTION.

in a garrison. It was on duty nineteen days and twenty-three hours. If molested by day the bells of the town were to be rung, if at night they were to be tolled. We have the names of those comprising the watch on November 29 and 30. They are:

For November 29. Captain, EDWARD PROCTOR.

Henry Bass.
Foster Condy.
John Lovell.
John Winthrop.
John Greenleaf.
Benjamin Alley.
Joshua Pico.
James Henderson.
Josiah Wheeler.
Joseph Edwards.
Jonathan Stodder.
Stephen Bruce.

Paul Revere.
Moses Grant.
Joseph Lovering.
Dr. Elisha Story.
Thomas Chase.
Benjamin Edes.
Joseph Pierce, Jr.
Captain Riordan.
John Crane.
John McFadden.
Thomas Knox, Jr.
Robert Hitchborn.

November 30. Captain, EZEKIEL CHEEVER.[1]

Thomas Urann.
William Dickman.
Samuel Peck.
Thomas Bolley.
John Rice.
Joseph Froude.
Obadiah Curtis.
George Ray.
Benjamin Ingerson.
Adam Collson.
Daniel Hewes.

Joseph Eayres.
William Sutton.
Ebenezer Ayres.
William Elberson.
Benjamin Stevens.
James Brewer.
Rufus Bant.
William Clap.
Nicholas Pierce.
Thomas Tileston.
Richard Hunnewell.

[1] Ezekiel Cheever, the great grandson of the famous schoolmaster of that name, in the early days of New England, was born in Charlestown, Mass., in May, 1720. He was by trade a sugar-baker (confectioner), and from 1752 to 1755

MAJOR GEN.^L JOSEPH WARREN
Slain at the Battle of Bunkers Hill June 17 1775

(Copied from the Boston print of 1782, it being from the London print previous to this date.)

"May our land be a land of liberty, the seat of virtue, the asylum of the oppressed, a name, a praise in the whole earth." — JOSEPH WARREN.
March 5, 1772.

INTRODUCTION.   XLIX

Hancock and Henry Knox were members of this volunteer guard. Volunteers were, after the first night, requested to leave their names at the printing-office of Edes and Gill; the duty of providing it having devolved upon the committee of correspondence.

Obadiah Curtis, born in Roxbury, Mass., in 1724; died in Newton, Mass., November 11, 1811. He was a wheelwright by trade, and his wife, Martha, kept an English goods store, at the corner of Rawson's Lane, (now Bromfield Street,) and Newbury (now Washington) Street, and accumulated a handsome estate. Becoming obnoxious to the British authorities, Mr. Curtis removed with his family to Providence, remaining there until after the evacuation of Boston. A person who saw him at this time thus describes his appearance: "He was habited according to the fashion of gentlemen of those days,—in a three-cornered hat, a club wig, a long coat of ample dimensions, that appeared to have been made with reference to future growth, breeches with large buckles, and shoes fastened in the same manner."

James Henderson was a painter, in Boston, at the beginning of this century.

Daniel Hewes, a mason by trade, resided on Purchase Street, where he died July 9, 1821; aged 77. He was a brother of George Robert Twelves Hewes.

Robert Hitchborn was a cooper, on Anne Street, in 1789.

Thomas Knox, Jr., a branch pilot, died in Charlestown, Mass., in April, 1817; aged 75. He joined the Masonic Lodge of St. Andrew in 1764. In 1789 his residence was on Friend Street.

Joseph Lovering was a tallow chandler. He lived on the corner of Hollis and Tremont Streets, opposite Crane and the Bradlees. Joseph Lovering, Jr., held the light by which Crane and others disguised themselves in Crane's carpenter's shop, on the evening of December 16. Lovering was a prominent member of the Charitable Mechanic Association, was many years a selectman and a fireward under the old town government of Boston, and was also a member of the first Board of Aldermen, under Mayor Phillips. He followed his father's business, and was some years a partner in the firm of J. Lovering & Sons.

was a selectman of Charlestown. Removing to Boston he joined the Sons of Liberty, and was active in the ante-revolutionary movements of the town, and prominent in its public meetings. He was appointed commissary of artillery in the army before Boston, May 17, 1775. He died a few years after the conclusion of the war. His brother, David, also a prominent Son of Liberty, was appointed moderator of the Old South meeting of December 14, but declined. Ezekiel was a member of the Committee that waited on the consignees and requested their resignation.

L   INTRODUCTION.

Joshua Pico, a cooper, on Sheaffe Street, residing on Clarke Street; died in January, 1807.
Joseph Pierce, Jr., was a merchant, at 58 Cornhill, in 1799.
Nicholas Pierce was a bricklayer, on Back (Salem) Street, in 1800.
John Rice was deputy-collector at Boston, 1789.
Benjamin Stevens was a tailor, at 33 Marlboro' Street, in 1789.
Jonathan Stodder was a member of St. Andrew's Lodge of Freemasons, in 1779.
Thomas Tileston, born September 21, 1735, was a carpenter on Purchase Street, in 1789. His father, Onesiphorous Tileston, also a housewright and a man of wealth, was captain of the Artillery Company in 1762.
John Winthrop resided in Cambridge Street, and died February 12, 1800; aged 53.

The power and influence of the Boston committee of correspondence, which played so important a part in the tea affair, can best be estimated by a glance at the list of names of its members. They were, Samuel Adams, James Otis, Joseph Warren, William Molineux, Dr. Benjamin Church, William Dennie, William and Joseph Greenleaf, Dr. Thomas Young, William Powell, Nathaniel Appleton, Oliver Wendell, Josiah Quincy, Jr., John Sweetser, Richard Boynton, John Bradford, William Mackay, Nathaniel Barber, Caleb Davis, Alexander Hill, and Robert Pierpont.

After the dissolution of the meeting of November 29, the committee met, and called on the committees from other towns to join them on all necessary occasions. Besides sending accounts of these events to all the towns, they also wrote to the committees of Rhode Island, New Hampshire, New York and Philadelphia, explaining their course, acting, as they said, "in the faith that harmony and concurrence in action uniformly and firmly maintained, must finally conduct them to the end of their wishes, namely, a full enjoyment of constitutional liberty." They received cheering replies and encouraging assurances from all quarters.

At the meeting next morning, a letter to John Scollay

INTRODUCTION.

from the consignees, containing their long-delayed proposals, was read. They expressed sorrow that they could not return satisfactory answers to the two messages of the town, as it was utterly out of their power to send the teas back, but said they were willing to store them until they could communicate with their constituents, and receive their further orders respecting them. This letter irritated the meeting, and it declined to take action upon it.

Before taking final leave of these obstinate gentlemen, I make a few citations from the recently published volume of "The Diary and Letters of Thomas Hutchinson." Writing to his son at the castle on November 30, Hutchinson says: "The gentlemen (consignees), except your uncle Clarke, all went to the castle yesterday. I hope they will not comply with such a monstrous demand." Hancock and Adams, he says, were two of the guard of the tea ship.

Thomas Hutchinson, Jr., to his brother Elisha:

"CASTLE WILLIAM, December 14, 1773.

. . . I imagine you are anxious to know what the poor banished commissioners are doing at the castle. Our retreat here was sudden, but our enemies do not say we came too soon. How long we shall be imprisoned 'tis impossible to say. . . . I hear there is a meeting of the *mobility* to day, but don't know the result. I hardly think they will attempt sending the tea back, but am more sure it will not go many leagues. The commissioners are all with us, and we are as comfortable as we can be in a very cold place, driven from our families and business, with the months of January and February just at hand.

P.S. — Our situation is rendered more agreeable by the polite reception we met with from Col. Leslie, and the other gentlemen of the army."

And on January 9, 1774, he writes:

"The Bostonians say we shall not return to town without making concessions. I suppose we shall quit the castle sometime this week, as we are all provided with retreats in the country. I have had a disagreeable six weeks of it, but am in hopes the issue will be well."

And again, on January 21, dated Milton:

"I wrote you some time ago I was in hopes our harassment was drawing to a close, and that we should leave the castle last week. Mr. Faneuil and myself coming off caused a supposition that we intended for Boston, which was the cause of Saturday's notification which I sent you.[1] Mr. Faneuil is since returned to the castle, and I am really more confined than if I was there, as I keep pretty close to my home. Mr. Jonathan Clarke sails in a few days for England, of which I am very glad, as it may prevent misapprehension of our conduct on that side of the water.

A proclamation from the governor was brought in to the meeting by Sheriff Greenleaf, which he begged leave of the moderator to read. Objection was made, but at the suggestion of Samuel Adams the meeting consented to hear it. The governor charged that the meeting of the previous day "openly violated, defied and set at naught the good and wholesome laws of the Province, and as great numbers were again assembled for like purposes, I warn," he said, "exhort and require you, and each of you, thus unlawfully assembled, forthwith to disperse, and to surcease all further unlawful proceedings at your peril." The reading was received with general and continued hisses, and a vote that the meeting would not disperse. Mr. Copley, the son-in-law of Mr. Clarke, inquired whether the meeting

---

[1] Probably the following handbill is referred to:

"Brethren and Fellow Citizens!

You may depend that those odious miscreants and detestable tools to ministry and government, the TEA CONSIGNEES, (those traitors to their country — butchers — who have done and are doing everything to murder and destroy all that shall stand in the way of their private interest,) are determined to come (from the castle) and reside again in the town of Boston! I therefore give you this early notice that you may hold yourselves in readiness on the shortest warning, to give them such a reception as such vile ingrates deserve.

(Signed),   JOYCE, Junior,
Chairman of the Committee for Tarring and Feathering.

☞ If any person shall be so hardy as to tear this down, he may expect my severest resentment.

J., Jun."

would hear the Messrs. Clarke, and whether they would be safe while coming to and returning from the meeting, and whether two hours would be allowed him in which to consult with them. The request of Copley, who was sincerely desirous of effecting a peaceful solution of the difficulty, was granted, and the meeting then adjourned until two o'clock.

The proceedings of this afternoon briefly stated were, the promise of Rotch, the owner, and Hall, the captain of the "Dartmouth," and the owners of the two other vessels expected with teas, that that article should not be landed, but should go back in the same ships, and the apology of Mr. Copley for the time he had taken, he having been obliged to go to the castle, where the consignees decided that it would be inexpedient for them to attend the meeting, but added to their former proposal that the tea should be submitted to the inspection of a committee, and also saying that as they had not been active in introducing the tea, they should do nothing to obstruct the people in returning it.

This was voted unsatisfactory. Resolves were then passed to the effect that all who imported tea were enemies to the country; that its landing and sale should be prevented, and that the tea should be returned to the place whence it came. And the meeting also voted to send these resolves to every seaport in the colonies and to England. The committee of correspondence was charged to make provision for the continuation of the watch, and "the brethren from the country" were thanked for their "countenance and union," and desired to afford their assistance on notice being given, and it was also declared to be "the determination of this body to carry their votes and resolves into execution at the risk of life and property."

Speaking of this meeting, Hutchinson says: "A more determined spirit was conspicuous in this body than in any of the former assemblies of the people. It was composed of the lowest as well, and probably in as great proportion, as of the superior ranks and orders, and all had an equal voice. No eccentric or irregular motions were suffered to take place. All seemed to have been the plan of a few, it may be of a single person."

And in a private letter, dated December 1, Hutchinson writes:

"While the rabble was together in one place, I was in another, not far distant, with his majesty's council, urging them to join with me in some measure to break up this unlawful assembly, but to no purpose. I hope the consignees will continue firm, and should not have the least doubt of it if it was not for the solicitation of the friends of Mr. Clarke. If they go the lengths they threaten, I shall be obliged to retire to the castle, as I cannot otherwise make any exertions in support of the king's authority."

The committee of correspondence omitted no step that prudence or caution could suggest to carry out the determination of the town. A letter from Philadelphia, just then received, said: "Our tea consignees have all resigned, and you need not fear, the tea will not be landed here nor at New York. All that we fear is that you will shrink at Boston. May God give you virtue enough to save the liberties of your country!"

A second and a third vessel soon arrived, and the selectmen gave peremptory orders, to prevent clandestine landing of the tea, and directed them to be anchored by the side of the "Dartmouth," at Griffin's Wharf. One guard answered for the three vessels. As the time drew near for the landing or return of the tea, the excitement of the community increased. "Where the present disorder will end," wrote

INTRODUCTION.

Hutchinson, "I cannot make a probable conjecture ; the town is as furious as in the time of the stamp act." "The flame is kindled," so wrote the wife of John Adams, "and like lightning, it catches from soul to soul. . . . My heart beats at every whistle I hear, and I dare not express half my fears."

Twenty days after her arrival in the port, a vessel was liable to seizure for the non-payment of duties on articles imported in her, nor on landing a portion of her cargo, could she be legally cleared. On official advice from the governor to Colonel Leslie, commander of the castle, and Admiral Montagu, the latter ordered the ships of war, "Active" and "King Fisher," to guard the passages to the sea, and permit no unauthorized vessels to pass. "The patriots," said Hutchinson, "now found themselves in a web of inextricable difficulties." "But where there is a will there is a way," and the patriots had more resources than the governor dreamed of.

Rotch, the owner of the "Dartmouth," was summoned before the committee (December 11), and was asked by Samuel Adams, the chairman, why he had not kept his pledge, to send his vessel and tea back to London. He replied that it was out of his power to do so. He was advised to apply for a clearance and a pass. "The ship must go," said Adams, "the people of Boston and the neighboring towns absolutely require and expect it."

The journals of the day are filled with items concerning the tea question. Little else was now thought of. They contained the resolves of the Massachusetts towns, encouraging Boston to stand firm, and assuring her of their support, and accounts from Philadelphia and New York of the determination to nullify the tea act, and of the declination of the consignees in the latter place.

The "Gazette," of December 13, editorially says: "The minds of the public are greatly irritated at the delay of Mr. Rotch, to take the necessary steps towards complying with their peremptory requisition." On this day an important session of the committee of the five towns already named took place at Faneuil Hall. "No business transacted matter of record," is the brief but suggestive entry as to its doings.

Dorchester, in legal town meeting, declared that, "should this country be so unhappy as to see a day of trial for the recovery of its rights by a last and solemn appeal to Him who gave them, they should not be behind the bravest of our patriotic brethren." Marblehead affirmed that the proceedings of the brave citizens of Boston, and of other towns, in opposition to the landing of the tea, were rational, generous and just; that they were highly honored for their noble firmness in support of American liberty, and that the men of the town were ready with their lives to assist their brethren in opposing all measures tending to enslave the country." Under date of December 3, the people of Roxbury voted that they were in duty bound to join with Boston, and other sister towns, to preserve inviolate the liberties handed down by their ancestors. Next day the men of Charlestown declared themselves ready to risk their lives and fortunes. Newburyport, Malden, Lexington, Leicester, Fitchburg, Gloucester, and other towns, also proferred their aid when needed.

The "Gazette," under date of Salem, December 7, has the following: "By what we can learn from private intelligence, as well as the public proceedings of a number of principal towns contiguous to the capital, the people, if opposed in their proceedings with respect to the tea, are determined upon hazarding a brush, therefore those who are willing to bear a part in it in preserving the rights of this country, would do well to get suitably prepared." This looked like business.

On the morning of December 14, the following handbill appeared in Boston:

Friends! Brethren! Countrymen! The perfidious act of your reckless enemies to render ineffectual the late resolves of the body of the people, demands your assembling at the Old South Meeting House, precisely at ten o'clock this day, at which time the bells will ring."

The meeting thus called was largely attended. Samuel Phillips Savage,[1] of Weston, was chosen moderator. Bruce, the master of the "Eleanor," promised to ask for a clearance for London, when all his goods were landed, except the tea, but said that, if refused, "he was loth to stand the shot of thirty-two pounders." Rotch, accompanied by Samuel Adams, Benjamin Kent, and eight others, applied to the collector of the port for a clearance, and reported, on his return, that the collector desired to consult with the comptroller, and promised an answer on the following morning. The meeting then adjourned until Thursday.

Next day Rotch, with the Committee, proceeded to the Custom House. Harrison, the Collector, and Comptroller

---

[1] A merchant and a former selectman of Boston, member of the Provincial Congress, President of the Massachusetts Board of War during the Revolution, and from Nov. 2, 1775, till his death, a Judge of the Court of Common Pleas for Middlesex County. He died at Weston in December, 1797; aged 79.

INTRODUCTION.

Hallowell, were both present. The owner said that he was required and compelled at his peril by the meeting to make the demand for the clearance of his vessel for London, with the tea on board, and one of the committee stated that they were present only as witnesses. The Collector unequivocally and finally refused to grant his ship a clearance until it should be discharged of the teas. The result was reported to the meeting on the following morning.

The eventful Thursday, December 16, 1773, a day ever memorable in the annals of the town, witnessed the largest gathering yet seen at the Old South Meeeting House. Nearly seven thousand persons constituted the assembly. Business was laid aside, and notwithstanding the rain, at least two thousand people flocked in from the country for twenty miles around. This time there was no need of handbills—there were none. No effort was required to bring together the multitude that quietly but anxiously awaited the outcome of the meeting. The gravity of the situation was universally felt. Immediate action was necessary, as the twenty days allowed for clearance terminated that night. Then the revenue officials could take possession, and under cover of the naval force land the tea, and opposition to this would have caused bloody work. The patriots would gladly have avoided the issue, but it was forced upon them, and they could not recede with honor.

The committee having reported the failure of its application for a clearance, Rotch was directed to enter a protest at the Custom House, and to apply to the governor for a pass to proceed on this day with his vessel on his voyage for London. He replied that it was impracticable to comply

INTRODUCTION. LIX

with this requirement. He was then reminded of his promise, and on being asked if he would now direct the "Dartmouth" to sail, replied that he would not. The meeting, after directing him to use all possible dispatch in making his protest and procuring his pass, adjourned until three o'clock.

At the afternoon meeting, information was given that several towns had agreed not to use tea. A vote was taken to the effect that its use was improper and pernicious, and that it would be well for all the towns to appoint committees of inspection "to prevent this accursed tea" from coming among them. "Shall we abide by our former resolution with respect to the not suffering the tea to be landed?" was now the question. Samuel Adams, Dr. Thomas Young and Josiah Quincy, Jr.,[1] an ardent young patriot devotedly attached to the liberties of his country, were the principal speakers. Only a fragment of the speech of Quincy remains. Counselling moderation, and in a spirit of prophecy, he said:

"It is not, Mr. Moderator, the spirit that vapors within these walls that must stand us in stead. The exertions of this day will call forth the events which will make a very different spirit necessary for our salvation. Whoever supposes that shouts and hosannas will terminate the trials of the day, entertains a childish fancy. We must be grossly ignorant of the importance and value of the prize for which we contend; we must be equally ignorant of the power of those who have combined against us; we must be blind to that malice, inveteracy and insatiable revenge which actuates our enemies, public and private, abroad and in our bosom, to hope that we shall end this controversy without the sharpest, the sharpest conflicts; to flatter ourselves that popular resolves, popular harangues, popular acclamations, and popular vapor will vanquish our foes. Let us consider the issue.

[1] Quincy visited England in 1774, and died on the passage home, in sight of his native land, April 26, 1775. He was a lawyer, and in conjunction with John Adams, defended the perpetrators of the "Boston Massacre."

LX   INTRODUCTION.

Let us look to the end. Let us weigh and consider before we advance to those measures which must bring on the most trying and terrific struggle this country ever saw."

But the time for weighing and considering the business in hand had passed. Time pressed and decisive action alone remained. "Now that the hand is at the plough," it was said, "there must be no looking back."

At half-past four it was unanimously voted that the tea should not be landed. An effort was now made to dissolve the meeting, but it was continued at the request of some of those present from the country, who wished to hear the result of Rotch's application to the governor.

It was an unusual time of the year to be at a country seat, but Governor Hutchinson was found at his Milton residence by Rotch, who renewed his request for a pass. Questioned by the governor as to the intentions of the people, Rotch replied that they only intended to force the tea back to England, but that there might be some who desired that the vessel might go down the harbor and be brought to by a shot from the castle, that it might be said that the people had done everything in their power to send the tea back. "Catching at this straw, with the instinct of a drowning man," Hutchinson offered Rotch a letter to Admiral Montagu, commending ship and goods to his protection, if Rotch would agree to have his ship haul out into the stream, but he replied that none were willing to assist him in doing this, and that the attempt would subject him to the ill will of the people. Hutchinson then sternly repeated his refusal of a pass,[1] as it would have been "a direct countenancing and encouraging the violation of the

[1] Lord Mahon, a candid British historian, thinks this concession unwisely denied.

"Who knows how tea will mingle with salt water?" — JOHN ROWE. *Old South Church, Boston, Dec. 16, 1773.*

INTRODUCTION.

acts of trade." Thus closed the last opportunity for concession.

It is only fair to say that the performance of what he honestly believed to be his duty was as vital a consideration with Thomas Hutchinson, the royal governor, as opposition to measures which he believed to be hostile to the liberties of his country was to Samuel Adams, the popular leader. We can at this day well afford to mete out this tardy justice to a man whose motives and conduct have been so bitterly and unscrupulously vilified and maligned as have been those of Thomas Hutchinson.

When Rotch returned and told the result of his application, it was nearly six o'clock. Darkness had set in, and the Old South, dimly lighted with candles, was still filled with an anxious and impatient multitude. "Who knows," said John Rowe,[1] "how tea will mingle with salt water?"

---

[1] John Rowe, a prominent merchant and patriotic citizen of Boston, died February 17, 1787; aged 72 years. He was many years a Selectman, Overseer of the Poor, and representative to the General Court, and was chairman of the committee chosen June 16, 1779, to fix the prices of merchandise, and to bring to punishment all offenders against the act against monopoly and forestalling. He was a member of the First Lodge of Freemasons, Boston, in 1740; master of the same Lodge in 1749, and fifth Provincial Grand Master in 1768. When, in 1766, Rowe was proposed for representative, Samuel Adams artfully suggested another, by asking — with his eyes on Mr. Hancock's house — " Is there not another John that may do better?" The hint took, and the wealth and influence of Hancock were secured on the side of liberty. Rowe's mansion,— subsequently that of Judge Prescott, father of the historian, — stood on the

INTRODUCTION.

The people hurrahed vehemently, and the cry arose, "A mob! a mob!" A call to order restored quiet. Dr. Young then addressed the meeting, saying that Rotch was a good man, who had done all in his power to gratify the people, and charged them to do no hurt to his person or property.

To the final question then put to him, whether he would send his vessel back with the tea in her, under the present circumstances, he replied, that he could not, as he "apprehended that a compliance would prove his ruin." He also admitted that if called upon by the proper persons, he should attempt to land the tea for his own security.

Adams then arose and uttered the fateful words, "This meeting can do nothing more to save the country." This was doubtless the preconcerted signal for action, and it was answered by the men who sounded the war-whoop at the church door. The cry was re-echoed from the gallery, where a voice cried out, "Boston harbor a tea-pot to-night; hurrah for Griffin's wharf!" and the "Mohawks" passed on to cut the Gordian knot with their hatchets.

Silence was again commanded, when the people, after "manifesting a most exemplary patience and caution in the methods they had pursued to preserve the property of the East India Company, and to return it safe and untouched to its owners," perceiving that at every step they had been thwarted by the consignees and their coadjutors, then dissolved the meeting, giving three cheers as they dispersed.

Meanwhile a number of persons, variously estimated at from twenty to eighty, (their number increasing as they

spot lately occupied by Dr. Robbins' church, in Bedford Street. A wharf and street once bore the name of this true friend of his country, but the wharf alone retains the title. Since 1856, Rowe Street has been absorbed in Chauncy Street.

INTRODUCTION.   LXV

advanced,) some of them disguised as Indians, and armed
with hatchets or axes, hurried to Griffin's (now Liverpool)
wharf, boarded the ships, and, warning their crews and the
customs officers to keep out of the way, in less than three
hours time had broken and emptied into the dock three
hundred and forty-two chests of tea, valued at £18,000. The
deed was not that of a lawless mob, but the deliberate and
well-considered act of intelligent, as well as determined,
men. So careful were they not to destroy or injure private
property, that they even replaced a padlock they had
broken. There was no noise nor confusion. They
worked so quietly and systematically that those on shore
could distinctly hear the strokes of the hatchets. As soon
as the people learned what was going forward, they made
their way to the scene of operations, covering the wharves
in the vicinity, whence they looked on in silence during the
performance. The night was clear, the moon shone brilliantly,
no one was harmed, and the town was never more quiet.
Next day, the Dorchester shore was lined with tea, carried
thither by the wind and tide. The serious spirit in which
this deed was regarded by the leaders, is illustrated by the
act of one who, after assisting his apprentice to disguise
himself, dropped upon his knees and prayed fervently for
his safety, and the success of the enterprise.

Among the spectators of the scene were Dr. John Prince,
of Salem; John Andrews, and Dr. Hugh Williamson, who
afterwards underwent an examination respecting the affair
before the British House of Commons.

Where is now the wide Atlantic Avenue, the old footpath
under Fort Hill, known as Flounder Lane, and afterwards
as Broad Street, wound around the margin of the water.

INTRODUCTION.

Sea Street was its continuation to Wheeler's Point (the foot of Summer Street). Opposite where Hutchinson (now Pearl) Street entered Flounder Lane, was Griffin's Wharf. The laying out of Broad Street and Atlantic Avenue, and the consequent widening and filling in, have resulted in obliterating Griffin's Wharf, although in Liverpool wharf it has a legitimate successor. The old dock logs were found near the centre of the avenue. The coal office of the Messrs. Chapin now occupies the site rendered memorable by the exploit of the Boston tea party.

The destruction of the tea is said to have been planned in the "Long Room," over Edes & Gills' printing-office, on the easterly corner of Franklin Avenue and Court Street, where the "Daily Advertiser" building recently stood. In their back office some of the party it is said were disguised.

Among the members of the "Long Room Club," as those who usually met here were styled, were Samuel Adams, Hancock, Warren, Otis, Church, Samuel Dexter, Dr. Samuel Cooper, and his brother, William Cooper, Thomas Dawes, Samuel Phillips Savage, Royal Tyler, Paul Revere, Thomas Fleet, John Winthrop, William Molineux, and Thomas Melvill.

A similar claim is also made for the "Green Dragon" tavern, then known as the "Freemasons' Arms," which stood near the northerly corner of Union and Hanover Streets, where the Masonic Lodge of St. Andrew held its meetings. The honor belongs equally to both. In both, the consultations of the popular leaders were undoubtedly held and their plans laid. Prominent members of this Lodge, who were also active "Sons of Liberty," and members of the tea

INTRODUCTION.

party were, Paul Revere, Edward Proctor, Thomas Chase, Adam Collson, Samuel Peck and Thomas Urann. Its later members, also identified with the tea party, were Samuel Gore, Daniel Ingersoll, Henry Purkitt, Amos Lincoln, James Swan, Robert Davis, Abraham Hunt, Eliphalet Newell and Nathaniel Willis. Other prominent Free Masons active in the tea affair were Dr. Warren and John Rowe. The tradition of the Lodge is, that the preliminaries of the affair were arranged here, and that the execution of them was committed mainly to the North End Caucus, with the cooperation of the more daring of the "Sons of Liberty." The committee of safety also met here. The record book of the lodge, under date of November 30, 1773, says:

"Lodge met and adjourned. N. B.— The consignees of the tea took the brethren's time."

And on the eventful 16th of December:

"The Lodge met and closed on account of the few members in attendance. Adjourned until to-morrow evening."

Three different parties, one or two of whom were disguised, had been prepared beforehand for this event, by the leaders. Certain it is that there were several squads in different parts of the town, who disguised themselves at their own or their neighbors' houses, and who then rendezvoused at points previously designated, before going to the wharf. Quite an Indian village was improvised at the junction of Hollis and Tremont Streets. John Crane, Joseph Lovering, and the Bradlees occupied opposite corners of this locality, the house and carpenter shop of Crane adjoining the refidence of the famous Dr. Mather Byles. Captain Thomas Bolter and Samuel Fenno, also of the tea party, were near neighbors of Crane, and like him, were carpenters.

INTRODUCTION.

Joseph Lovering, Jr., related that he held the light for Crane and some of his neighbors, to disguise themselves, in Crane's shop. The four brothers Bradlee, and a brother-in-law, were prepared for the occasion at their house opposite.

Perhaps the best contemporaneous account of the affair is the following, from the "Massachusetts Gazette," of December 23:

"Just before the dissolution of the meeting," says the 'Gazette,' a number of brave and resolute men, dressed in the Indian manner, approached near the door of the assembly, and gave a war-whoop, which rang through the house, and was answered by some in the galleries, but silence was commanded, and a peaceable deportment enjoined until the dissolution. The Indians, as they were then called, repaired to the wharf, where the ships lay that had the tea on board, and were followed by hundreds of people, to see the event of the transactions of those who made so grotesque an appearance. The Indians immediately repaired on board Captain Hall's ship, where they hoisted out the chests of tea, and when on deck stove them and emptied the tea overboard. Having cleared this ship, they proceeded to Captain Bruce's, and then to Captain Coffin's brig. They applied themselves so dexterously to the destruction of this commodity, that in the space of three hours they broke up three hundred and forty-two chests, which was the whole number in these vessels, and discharged their contents into the dock. When the tide rose it floated the broken chests and the tea insomuch that the surface of the water was filled therewith a considerable way from the south part of the town to Dorchester Neck, and lodged on the shores. There was the greatest care taken to prevent the tea from being purloined by the populace; one or two being detected in endeavoring to pocket a small quantity were stripped of their acquisitions and very roughly handled. It is worthy of remark that although a considerable quantity of goods were still remaining on board the vessel, no injury was sustained. Such attention to private property was observed, that a small padlock belonging to the captain of one of the ships being broke, another was procured and sent to him. The town was very quiet during the whole evening and the night following. Those who were from the country went home with a merry heart, and the next day joy appeared in almost every countenance, some on account of the destruction of the tea, others on account of the quietness with which it was effected. One of the Monday's papers says the masters and owners are well pleased that their ships are thus cleared,"

INTRODUCTION. LXIX

Another Boston paper says:

"The people repaired to Griffin's wharf, where the tea vessels lay, proceeded to fix tackles and hoist the tea upon deck, cut the chests to pieces, and throw the tea over the side. . . . They began upon the two ships first, as they had nothing on board but the tea, then proceeded to the brig, which had hauled to the wharf but the day before, and had but a small part of her cargo out. The captain of the brig begged they would not begin with his vessel, as the tea was covered with goods belonging to different merchants in the town. They told him 'the tea they wanted, and the tea they would have, but if he would go into his cabin quietly, not one article of his goods should be hurt.' They immediately proceeded to remove the goods, and then to dispose of the tea."

From the "Evening Post" of Monday, December 20, 1773:

"Previous to the dissolution, a number of persons, supposed to be the aboriginal natives, from their complexion, approaching the door of the assembly, gave the war-whoop, which was answered by a few in the galleries of the house, where the crowded assembly was convened. Silence was commanded, and prudent and peaceable deportment again enjoined. The savages repaired to the ships which contained the pestilential tea, and had begun their ravages previous to the dissolution of the meeting."

Extract from the log-book of the "Dartmouth:"

"Thursday, December 16. This twenty-four hours rainy weather, terminating this day. Between six and seven o'clock this evening, came down to the wharf a body of about one thousand people, among them were a number dressed and whooping like Indians. They came on board the ship, and after warning myself and the custom-house officers to get out of the way, they undid the hatches and went down the hold, where was eighty whole, and thirty-four half chests, of tea, which they hoisted upon deck, and cut the chests to pieces, and hove the tea all overboard, where it was damaged and lost."

John Andrews, an eye-witness, in a letter to a friend relates particulars not elsewhere mentioned. While drinking tea at his house he heard "prodigious shouts," and went to the Old South Meeting House to ascertain the cause:

"The house was so crowded," he says, "that I could get no further than the porch, when I found the moderator was just declaring the meeting to be dissolved, which caused another general shout out-doors and in, and three cheers. What with that and the consequent noise of breaking up the meeting, you'd thought

INTRODUCTION.

the inhabitants of the infernal regions had broke loose. For my part, I went contentedly home and finished my tea, but was soon informed what was going forward. Not crediting it without ocular demonstration, I went and was satisfied. They mustered, I'm told, upon Fort Hill, to the number of about two hundred, and proceeded, two by two, to Griffin's wharf, where Hall, Bruce and Coffin lay. . . . The latter arrived at the wharf only the day before, and was freighted with a large quantity of other goods, which they took the greatest care not to injure in the least, and before nine o'clock in the evening every chest on board the three vessels was knocked to pieces and flung over the sides. They say the actors were Indians from Narragansett; whether they were or not, to a transient observer they appeared as such, being clothed in blankets, with their heads muffled, and copper-colored countenances, being each armed with a hatchet or axe, or pair of pistols, nor was their dialect different from what I conceive these geniuses to speak, as their jargon was unintelligible to all but themselves. Not the least insult was offered to any person save one Captain Connor, a letter of horses in this place, not many years since removed from dear Ireland, who had ript up the lining of his coat and waistcoat under the arms, and watching his opportunity, had nearly filled them with tea, but being detected, was handled pretty roughly. They not only stripped him of his clothes, but gave him a coat of mud, with a severe bruising into the bargain, and nothing but their utter aversion to making any disturbance prevented his being tarred and feathered."

Many interesting details are supplied by the reminiscences of the actors themselves, long afterwards. In the "Recollections of a Bostonian," published in the "Centinel," in 1821-22, the writer says he spent the night but one before the destruction of the tea as one of the guard detached from the new grenadier corps, in company with Gen. Knox, then one of its officers, on board one of the tea ships. He heard John Rowe suggest to the meeting in the Old South, "Who knows how tea will mingle with salt water?" a suggestion received with great applause. He further states that when the answer of the governor was reported to the meeting —

"An Indian yell was heard from the street. Mr. Samuel Adams cried out that it was a trick of their enemies to disturb the meeting, and requested the people to keep their places, but the people rushed out and accompanied the

Indians to the ships. The number of persons disguised as Indians is variously stated,—none put it lower than sixty, nor higher than eighty. The destruction was effected by them, and some young men who volunteered. One of the latter collected the tea which fell into the shoes of himself and companions, and put it in a phial and sealed it up,—now in his possession. . . . The hall of council is said to have been in the back room of Edes' printing-office, at the corner of the alley leading to Brattle Street Church, from Court Street."

In 1827, Joshua Wyeth, of Cincinnati, related the following particulars of the affair to Rev. Timothy Flint. Wyeth, then sixteen years old, was a journeyman blacksmith in the employ of Watson and Gridley. He says:

"Our numbers were between twenty-eight and thirty. Of my associates I only remember the names of Frothingham, Mead, Martin and Grant. Many of them were apprentices and journeymen, not a few, as was the case with myself, living with Tory masters. I had but a few hours warning of what was intended to be done. We first talked of firing the ships, but feared the fire would communicate to the town. We then proposed sinking them, but dropped that project through fear that we should alarm the town before we could get through with it. We had observed that very few persons remained on board the ships, and we finally concluded that we could take possession of them, and discharge the tea into the harbor without danger or opposition. One of the ships laid at the wharf, the others a little way out in the stream, with their warps made fast to the wharf. To prevent discovery, we agreed to wear ragged clothes and disfigure ourselves, dressing to resemble Indians as much as possible, smearing our faces with grease and lamp black or soot, and should not have known each other except by our voices. Our most intimate friends among the spectators had not the least knowledge of us. We surely resembled devils from the bottomless pit rather than men. At the appointed time we met in an old building at the head of the wharf, and fell in one after another, as if by accident, so as not to excite suspicion. We placed a sentry at the head of the wharf, another in the middle, and one on the bow of each ship as we took possession. We boarded the ship moored by the wharf, and our leader, in a very stern and resolute manner, ordered the captain and crew to open the hatchways, and hand us the hoisting tackle and ropes, assuring them that no harm was intended them. The captain asked what we intended to do. Our leader told him that we were going to unload the tea, and ordered him and the crew below. They instantly obeyed. Some of our number then jumped into the hold, and passed the chests to the tackle. As they were hauled on deck others knocked them open with axes, and others raised them to the railing and discharged their contents overboard. All who were not needed

INTRODUCTION.

for discharging this ship went on board the others, warped them to the wharf, when the same ceremonies were repeated. We were merry, in an undertone, at the idea of making so large a cup of tea for the fishes, but were as still as the nature of the case would admit, using no more words than were absolutely necessary. We stirred briskly in the business from the moment we left our dressing-room. I never worked harder in my life. While we were unloading, the people collected in great numbers about the wharf to see what was going on. They crowded around us so as to be much in our way. Our sentries were not armed, and could not stop any who insisted on passing. They were particularly charged to give us notice in case any known Tory came down to the wharf. There was much talk about this business next morning. We pretended to be as zealous to find out the perpetrators as the rest, and were all so close and loyal, that the whole affair remained in Egyptian darkness."

In 1835, a small volume appeared, entitled "Traits of the Tea Party," with a memoir of G. R. T. Hewes. From it we glean the following incidents.

Mr. Hewes thinks that among the speakers at the meeting on the afternoon of December 16, was John Hancock, who said that "the matter must be settled before twelve o'clock that night." Hewes positively affirms that he recognized Hancock, who worked by his side in the destruction of the tea, not only by his ruffles, which were accidentally exposed, and by his figure and gait, but by his voice and features, notwithstanding his paint, and the loosened club of hair behind. In this he was undoubtedly mistaken. Neither Hancock, Adams nor Warren were among the disguised Indians. There were enough who were competent for the business without them.

Just before the meeting dissolved, some one in the galleries (Mr. Pierce thinks it was Adam Collson) cried out with a loud voice, "Boston harbor a tea-pot to-night! Hurrah for Griffin's wharf!" This is probably the disorder checked by the chairman, and which was in response to the war-whoops outside. Three cheers were given by the meeting as it broke up.

The disguise of the Indians was hastily prepared. Many of them arrayed themselves in a store on Fort Hill. The original number of one of the parties was fifteen or twenty. Many others joined in the act of breaking up the boxes, who disguised themselves as best they could, and some, chiefly extempore volunteers, were not disguised at all. Hewes himself, while the crowd rushed down Milk Street, made his way to a blacksmith's shop, on Boylston's wharf, where he hastily begrimmed his face with a *soot*-able preparation, thence to the house of an acquaintance near Griffin's, where he got a blanket, which he wrapped around his person.

When he reached the wharf, there were many there, but no crowd. The moon shone brightly. From one hundred to one hundred and fifty were engaged. The whole were divided into three equal divisions, with a captain and boatswain for each. Hewes's whistling talent — a matter of public notoriety — procured him the position of boatswain in the party, under Captain Lendall Pitts, which boarded the brig. Many were fantastically arrayed in old frocks, red woolen caps or gowns, and all manner of like habiliments.

One of Pitts's first official acts was to send a message to the mate, who was in his cabin, for the use of a few lights and the brig's keys, so that as little damage as possible might be done to the vessel. The keys were handed over without a word, and he also provided candles. The three parties finished their separate tasks nearly at the same time, and without unnecessary delay. A number of sailors and others had joined them from time to time, and aided them in hoisting the chests from the hold.

INTRODUCTION.

Collecting on the wharf, which was now covered with spectators, a fresh inspection was instituted, and all the tea men were ordered to take off their shoes and empty them, which was supposed to be done. Pitts, who was a military man, and a prominent Son of Liberty, was appointed commander-in-chief; the company was formed in rank and file by his directions, with the aid of Barber, Proctor, and some others, and "shouldering arms,"—such as they had, tomahawks included,—they marched up the wharf, to what is now the east end of Pearl Street, back into town, and then separated and went quietly home.

All was done in plain sight of the British squadron, which lay less than a quarter of a mile distant. Admiral Montagu witnessed most of the affair from a more convenient point—the house of a Tory, named Coffin, on Atkinson Street, near the head of the wharf. Raising the window as they came along, he said, "Well, boys, you have had a fine, pleasant evening for your Indian caper, haven't you? But mind, you have got to pay the fiddler yet!"

"Oh, never mind!" shouted Pitts, "never mind, squire! Just come out here, if you please, and we'll settle the bill in two minutes." This caused a shout, the fife struck up a lively air, the admiral put the window down in a hurry, and the company marched on.

When Hewes reached home he told his wife the story. "Well, George," said she, "Did you bring me home a lot of it?" The only tea known to have been brought that night from the wharf was in the shoes of Thomas Melvill. A sample gathered on the Dorchester shore by Dr. Thaddeus M. Harris, is now preserved in the cabinet of the Antiquarian Society, at Worcester.

DIAGRAM SHOWING THE ROUTE TAKEN FROM THE OLD SOUTH CHURCH TO THE WHARF. *(See dotted lines.)*

One O'Connor, an Irishman, formerly a fellow apprentice with Hewes, attempted to secrete some of the tea. Hewes noticed a suspicious movement of his hands along the lining of his coat, and informed Pitts. Catching him by the skirts of his coat, he pulled him back as he was trying to escape, and he was quickly relieved of his cargo, as well as the apparel which contained it, and a few kicks were applied to hasten his retreat.

Early on the morning of the 17th, a long windrow of tea, "about as big as you ever saw of hay," was seen extending from the wharves down to the castle. A party of volunteers soon turned out in boats, and stirred it up in the "pot" pretty effectually

Those who undertook to preserve any of the poisonous herb were sharply looked after by the patriots. A Boston paper of January 3, 1774, says:

"Whereas, it was reported that one Withington, of Dorchester, had taken up and partly disposed of a chest of the East India Company's tea, a number of the Cape or Narragansett Indians went to the house of Captain Ebenezer Withington, and his brother Phillip, last Friday evening, and thoroughly searched their houses, without offering the least offence to any one. Finding no tea, they proceeded to the house of old Mr. Ebenezer Withington, at a place called Sodom, below Dorchester Meeting House, where they found part of a half-chest, which had floated, and was cast up on Dorchester Point. This they seized and brought to Boston Common, where they committed it to the flames."

Benjamin Simpson, a bricklayer's apprentice, says:

"After the meeting in the Old South was over, there was a cry in the gallery of 'every man to his tent.' We repaired to the wharf. I went on board both ships, but saw no person belonging to them. In a few minutes a number of men came on the wharf, (with the Indian pow-wow,) went on board the ships, then lying at the side of the wharf, the water in the dock not more than two feet deep. They began to throw the tea into the water, which went off with the

lxxviii   INTRODUCTION.

tide till the tea grounded. We soon found there was tea on board the brig also. A demand being made of it, the captain told us the whole of his cargo was on board; that the tea was directly under the hatches, which he would open if we would not damage anything but the tea, which was agreed to. The hatches were then opened, a man sent down to show us the tea, which we hoisted out, stove the chests and threw tea and all overboard. Those on board the ships did the same. I was on board the ships when the tea was so high by the side of them as to fall in, which was shovelled down more than once. We on board the brig were not disguised. I was then nineteen years old; I am now (1830) seventy-five."

Peter, the son of Benjamin Edes, the printer, in a letter to his grandson, Benjamin C. Edes, written in 1836, says of the tea party:

"I know but little about it, as I was not admitted into their presence, for fear, I suppose, of their being known. . . . I recollect perfectly well that in the afternoon preceding the evening of the destruction of the tea, a number of gentlemen met in the parlor of my father's house, — how many I cannot say. As I said before, I was not admitted into their presence; my station was in another room, to make punch for them, in the bowl[1] which is now in your possession, and which I filled several times. They remained in the house till dark, — I suppose to disguise themselves like Indians, — when they left the house, and proceeded to the wharves where the vessels lay. Before they reached there they were joined by hundreds. I thought I would take a walk to the wharves as a spectator, where was collected, I may say, as many as two thousand persons. The Indians worked smartly. Some were in the hold immediately after the hatches were broken open, fixing the ropes to the tea-chests, others were breaking open the chests, and others stood ready with hatchets to cut off the bindings of the chests and cast them overboard. I remained till I was tired, and fearing some disturbance might occur, went home, leaving the Indians working like good, industrious fellows. This is all I know about it."

The account given by General Ebenezer Stevens to his son, Horatio Gates Stevens, is as follows:

"I went from the Old South Meeting House just after dark. The party was about seventy or eighty. At the head of the wharf we met the detachment of

[1] This punch bowl is now in the possession of the Massachusetts Historical Society.

INTRODUCTION. LXXIX

our company (Paddock's Artillery) on guard, who joined us. I commenced with a party on board the vessel of which Hodgdon[1] was mate, (the 'Dartmouth') and as he knew me, I left that vessel with some of my comrades and went aboard another vessel, which lay at the opposite side of the wharf. Numbers of others took our places on board Hodgdon's vessel. We commenced handing the boxes of tea on deck, and first began breaking them with axes, but found much difficulty, owing to the boxes of tea being covered with canvas,— the mode that the article was then imported in. I think that all the tea was destroyed in about two hours. We were careful to prevent any being taken away. None of the party were painted as Indians, nor, that I know of, disguised, excepting that some of them stopped at a paint shop on the way, and daubed their faces with paint."

Robert Sessions, of South Wilbraham, (now Hampden) Mass., another actor in the scene, says:

"I was living in Boston at the time, in the family of a Mr. Davis, a lumber merchant, as a common laborer. On that eventful evening, when Mr. Davis came in from the town meeting, I asked him what was to be done with the tea. 'They are now throwing it overboard,' he replied. Receiving permission, I went immediately to the spot. Everything was as light as day, by the means of lamps and torches; a pin might be seen lying on the wharf. I went on board where they were at work, and took hold with my own hands. I was not one of those appointed to destroy the tea, and who disguised themselves as Indians, but was a volunteer; the disguised men being largely men of family and position in Boston, while I was a young man, whose home and relations were in Connecticut. The appointed and disguised party proving too small for the quick work necessary, other young men, similarly circumstanced with myself, joined them in their labors. The chests were drawn up by a tackle,— one man bringing them forward, another putting a rope around them, and others hoisting them to the deck and

Alex.ⁿ Hodgdon

[1] Alexander Hodgdon, mate of the "Dartmouth," was subsequently (1787-92) Treasurer of the State of Massachusetts. Stevens was at that time courting his sister (they were afterwards married), and was naturally desirous not to compromise himself or his friend.

carrying them to the vessel's side. The chests were then opened, the tea emptied over the side, and the chests thrown overboard. Perfect regularity prevailed during the whole transaction. Although there were many people on the wharf, entire silence prevailed, — no clamor, no talking. Nothing was meddled with but the teas on board. After having emptied the whole, the deck was swept clean, and everything put in its proper place. An officer on board was requested to come up from the cabin and see that no damage was done except to the tea. At about the close of the scene, a man was discovered making his way through the crowd with his pockets filled with tea. He was immediately laid hold of, and his coat skirts torn off, with their pockets, and thrown into the dock with the rest of the tea. I was obliged to leave the town at once, as it was of course known that I was concerned in the affair."

William Tudor, then a law student in the office of John Adams, and acquainted with some of the members of the tea party, gives in his "Life of James Otis," the following account of it:

"A band of eighteen or twenty young men (no one of whom was in any disguise), who had been prepared for the event, went by the Meeting House giving a shout. It was echoed by some within; others exclaimed, 'the Mohawks are come!;' the assembly broke up and a part of it followed this body of young men to Griffin's wharf. Three different parties, composed of trust-worthy persons, many of whom were in after life among the most respectable citizens of the town, had been prepared, in conformity to the secret resolves of the political leaders, to act as circumstances should require. They were seventy or eighty in all, and when every attempt to have the tea returned had failed, it was immediately made known to them, and they proceeded at once to throw the obnoxious merchandise into the water. One, if not two of these parties, wore a kind of Indian disguise. Two of these persons, in passing over Fort Hill to the scene of operations, met a British officer who, on observing them, naturally enough drew his sword. As they approached, one of the Indians drew a pistol, and said to the officer, 'The path is wide enough for us all; we have nothing to do with you, and intend you no harm; if you keep your own way peaceably, we shall keep ours.'"

Henry Purkitt,, Samuel Sprague and John Hooten, (all living in 1835,) were apprentices of about the same age. Purkitt and Dolbear were apprentices with Peck, the cooper, in Essex Street. While at their work they heard a loud

INTRODUCTION.   LXXXI

whistle, which startled them, and which they followed till it brought them to the wharf. Their part of the play was on the flats, by the side of one of the vessels, — for it was nearly low tide, — and with other boys, by direction of the commander, to break up more thoroughly the fragments of chests and masses of tea thrown over in too great haste. They found their return upon deck much facilitated by the immense pile which had accumulated beneath and around them. The commander acted as an interpreter for those persons, — apparently five or six aboard each vessel, — who especially assumed the Indian guise. These were no doubt among the principal directors of the whole affair. They affected to issue their orders from time to time in an Indian jargon, the interpreter communicating what the chiefs said; attended to the procuring of keys and lights, the raising of the derricks, trampling the tea into the mud, sweeping the decks at the close of the scene, calling up the mate to report whether everything (except, of course, the tea) was left as they found it, etc.

Purkitt and Dolbear went home early. Peck, who was believed to be one of the chiefs, came in rather softly, at one o'clock in the morning. The boys noticed some indications of red paint behind his ears, next day. The only tools they used were staves, which they made before starting.

David Kinnison, the last survivor of the tea party, died at Chicago in 1852, at the great age of one hundred and fifteen. He was one of seventeen inhabitants of Lebanon, Maine, who had associated themselves together as a political club, and who had determined, at all hazards, to destroy the tea, whether assisted or not. Some of them repairing to Boston, joined the party, and twenty-four, disguised as Indians, hastened on board the ships, twelve armed with muskets and bayonets, the rest with tomahawks and clubs. They expected to have a fight, not doubting that an effort would be made for their arrest, and agreed at the outset to stand by each other to the last. They also pledged themselves not to reveal the names of the party. Owing to the great age of Kinnison, when this relation was made to Mr. Lossing, it is possibly in some particulars erroneous, and is given only as a piece of original evidence, and simply for what it is worth.

With a British squadron and British troops so near at hand, it seems strange that the party was not interrupted. The probable reason is, that something far more serious was expected on any attempt to land the tea, and that the authorities, the owners of the ships, the consignees of the tea, and all others concerned, were glad to be thus extricated from a serious dilemma. They, however, could not be called upon to interfere, except by the civil authorities, in case of a riot.

Governor Hutchinson says "the tea could have been secured in the town in no other way than by landing marines from the men-of-war, or bringing to town the regiment which was at the castle, to remove the guards from the ships and to take their places." This would have brought on a greater convulsion than there was any danger of in 1770, and it would not have been possible, when two regiments were forced out of the town, for so small a body of troops to have kept possession of the place. He did not suppose such a measure would be approved of in England, nor was he sure of support from any one person in authority. There was not a justice of peace, sheriff, constable or peace officer in the province who would venture to take cognizance of any breach of law against the general bent of the people. So many of the actors were universally known that a proclamation, with a reward for discovery, would have been ridiculed. Hutchinson submitted the consideration of the affair to the council, and that body promised to give it attention, but nothing came of it. "Of the thousands concerned in the transaction," wrote General Gage to the historian Chalmers, "or who were spectators of it, only one witness could be procured to give testimony against them, and that one conditionally that the delinquents should be tried in England." So far as is known, only a single person was arrested,—a Mr. Eckley, and he was never brought to trial.

A fourth tea-ship, destined for Boston, was wrecked on Cape Cod. The few chests of tea saved from her cargo were, by the governor's order, placed in the castle. Twenty-eight chests, brought a little later by another vessel from London, on the joint account of Boston merchants, were destroyed by a disguised party, on March 7, 1774. The people of Charlestown destroyed, in the market place, all the tea they could find in the town, paying the owners its value. Other towns did the same.

An account of the transaction, drawn up by the Boston committee, was carried by Paul Revere, to New York and Philadelphia. When the news reached New York, vast numbers of the people collected. They were in high spirits, one and all declaring that the ships with tea on board, designed for that port, should on arrival be sent back, or the tea destroyed. They highly extolled the Bostonians for what the people had done, and immediately forwarded the news to Philadelphia. When Revere, on his return, brought word that Governor Tryon had engaged to send the New York tea-ships back, all the bells in Boston were rung next morning.

Extract from a letter to the Sons of Liberty, in New York, dated Boston, December 17, 1773:

"The bearer is chosen by the committee from a number of gentlemen, who volunteered to carry you this intelligence. We are in a perfect jubilee. Not a Tory in the whole community can find the least fault with our proceedings. . . . The spirit of the people throughout the country is to be described by no terms in my power. Their conduct last night surprised the admiral and English gentlemen, who observed that these were not a mob of disorderly rabble, (as they have been reported,) but men of sense, coolness and intrepidity."

The tea shipped to South Carolina (two hundred and fifty-seven chests) arrived on the second of December. So strenuous was the opposition to its being landed, that the consignees were persuaded to resign. Though the collector, after the twentieth day, seized the dutiable article, as no one would sell it or pay the duty, it perished in the damp cellars where it was stored.

On December 25, news reached Philadelphia that its tea-ship was at Chester. The Delaware pilots had been warned, by printed handbills, not to conduct any tea-ships into the harbor, as they were only sent for the purpose of enslaving and poisoning the Americans. Four miles below the town it came to anchor. On the 27th, news of what had occurred in Boston having arrived, five thousand men collected in town meeting at an hour's notice. At their suggestion, the consignee, who came as passenger, resigned, and the captain agreed to take his ship and cargo back to London the very next day.

The ship "Nancy," Captain Lockyer, destined for New York, having been blown off the coast, refitted at Antigua, and proceeding thence to New York, arrived there April 18,

1774. Some of the committee went on board and prevented her coming up to the city, but the captain was allowed to procure some necessary stores, and then, by the advice of the consignees, returned to London without breaking bulk. A quantity of tea — private property — was imported from London, and an application from the consignee to have it returned to England was refused by the custom-house officers. A number of "Mohawks" then took charge of the business, and emptied the whole of it into the sea.

A few days later, Captain Chambers, master of the ship "London," trading to New York, who had on a former occasion received the thanks of her citizens for refusing to bring the East India Company's tea, was detected in introducing eighteen boxes of fine tea, curiously concealed between blankets, etc., which he intended to smuggle, but the people having discovered it, immediately threw it into the sea, and the captain, to escape the wrath of the people, took refuge in Captain Lockyer's vessel, and sailed for England.

Opposition to the obnoxious tea duty had by no means subsided, when, in October, 1774, the brigantine "Peggy Stewart" approached Annapolis, Maryland, with a cargo of tea on board. At once there was a great commotion. Terror seized the owners. They applied to Charles Carroll for advice. He told them there was but one way to save their persons and property from swift destruction, and that was to burn their vessel and cargo instantly, and in sight of the people. It was done, and the flames did for Annapolis what the "Mohawks" had done for Boston.

"This," said Hutchinson, referring to the action of Boston,

"was the boldest stroke that had been struck in America." Writing to Sir Francis Bernard, he spoke of it as "an unfortunate event, and what every body supposed impossible after so many men of property had made part of the meetings, and were in danger of being liable for the value of it. It would have given me a much more painful reflection," he continued, "if I had saved it by any concession to a lawless and highly criminal assembly of men, to whose proceedings the loss must be consequently attributed, and the probability is that it was a part of their plan from the beginning."

"We do console ourselves," wrote John Scollay, chairman of the Selectmen of Boston, and prominent in the affair, "that we have acted constitutionally."

"The most magnificent movement of all," wrote John Adams in his diary. "There is a dignity, a majesty, a solemnity in this last effort of the patriots that I greatly admire. This destruction of the tea is so bold, so daring, so firm, so intrepid and inflexible, and it must have so important consequences, and so lasting, that I cannot but consider it as an epoch in history. The question is whether the destruction of the tea was necessary? I apprehend it was absolutely and indispensably so. . . . 'To let it be landed would be giving up the principle of taxation by Parliamentary authority, against which the continent has struggled for ten years. . . . But, it will be said, it might have been left in the care of a committee of the town, or in Castle William. To this many objections may be urged."

The historian Ramsay says: "If the American position was right in relation to taxation, the destruction of the tea was warranted by the great law of self-preservation. For it was not possible for them by any other means within the compass of probability to discharge the duty they owed to their country."

"I cannot but express my admiration of the conduct of this people," writes an 'Impartial Observer' in the "Boston Evening Post" of December 20, 1773. . . . "I shall return home doubly fortified in my resolution to prevent that deprecated calamity, the landing the tea in Rhode Island, and console myself with the happier assurance that my brethren have not less resolution than their neighbors."

"It became," says Hon. Robert C. Winthrop, "a simple question, which should go under, British tea or American liberty? That volunteer band of Liberty Boys performed their work 'better than they knew,' averting contingencies which must have caused immediate bloodshed, and accomplishing results of the greatest importance to the American cause."

. Wm. C. Rives, in his Life of James Madison, says: "This memorable occurrence was undoubtedly, in the immediate sequence of the events which it produced, the proximate cause of the American Revolution."

A Tory pamphleteer of the time gives us the Loyalist view of the affair. He says: "Now the crime of the Bostonians was a compound of the grossest injury and insult. It was an act of the highest insolence towards government, such as mildness itself cannot overlook or forgive. The injustice of the deed was also most atrocious, as it was the destruction of property to a vast amount, when it was known that the nation was obliged in honor to protect it."

We subjoin some of the comments of candid British writers respecting the affair. Mr. Massey says: "The question of taxation was virtually settled by this signal

INTRODUCTION.

failure to enforce the law, or rather by the absence of any attempt to protect the property of merchants who had made their ventures by the express authority, if not at the instance of the British government."

While speaking of the destruction of the tea as the "crowning outrage," Lecky says, "It will probably strike the reader that every argument which shewed that the tea duty was not a grievance, was equally powerful to show that it was perfectly useless as a means of obtaining a revenue. It would be difficult indeed to find a more curious instance of legislative incapacity than the whole transaction displayed."

Hear Carlyle:

"Thursday, December 16, 1773. What a contention is going on far over seas at Boston, New England. The case is well known and still memorable to mankind. British parliament, after nine years of the saddest haggling, and baffling to and fro under constitutional stress of weather, and such east winds and west winds of parliamentary eloquence as seldom were, has made up its mind that America shall pay duty on their teas before infusing them, and America, Boston more especially, is tacitly determined that it will not, and that to avoid mistakes the teas shall never be landed at all. . . .

"Rotch's report done, the chairman (an Adams 'American Cato,' subsequently so called,) dissolves the sorrowful seven thousand, with these words, 'The meeting declares it can do nothing more to save the country," we'll naturally go home then and weep. Hark however! almost on the instant, in front of the Old South Meeting House, a terrific war-whoop, and about fifty Mohawk Indians, with whom Adams seems to be acquainted, and speaks without interpreter: Aha !

"And sure enough, before the stroke of seven these fifty painted Mohawks are forward without noise to Griffin's wharf, have put sentries all round them, and in a great silence of the neighborhood, are busy in three gangs upon the dormant tea ships, opening their chests and punctually shaking them out into the sea. Listening from the distance you could hear distinctly the ripping open of the chests and no other sound. About ten P.M. all was finished, . . . the Mohawks gone like a dream, and Boston sleeping more silently even than usual."

In England, the news of the destruction of the tea at Boston was received with astonishment, not unmixed with anger. Men of all parties were swept into the hostile

INTRODUCTION.   LXXXIX

current. Coercive measures were at once brought forward in parliament. In the debates that ensued, a member said, "The town of Boston ought to be knocked about their ears and destroyed." Moderate and judicious men made a gallant stand against the bill shutting up the port of Boston, but the current was irresistible; and the measure, with others of like character, passed by overwhelming votes. Burke, on the question of the repeal of the tea tax, made one of his noblest efforts. Colonel Barré told the House that if they would keep their hands out of the pockets of the Americans they would be obedient subjects. Johnstone, formerly governor of Florida, who had before predicted to the East India Company, that exporting tea on their own account was absurd and would end in loss, now predicted that the Port Bill would, if passed, be productive of a general confederacy to resist the power of Britain, and end in a general revolt. His utterances were prophetic indeed. These measures did unite the colonies, and produced a general revolt ending in American independence.

Accounts vary greatly as to the number and appearance of the tea party. The original body which arrived so opportunely at the door of the "Old South," and which may have included Molineux, Revere, and the more prominent leaders, was probably not numerous. They, however, had passed the word, and trusty coadjutors were not long in following them. Colonel Tudor and Colonel Stevens say they were not disguised, but all other accounts state that they were in the Indian dress, or something resembling it.

The historian, Gordon, places their number at seventeen, "though judged to be many more as they ran across Fort Hill." "Our number was between twenty-eight and thirty,"

INTRODUCTION.

says Wyeth, one of the party. Hutchinson says about fifty, and many have since adopted his statement. Tudor, in his "Life of Otis," says seventy or eighty. Colonel Ebenezer Stevens agrees with him. "None put the number lower than sixty, nor higher than eighty," is the recollection of "a Bostonian," fifty years after the event. John Andrews was told that they mustered on Fort Hill to the number of about two hundred. "From one hundred to one hundred and fifty being more or less actively engaged" thought Hewes, one of the actors. "Two or three hundred dressed like Indians," wrote Dr. Cooper to Dr. Franklin.

These varying estimates may be accounted for in this way. Those who report the smaller number either repeated what they were told, or saw only one of the parties on its way to the ships, while the others speak of the entire body after its separate parts had united at the wharf. Some may mean only such of the party as were in Indian dress. If we place the number on board the ships at fifty or sixty, and estimate those at work by the sides of the vessels at sixty or seventy, we shall probably not be far out of the way, the whole number then aggregating from one hundred and ten to one hundred and thirty. The names of more than one hundred of these have been preserved.

Who were these men? "Depend upon it," said John Adams to Hezekiah Niles in 1819, "These were no ordinary Mohawks. The profound secrecy in which they have held their names, and the total abstinence of plunder, are proofs of the character of the men." But two of the recognized leaders of the people were there, — Dr. Young and Thomas Molineux. Most of them were mechanics and apprentices, but they were mechanics of the stamp of

Revere, Howard, Wheeler, Crane and Peck, men who could restrain and keep in due subordination the more fiery and dangerous element, always present in popular demonstrations. That element was not wholly absent on this occasion, for Mackintosh, the leader in the Stamp Act riots, was present with "his chickens," as he called them, and active in destroying the tea. There were also professional men, like Dr. Young and Dr. Story, and merchants, such as Molineux, Proctor, Melvill, Palmer, May, Pitts and Davis, men of high character and standing, so that all classes were fairly represented. As might be expected, those appointed for the work, and who were in Indian dress, were largely men of family and position in Boston.

A writer in the American Magazine of History attempts to discredit the statement that the party were in Indian dress, intimating that it was an afterthought, intended to deceive the authorities, and lead them to the belief that the disguise was too complete to allow of identification for arrest or punishment. Cavils like this are superfluous in view of the abundant testimony to the contrary. The sworn protest of Captain Bruce, of the "Eleanor," one of the tea-ships, given on a subsequent page in this volume, is of itself sufficient evidence upon this point. The number of those who, prepared as they were, on the spur of the moment, really bore any very great resemblance to Indians, was no doubt small. A large number of the actors hastily assumed such disguises as were nearest at hand.

No doubt the principals in this transaction pledged one another to keep their connection with it a profound secret, and they did so, but the young apprentices and volunteers, who, without premeditation, joined the party on its way to the wharf, were under no such restraint, and we can only wonder that they made no revelation concerning an event of such importance. It was not until a very late period of their lives that any of them opened their lips publicly about it, and when more than half a century had elapsed since it occurred.

The names of fifty-eight of these men, given below, are taken from Thatcher's "Traits of the Tea Party," published in 1835, while nine or ten of them were yet living, the source whence all later lists have been derived. Possibly this list is identical with that mentioned as having once been in the possession of Peter, the son of Benjamin Edes, the printer. Of this list it is safe to say that, while far from being complete, it is correct as far as it goes. The names that follow the list of 1835, have been gleaned from a great variety of sources, principally family tradition.

"List of the tea party, furnished in 1835, by an aged Bostonian, well acquainted with the subject, of the persons generally supposed, within his knowledge, to have been more or less actively engaged." Those starred were then living:

*George R. T. Hewes.	Nathaniel Green.
Joseph Shed.	*Benj. Simpson.
John Crane.	Joseph Eayres.
Josiah Wheeler.	Joseph Lee.
Thomas Urann.	William Molineux.
Adam Collson.	Paul Revere.
S. Coolidge.	John Spurr.
Joseph Payson.	Thomas Moore.
James Brewer.	Samuel Howard.
Thomas Bolter.	Matthew Loring.
Edward Proctor.	Thomas Spear.
Samuel Sloper.	Daniel Ingoldson.
Thomas Gerrish.	Richard Hunnewell.

INTRODUCTION.

*John Hooton.
*Jonathan Hunnewell.
Thomas Chase.
Thomas Melvill.
*Henry Purkitt.
Edward C. Howe.
Ebenezer Stevens.
Nicholas Campbell.
John Russell.
Thomas Porter.
William Hendley.
Benjamin Rice.
Samuel Gore.
Nathaniel Frothingham.
Moses Grant.
*Peter Slater.

James Starr.
Abraham Tower.
*William Pierce.
William Russell.
T. Gammell.
—— McIntosh.
Dr. Thomas Young.
Joshua Wyeth.
Edward Dolbear.
—— Martin.
Samuel Peck.
Lendall Pitts.
*Samuel Sprague.
Benjamin Clarke.
Richard Hunnewell, Jr.
*John Prince.

Additional names of the tea party, derived principally from family tradition:

Nathaniel Barber.
Samuel Barnard.
Henry Bass.
Edward Bates.
Nathaniel Bradlee.
David Bradlee.
Josiah Bradlee.
Thomas Bradlee.
Seth Ingersoll Brown.
Sephen Bruce.
Benjamin Burton.
George Carleton.
Gilbert Colesworthy.
John Cochran.
Gershom Collier.
James Foster Condy.
Samuel Cooper.
Thomas Dana, Jr.
Robert Davis.
Joseph Eaton:
—— Eckley.

William Etheridge.
Samuel Fenno.
Samuel Foster.
John Fulton.
Samuel Hammond.
John Hicks.
Samuel Hobbs.
Thomas Hunstable.
Abraham Hunt.
David Kinnison.
Amos Lincoln.
Thomas Machin.
Archibald Macneil.
John May.
—— Mead.
Anthony Morse.
Eliphalet Newell.
Joseph Pearse Palmer.
Jonathan Parker.
John Peters.
Samuel Pitts.

Henry Prentiss. John Truman.
John Randall. Isaac Williams.
Joseph Roby. David Williams.
Phineas Stearns. Jeremiah Williams.
Robert Sessions. Thomas Williams.
Elisha Story. Nathaniel Willis.
James Swan.

BIOGRAPHICAL NOTICES

OF THE

Boston Tea Party.

MAJOR NATHANIEL BARBER,

A prominent merchant and patriot of Boston, was one of the famous "Whig Club" of ante-revolutionary days, in which were James Otis, Dr. Church, Dr. Warren and other leaders of the popular party. In it Civil Rights and the British Constitution were standing topics for discussion. He was one of the committee of correspondence, from its creation in 1772, and afterwards of the committee of safety, and was naval officer of the port of Boston in 1784. He joined St. Andrew's Lodge of Freemasons in 1780, and died at his house, in Bear Lane, (Richmond Street,) October 13, 1787; aged 59. Before the Revolution he kept an insurance office in Fish (now North) Street.

SAMUEL BARNARD,

A major in the Revolutionary army, was born in Watertown, Mass., June 19, 1737; died August 8, 1782.

HENRY BASS,

A prominent "Son of Liberty," a merchant on Orange Street, residing in Rawson's Lane, (Bromfield Street,) died June 5, 1813; aged 74. He was the first volunteer on the roll of the guard of the tea-ship, November 29, 1773. Drake ("Old Landmarks of Boston,") says Samuel Adams and Major Melvill often passed a convivial evening, and ate a Sunday dinner, at his house.

Henry Bass [signature]

Captain THOMAS BOLTER,

A housewright, residing on Nassau (now Tremont) Street, died in August, 1811; aged 76. Mary, his widow, died May 30, 1813; aged 76.

DAVID, THOMAS, NATHANIEL, AND JOSIAH BRADLEE,

Were brothers, who lived in the house yet standing, on the southerly corner of Hollis and Tremont Streets. Their sister, Sarah, assisted her husband, John Fulton, and her brothers, to disguise themselves, having made preparations for the emergency a day or two beforehand, and afterwards followed them to the wharf, and saw the tea thrown into the dock. Soon returning, she had hot water in readiness

"Owe no man anything. Be true to thyself, to thy country, and to thy God."
— C. D. BRADLEE, Blackstone Square, Boston.

for them when they arrived, and assisted in removing the paint from their faces. As the story goes, before they could change their clothes, a British officer looked in to see if the young men were at home, having a suspicion that they were in the tea business. He found them in bed, and to all appearance asleep, they having slipped into bed without removing their "toggery," and feigning sleep. The officer departed satisfied. Mrs. Fulton helped to dress the wounds of the soldiers who were in the battle of Bunker Hill. She died in Medford, Mass., in 1836, and is the authority for the above statement. Of the brothers, —

David, was born November 24, 1742; died March 10, 1811.

Thomas, born December 4, 1744; died Oct. —, 1805.
Nathaniel, born February 16, 1746; died May 8, 1813.
Josiah, born March 24, 1754; died October 2, 1798.

The old house, built by Nathaniel, in 1771, is now the residence of his grandson, Nathaniel Bradlee Doggett, to whose son, Samuel Bradlee Doggett, I am indebted for the above facts.

JAMES BREWER,

Pump and blockmaker, in Summer Street, died in April, 1805. He took an active part in the early movements of the Revolution; was one of the volunteer guard on the "Dartmouth," November 30, 1773, and prominent in the destruction of her cargo, and was also one of the young men who removed at noon-day, and while it was under guard, the cannon from the gun-house on West Street, which afterwards found its way to Washington's camp. Some of the tea party met at his house, and were assisted in preparing themselves by his wife and daughter, who blackened their faces with burnt cork. He was a confidential messenger between Governor Hancock and Washington, and was afterwards a prisoner of war, having been taken in a privateer, in 1781. He was an early member of the Massachusetts Charitable Mechanic Association, and was also a member of the Massachusetts Lodge of Freemasons in 1792. His son, Thomas, a member of the City Council of Boston in 1825-26, died June 4, 1859; aged 78.

SETH INGERSOLL BROWN

Was born in Cambridge, Mass., March 13, 1750. He was the son of William Brown, born in 1683. Mr. Brown's trade was that of a house carpenter. In the lower part of his shop, in Charlestown, was stored the ammunition afterwards used in the battle of Bunker Hill. He was in full sympathy with the cause of liberty; was one of the "Mohawks" on the memorable 16th of December, and on that occasion was masked and painted, and bore a club. He used to relate to his daughters, that on returning home from the scene of destruction, he had to fight his way through the excited crowd, with his back to the houses, to avoid discovery. They kept his connection with the affair a profound secret many years, and when it was spoken of in their old age, excused their silence regarding it on the ground that they thought it was a disgrace, like a riot or a mob, and ought not to be told. At Bunker Hill he was

INTRODUCTION. xcix

wounded in the leg, and also received an injury to his eye. He said he should never forget the cry that went up during the battle, of "No ammunition ! no ammunition !" Mr. Brown served as an assistant commissary during the siege of Boston, and continued with the army until the war closed. He was paid off in worthless Continental money — there was no other — and it is related that his spunky little wife, indignant at the poor reward of such sacrifices as her husband had made, on receiving it from him, threw it all into the fire. She is described as short, stout and handsome, with long, straight, black hair, that fell almost to her feet.

After the war, Mr. Brown, with impaired health and eyesight, kept a tavern successively in Charlestown, Cambridge, Newton Corner, the Punch Bowl in Roxbury, and finally the Sun tavern, in Wing's Lane, (Elm Street,) Boston. He died in Charlestown, Mass., March 9, 1809, leaving several children by his second wife, Sarah Godding, of Cambridge. Three of his daughters, Cynthia, Harriet and Angeline — lived to be over eighty, — retained their memories and their mental faculties to the last, and preserved many interesting reminiscences of their father's revolutionary career. Mr. Brown was a good singer, and they recall this verse of a song, having reference to the battle of Bunker Hill:

> "We marchèd down to Charlestown ferry,
> And there we had our battle ;
> The shot it flew like pepper and salt,
> And made the old town rattle."

The name of Seth Ingersoll Brown is recorded on the monument, in Hope Cemetery, Worcester, Mass., erected in

INTRODUCTION.

1870, to the memory of Captain Peter Slater, and his associates of the Boston tea party. He is buried in the Granary burying-ground.

Of Mr. Brown's descendants, known in public life, may be mentioned Rev. John W. Hanson, D.D., of Chicago, Ill.; Rev. Warren H. Cudworth, D.D., formerly of East Boston; Harriet H. Robinson, who married William S. Robinson, ("Warrington,") journalist, and clerk of the Massachusetts House of Representatives from 1862 to 1873, and their elder daughter, Harriet R. Shattuck.

"Though none of his descendants will continue to bear his name, — the male branch being extinct in the third generation," writes his grand-daughter, Mrs. H. H. Robinson, "some of them have inherited his spirit of resistance to laws that compel them — his only surviving representatives, — "to submit to taxation without representation." To this lady we are indebted for the materials from which this notice is derived.

Some lines, written in 1773, by Susannah Clarke, "Warrington's" great grandmother's sister, serve to manifest the spirit that pervaded the country when non-tea drinking was held to be a religious duty by American women:

"We 'll lay hold of card and wheel,
And join our hands to turn and reel;
We 'll turn the tea all in the sea,
And all to keep our liberty.

We'll put on home-spun garbs,
And make tea of our garden herbs;
When we are dry we'll drink small beer,
And FREEDOM shall our spirits cheer."

STEPHEN BRUCE

Was a merchant, doing business at 28 State Street, and was one of the volunteer guard on the "Dartmouth." He was the first inspector of beef and pork, appointed by the State of Massachusetts, and was a man of sound judgment and inflexible integrity. He became a member of the Masonic Lodge of St. Andrew in 1779, and master in 1782. He died July 26, 1801.

Colonel BENJAMIN BURTON

Was born in the old Burton House, Thomaston, Maine, December 9, 1749, and died in Warren, Maine, May 23, 1835. Happening to be in Boston on a visit on the memorable 16th of December, 1773, he went with the crowd to the Old South Meeting House, and at the close of the meeting, heard the cry "Tea party! tea party!" Joining the party that boarded the tea-ships, he labored with all his might in throwing the tea into the water. It being about low tide, the tea rested on the bottom, and when the tide rose it floated, and was lodged by the surf along the shore. He was subsequently an officer in the Revolutionary army; was present at the surrender of Burgoyne, and himself fell into the hands of the enemy, in February, 1781, sharing in the imprisonment of General Peleg Wadsworth, at Castine, and in the daring escape of that officer. After the war, he was eight years a magistrate, and was often a member of the legislature.

NICHOLAS CAMPBELL

A native of the Island of Malta, died in Warren, R. I., July 23, 1829; aged ninety-seven. He came to this country just previous to the Revolution, during a great part of which he was employed in the marine service, and by many deeds of noble daring, aided the cause of liberty, and evinced his attachment to his adopted country. He had been a resident of Warren fifty-four years.

THOMAS CHASE,

One of the most active of the "Sons of Liberty," was a distiller, near the famous Liberty Tree, at the junction of Orange, Essex and Newbury Streets. In the office of Chase & Speakman the meetings of the committee of the "Sons" were held, of one of which John Adams has left an account. Chase was one of those who prepared and suspended the effigies of Bute and Oliver from Liberty Tree, on August 14, 1765. He was one of the volunteer guard on the "Dartmouth," on the night of November 29, 1773; was a member of the "Anti-Stamp Fire Society," formed soon after the passage of the Stamp Act, in 1765, and joined St. Andrew's Lodge of Freemasons in 1769.

BENJAMIN CLARKE

Was a cooper, in Ship Street, and in 1807 resided in Prince Street. He became a member of the Massachusetts Charitable Mechanic Association in 1801; of the Ancient and Honorable Artillery Company in 1806, and died in 1840.

JOHN COCHRAN,

Born in East Boston, in 1750; died in Belfast, Maine, October 30, 1839. The monument there erected to his memory bears the following inscription: "He was one of the memorable tea party at Boston, December 16, 1773." His only surviving son, of the same name, now (1884) resides at Belfast, at the age of eighty-three

GILBERT COLESWORTHY,

Born in Boston, December 23, 1744, removed to Nantucket, Mass., and died there in 1818.

GERSHOM COLLIER,

Of Chesterfield, Mass., died about the year 1825.

ADAM COLLSON

Was a leather dresser, near the "Great Trees," on Essex Street, as we learn by his advertisement soon after the passage of the Stamp Act, in which he says: "Understanding that many worthy tradesmen had agreed to wear nothing but leather for their working habits, 'he offers' to dress all sorts of skins suitable for that purpose." Collson was one of the volunteer guard on the "Dartmouth" on the night of November 30, 1773, and was said to be the person who, at the close of the meeting of December 16th, at the Old South, shouted from the gallery, "Boston harbor a tea-pot to-night!" He became a member of St. Andrew's Lodge of Freemasons in 1763, and at the time of his death, February 16, 1798, aged sixty, resided at 59 Marlboro' (Washington) Street. He was a member of the "Long Room" Club.

JAMES FOSTER CONDY,

A bookseller in Boston before the Revolution, doing business in Union Street, "opposite the cornfields," died in Haverhill, Mass., July 12, 1809.

SAMUEL COOPER

Was born in Boston, in 1755, and was living in Georgetown, D.C., in 1838. He was commissioned second lieutenant in Crane's artillery regiment, February 1, 1777;

INTRODUCTION.

quartermaster 14th May, 1778; lieutenant and adjutant in 1783. He was inspector of pot and pearl ashes in New York city and county, from 1808 to 1830. Adjutant-General Samuel Cooper, of the United States army, afterwards a general in the Confederate army, who died in 1877, was his son.

JOHN CRANE,

Colonel of the Massachusetts regiment of artillery in the Continental line of the Revolutionary army, was born in Milton, Mass., 7th December, 1744, and died in Whiting, Maine, 21st August, 1805. His education was scanty. In 1759, when only fifteen years of age, his father, Abijah was drafted as a soldier in the French war. John offered to go in his father's stead, and was laughed at on account of his youth. Nevertheless, the boy went and proved himself a brave lad, saving the life of a lame fellow-soldier, who had fallen when pursued by a party of Indians, at St. John's. He came to Boston in early life, married, and established himself in business as a house carpenter, — his house and shop being in Tremont Street, opposite Hollis. He assisted Major Paddock in setting out the elm trees on the Tremont Street mall, about the year 1765. These trees were old acquaintances of Crane's, having, like him, been transplanted from Milton. Naturally enough, in one of his ardent temperament, he at once identified himself with the active Sons of Liberty. One of the famous tea party, his career came near being permanently ended by the fall of a derrick, used in hoisting out the tea, which, falling upon him,

INTRODUCTION.

knocked him senseless. His comrades, supposing him killed, bore him to a neighboring carpenter's shop, and secreted the body under a pile of shavings. They afterwards took him to his home, where good nursing and a strong constitution, soon brought him round. The late Colonel Joseph Lovering, who lived opposite to Crane, used to relate that he held the light on that memorable evening, while Crane, and other young men, his neighbors, disguised themselves for the occasion. House building and other branches of industry having been paralyzed by the "Boston Port Bill," Crane, with his partner, Ebenezer Stevens, (also one of the tea party,) went to Providence, R.I., where they followed their business with success, until the war broke out. Both had been members of Paddock's artillery company, a corps famous for having furnished a large number of valuable officers to that arm of the service in the Revolutionary army, among whom may be named John Crane, Ebenezer Stevens, William Perkins, Henry Burbeck, John Lillie, and David Bryant. Crane had been commissioned by Governor Wanton, captain-lieutenant of the train of artillery of the colony of Rhode Island, December 12, 1774, (barely one year after the destruction of the tea,) and immediately after receiving the news of the battle of Lexington, he was made captain of the train attached to the Rhode Island "Army of Observation," commanded by General Nathaniel Greene. Crane's command, "all well accoutred, with four excellent field-pieces marched, in the latter part of May, to join the American army near Boston. . They made a very military appearance, and are, without exception, as complete a body of men as any in the king's dominions." Stevens was a lieutenant in this company. Possessing a remarkably keen vision, Crane was exceedingly skilful as an artillerist, a talent he had frequent opportunities to display during the siege of Boston. Early in the morning of July 8, 1775, Majors Tupper and Crane, with a number of volunteers, attacked the British advance guard at Brown's House, on Boston Neck, (near the corner of Newton Street and Blackstone Square.) routed them, and burned two houses. This was regarded as a brave and well-executed affair, and is noteworthy as being the only hostile encounter that has ever taken place in the old limits of Boston. During the siege he was stationed at the Roxbury line, and was engaged in several skirmishes on the islands in the harbor. Commissioned major of Knox's regiment, January 1, 1776, he accompanied the army to New York, and while cannonading a British frigate which was passing his batteries at Corlaers Hook, was severely wounded by a cannon ball, which carried off a part of his foot, disabling him for several months, and finally causing his death—the wound having closed. He raised in Massachusetts, in 1777, the 3d regiment of Continental artillery, which he commanded till the war ended, when he was brevetted a brigadier-general, (October 10, 1783,) his commission as colonel dating from January 1, 1777. This corps, officered chiefly from those who had been trained under Paddock, Gridley and Knox, was not exceeded in discipline, valor, and usefulness by any in the service. It was principally employed with the main army, and was an essential auxiliary in the most important operations. Portions of it were also with Sullivan in the Rhode Island campaign, with Gates at Saratoga, and in the heroic defence of Red Bank, on the Delaware. After the peace, Crane formed a partnership with Colonel Lemuel Trescott, in the lumber business, in

Passamaquoddy, Maine, in which they were unsuccessful. The connection was soon dissolved, and Crane finally settled in Whiting, Washington County, Maine, where he had a grant of two hundred acres of land, for his Revolutionary services, from the legislature of Massachusetts. Colonel Crane was five feet eight inches in height, stout and thick set. He possessed great energy, resolution and courage, and at critical moments was perfectly cool. In 1790, he was commissioned judge of the Court of Common Pleas, by Governor Hancock. While at the lines on Boston Neck, Crane aimed a ball at a house near his own, belonging to Rev. Dr. Byles, the Tory, but succeeded only in knocking the ridge pole from his own dwelling. He became a Freemason in 1781, joining an army lodge at West Point, and was also a member of the Massachusetts Society of the Cincinnati. Colonel Crane, in 1767, married Mehitabel Wheeler, believed to have been a sister of Captain Josiah Wheeler, a member of the tea party. His three daughters married three sons of Colonel John Allan, who, with his Indian allies, rendered valuable service to the patriot cause in protecting throughout the Revolutionary war, the exposed north-eastern frontier. William Allan, who married Alice Crane, was the grandfather of George H. Allan, of Boston, from whom many of the above facts have been derived, and who has made extensive collections relative to the Allan and Crane families.

Major ROBERT DAVIS,

Merchant, importer of groceries, wines and liquors, did business at No. 1 Cornhill, and resided in Orange Street. He was the son of Joshua and Sarah (Pierpont) Davis, and was born 24th January, 1747. He was a Son of Liberty, and as an officer in Crafts's artillery regiment, took part in the expulsion of the British fleet from Boston harbor, ultimately attaining the rank of major. Member of the Ancient and Honorable Artillery Company in 1786. His brothers, Caleb and Amasa, were also prominent Revolutionary characters, — the latter having been forty years quartermaster-general of Massachusetts. Robert Davis became a member of St. Andrew's Lodge of Freemasons in 1777, and died in November, 1798. His daughter, Clarissa, widow of William Ely, was living in Hartford in 1873, at the age of eighty-two.

EDWARD DOLBEAR

Was a fellow-apprentice, and afterwards a partner with Henry Purkitt, in the business of a cooper, in South Street. His residence was near Dr. Eliot's Meeting House, where he died, in April, 1796.

Captain JOSEPH EATON

Was an eccentric and excitable, but patriotic citizen, a hatter by trade. He claimed to have hauled down the first British colors at the outset of the Revolution, and to have loaded a cannon in State Street to prevent the regulars from landing, in 1774. He was a member of the Ancient and Honorable Artillery Company; was an ardent democrat, and late in life wore a cocked hat, and styled himself "general."

JOSEPH EAYRES

Was one of the volunteer guard on the "Dartmouth" on the night of November 30, 1773. He was a housewright in Essex Street, in 1789.

———— ECKLEY,

A barber, was informed against for his participation in the destruction of the tea, and committed to prison. The Sons of Liberty supported him while in confinement, and also provided for his family. He was finally liberated, and the person who informed against him was tarred and feathered, and paraded through the town with labels on his breast and back bearing his name, and the word "INFORMER" in large letters.

WILLIAM ETHERIDGE,

Who was a mason, while engaged in throwing the tea overboard, was recognized by his apprentice, Samuel Sprague.

SAMUEL FENNO,

A housewright, was born in Boston, in 1745, and died in 1806. He lived in a large wooden house on Tremont

INTRODUCTION.

Street, near Hollis Street, and was a near neighbor of Crane, Lovering and the Bradlees. He was a man of unusual reticence, but noted for courage and patriotism. From 1773 till his death, he kept a vow never to drink tea. In 1797 he married Mary, the sister of Joseph Hiller, the first collector of the port of Salem, and was the father of Captain John Fenno, a pioneer in the China trade.

CAPTAIN SAMUEL FOSTER,

Of Roxbury, was a sergeant in Captain Moses Whiting's minute company, at Lexington, and as a captain in Greaton's regiment, served at Ticonderoga, and in other campaigns of the Revolutionary war.

NATHANIEL FROTHINGHAM,

A coachmaker, at No. 5 West Street, died January 22, 1825; aged seventy-nine.

Nath'l Frothingham

JOHN GAMMELL

Was of Scotch descent, his father bearing the same name, having come to Boston about the year 1740. The son was born in Boston, in 1749, and died there in 1827. His trade was that of a carpenter, in which capacity he served seven years in the construction department of the Revolutionary army. He was a participant in the Stamp Act riots, and in the destruction of the tea, and in his later years used to describe the latter affair, with great minuteness, in the presence of his family, and on the anniversary of the day would act over again the part he then performed. He married Margaret Urann, by whom he had fifteen children. As the initials J and T were in old times interchangeable, there is no doubt but this is the person mentioned in the list of 1835.

<small>Communicated by Prof. Wm. Gammell, of Brown University, and Rev. Sereno Dwight Gammell, of Wellington, O., grandsons of John Gammell.</small>

SAMUEL GORE,

Born in Boston, February 6, 1751; died November 16, 1831. Captain John Gore, his father, a lieutenant in the Ancient and Honorable Artillery Company, in 1753, had, by industry, acquired considerable wealth. Being a Tory, he left Boston with the British army in 1776, but afterwards returned. Samuel followed his father's trade, that of a painter, in Court Street, at the corner of Gore's Alley, (Brattle Street,) but, unlike him, was an ardent patriot. He was one of the party of young men who, at noon-day, and under the eyes of the British guard, carried off and secreted the cannon from the gun-house that stood opposite the mall at the corner of West Street. His companions in this daring feat were Nathaniel Balch, James Brewer, Moses Grant, Jeremiah Gridley and —— Whiston. Mr. Gore was one of those who established the glass-works in Essex Street, a speculation by which he unfortunately lost all the accumulations of many years of untiring industry. He was a member of the Masonic Lodge of St. Andrew, in 1778, and was the first treasurer of the Massachusetts Charitable Mechanic Association. Governor Christopher Gore was a younger brother. He was a man of superior intelligence, kindness of heart, and courtesy of manner.

MOSES GRANT,

Son of Samuel, and father of Deacon Moses Grant, was born in Boston, March 13, 1743; died December 22, 1817. He was an upholsterer, on Union Street, and his son, Moses, was a partner with him until his death. He was an ardent patriot; was one of the volunteer guard on the "Dartmouth," on the night of November 29, 1773; was one of those who seized and carried off the cannon from the gunhouse, on West Street, and one of the renowned "tea party." Member of the company of cadets, and a deacon of Brattle Street church.

NATHANIEL GREENE

Was in 1789 register of deeds, at 42 Cornhill. He was an ardent Son of Liberty, and was present at the public celebration in Dorchester, where three hundred of them gathered, August 14, 1769.

Nath'l Greene

SAMUEL HAMMOND,

One of the tea party, died at Wadsborough, Vt., January 4, 1842; aged ninety-three. In 1774, he began a settlement near Otter Creek, N.Y., but the hostility of the Indians drove him to Vermont, and he fixed his residence at Wadsborough. He was an industrious farmer, and an active patriot.

WILLIAM HENDLEY,

A Revolutionary pensioner, formerly of Roxbury, died at Waldoborough, Me., in February, 1830; aged eighty-two. He was a mason, on Newbury Street, Boston, in 1796.

GEORGE ROBERT TWELVES HEWES,

Born in Boston, September 5, 1742, died at Richfield, Otsego County, N.Y., November 5, 1840, at the great age of ninety-eight. His education was scanty; farming, fishing, and shoemaking being his chief occupations. Excitable and patriotic, he took part in numerous ante-Revolutionary disturbances in Boston, and engaged in the naval, and afterwards in the military, service of his country during the war. His residence was at the Bulls Head, an old house that stood on the north-east corner of Congress and Water Streets. The most detailed account we have of the destruction of the tea in Boston, was given by him, in "Traits of the Tea Party," by B. B. Thatcher, published in New York, in 1835. An oil portrait of Hewes is in the possession of his grandson, Mr. Henry Hewes, of West Medford, Mass.

JOHN HICKS,

Born in Cambridge, May 23, 1725, was one of the earliest martyrs to the cause of American liberty, having been killed by the British on their retreat from Lexington, April 19, 1775. John, his son, was a printer, and became in 1773, a partner with Nathaniel Mills, in the publication of the "Post Boy," a Tory sheet.

SAMUEL HOBBS,

Born in Lincoln, Mass., in 1750, died at Sturbridge, Mass., in May, 1823. While in the employ of Simeon Pratt, a tanner, of Roxbury, he aided in throwing the tea overboard, and afterwards said that chests of Bohea, weighing three hundred and sixty pounds, were rather heavy to lift. He settled in Sturbridge, as a farmer, also carrying on his trade of tanner and currier. By his wife, Lucy Munroe, of Lexington, he had four children.

JOHN HOOTON,

An apprentice, while at work on the tea, saw a person who looked like a countryman, coming up with a small boat to the ship's side, evidently intending to secure a cargo for his own use. He, and three or four other "North Enders," as full of spirit as himself, being directed to dislodge the interloper, jumped over and beat the canoe from under him "in the twinkling of an eye." Hooton was an oarmaker, at Hooton's wharf, Fish Street, in 1789. In 1806, he was a wood-wharfinger, on North Street, residing in Prince Street. In 1838, his residence was in Chelsea, Mass.

SAMUEL HOWARD,

A Boston shipwright, resided at the "Mansion House," as it was called, which stood on the site of the Mariner's Church, North Square. He died here in January, 1797, at the age of forty-five, and was buried in Copp's Hill. His wife, Anna Lillie, the sister of Major John Lillie, of the Revolutionary army, died in North Andover, in 1804. Two of our well-known fellow citizens, Henry Lillie Pierce and Edward L. Pierce, are grandsons of Major Lillie. Theophilus Lillie, the Tory trader, who was mobbed during the tea excitement, was Major Lillie's uncle. Caroline, the youngest child of Samuel and Anna Lillie Howard, born October 3, 1794, married Rev. Samuel Gilman, D.D., of Charleston, S.C. She is still living, at the age of ninety, and resides at Tiverton, R.I., with a daughter Mrs. Bowen.

GEORGE ROBERT TWELVES HUGHES.

EDWARD C. HOWE,

Ropemaker, died in September, 1821, aged seventy-nine. E. C. Howe & Son (Joseph) dissolved partnership August 1, 1800. Howe's rope-walk was one of seven, on the west side of Pearl Street, all of which were burnt in July, 1794.

JONATHAN HUNNEWELL,

The son of Richard, followed his father's trade, of a mason. He was born in Boston, May 19, 1759; died in April, 1842. He was several times a selectman of Boston, and member of both branches of the legislature; was connected with many benevolent institutions, and was for nine years president of the Massachusetts Charitable Mechanic Association. He was one of the principal agents in the establishment of the glass-works, in Boston and Chelmsford, and its failure, in 1822, made him a poor man. For many years he had a country residence at Newton, which was the seat of a generous hospitality. The latter part of his life was passed in seclusion, at Roxbury, where, in 1800, he married the widow Theoda Davis. Jonathan, his brother, and Richard, his father, were also in the tea party.

RICHARD HUNNEWELL.

A mason, member of the Massachusetts Charitable Mechanic Association, died in October, 1805. He resided in Essex Street; was an active Son of Liberty, and was one of the volunteer guard on the "Dartmouth," on the night of

November 30, 1773. His two sons, fourteen and sixteen years of age, were with him at the throwing overboard of the tea.

THOMAS HUNSTABLE

Was born in 1753. He lived for many years on Brighton Street, and was a Freemason.

Colonel ABRAHAM HUNT

Was born in Braintree, Mass., June 2, 1748; died December 5, 1793. He was apprenticed, in 1763, to Edmund Quincy, who kept a wine-store, and was afterwards connected with him in the trade. In 1789, his place of business was in Middle (Hanover) Street, and his residence on Federal Street. He served as lieutenant and adjutant at the siege of Boston; was in the Ticonderoga campaign, remaining some years in the service, which he quitted with the rank of captain. June 24, 1781, he was agent for the privateer "Buccaneer," Captain Hoysted Hacker. For a time he was inspector of the ports of Boston and Charlestown. In 1777, he became a member of St. Andrew's Lodge of Freemasons. October 15, 1771, he married Mary St. Leger. His orderly books for June and July, 1775, are in the possession of his grandson, —— Urann, Esq.

DANIEL INGERSOLL,

Housewright, formerly of Boston, died in Keene, N.H., October 17, 1829, aged seventy-nine. He was a member of St. Andrew's Lodge, in 1782.

DAVID KINNISON,

The last of the tea party, born in Old Kingston, near Portsmouth, Maine, November 17, 1736; died in Chicago, February 24, 1852; aged one hundred and fifteen years. Up to the Revolution he was a farmer, at Lebanon, whence, with a few comrades, members of a political club, he went to Boston, with the express purpose of destroying the tea. He was in active service during the war, participating in many battles, and was a prisoner among the Indians at its close. He was a farmer, at Wells, Maine, when the war of 1812 broke out, and was in the battles at Sackett's Harbor and Williamsburg, and in the latter was badly wounded in the hand, by a grape-shot. He afterwards lived at Lyme, and at Sackett's Harbor, N. Y., and in July, 1845, went to Chicago. At Lyme, while felling a tree, he was struck down by a limb, which fractured his skull, broke his collar bone, and two of his ribs. While engaged in discharging a cannon, at a training at Sackett's Harbor, both legs were broken and badly shattered. Up to 1848 he had always made something by his labor, and was the father of twenty-two children. He learned to read when past sixty. A daughter, who survived in 1848, was made acquainted in that year with her father's existence, by the publication of Mr. Lossing's "Field Book of the Revolution." Hastening to him, she smoothed the patriarch's pillow in his passage to the grave.

JOSEPH LEE,

Merchant, on Long Wharf, afterwards at 9 Doane Street, was a member of Massachusetts Lodge of Freemasons, in 1773, and died February 6, 1831; aged eighty-six.

Joseph Lee

AMOS LINCOLN,

Born in Hingham, Mass., March 17, 1753, died at Quincy, Mass., January 15, 1829. He was apprenticed to a Mr. Crafts, at the North End, who, on the evening of December 16, 1773, secretly procured for him an Indian disguise, dressed him in his own chamber, — darkening his face to the required tint, — and then, dropping on his knees, prayed most fervently that he might be protected in the enterprise in which he was engaged. Joining Stark's New Hampshire regiment, he was in the battle of Bunker Hill; was afterwards a captain in Craft's artillery regiment, and was at one time in charge of the castle, in Boston harbor. When Shays' insurrection broke out, he assisted in its suppression. He was a housewright of much skill. The wood-work of the State House was under his charge, and evinces the grace and beauty of his workmanship. He married a daughter of Paul Revere. His grandson, Frederick W. Lincoln, has been mayor of Boston. He joined St. Andrew's

Lodge of Freemasons, in 1777. Governor Levi Lincoln, of Massachusetts, and Governor Enoch Lincoln, of Maine, were nephews of Captain Amos Lincoln.

Amos Lincoln

MATTHEW LORING

Was a cordwainer, on Devonshire Street, residing on Brattle Street. He died November 7, 1829; aged seventy-nine.

THOMAS MACHIN

Was born in Staffordshire, England, 20th March, 1744; was employed by Brindley in canal construction, and in 1772 came to America, and settled in Boston. He was wounded at Bunker Hill, while acting as lieutenant of artillery; 18th January, 1776, was commissioned second lieutenant in Col. Knox's artillery regiment, and was employed from April to June in that year in laying out the fortifications for the defence of the town and harbor of Boston; from July, 1776, to 1781, he was employed in constructing the fortifications which were to render the Hudson impassable to British vessels. In October, 1777, when Forts Montgomery and Clinton were taken by the British, Captain Machin was wounded by a musket-ball, which entered his breast and passed out under his right shoulder. In April, 1779, he accompanied Colonel Van Schaick's expedition against the Onondagas, of which he kept a journal, and in June joined Sullivan's expedition to the Genesee Valley, as engineer. A map of this expedition, executed by him, was in the possession of his son, Captain Thomas Machin. In the fall of 1781, he aided in laying out the works of the American army, then besieging Yorktown. In 1783, he began a settlement at New Grange, Ulster County, and in the following year erected several mills at the Great Pond, a few miles west of Newburgh. March 12, 1793, he was commissioned a captain, to take rank as such from 21st August, 1780. In January, 1797, he removed to Montgomery County, N.Y., where he practised surveying, and where he died, at his residence in Charleston, a part of the old town of Mohawk, 3d April, 1816; Member of Army Lodge, West Point, 1782.

ARCHIBALD MACNEIL,

Died in Scituate, Mass., February 1, 1840; aged ninety.

CAPTAIN MACKINTOSH

Was a tradesman of Boston, who acquired great prominence in the local disturbances of the town, prior to the outbreak of the Revolution, but who disappears from her history after that period. He first came into notice as the leader of the South End party, in the celebration of Pope Day, which took place on the 5th of November, in commemoration of the discovery of the gunpowder plot. In 1765, the two factions of the North and South Ends harmonized, and after a friendly meeting in King (now State) Street, marched together to Liberty Tree. The leaders, — Mackintosh of the South, and Swift of the North End, — appeared in military habits, with small canes resting on their left arms, having music in front and flank. All the property used on such occasions was afterwards burnt on Copp's Hill. Mackintosh was a ringleader in the riot of August 26, 1765, when Lieutenant-Governor Hutchinson's house was destroyed, and was arrested in King Street next day, but was immediately released by the sheriff, on the demand of a number of merchants, and other persons of character and property.

From the Diary and Letters of Thomas Hutchinson, we take the following passage :

"The Governor had summoned a council the day after the riot. The sheriff attended, and upon enquiring, it appeared that one Mackintosh, a shoemaker, was among the most active in destroying the Lieutenant-Governor's house and furniture. A warrant was given to the sheriff to apprehend him by name, with divers others. Mackintosh appeared in King Street, and the sheriff took him, but soon discharged him, and returned to the council chamber, where he gave an account of his taking him, and that Mr. Nathaniel Coffin, and several other gentlemen, came to him and told him that it had been agreed that the cadets, and many other persons, should appear in arms the next evening, as a guard and security against a fresh riot, which was feared, and said to have been threatened, but not a man would appear unless Mackintosh was discharged. The Lieutenant-Governor asked, 'And did you discharge him?' 'Yes.' 'Then you have not done your duty.' And this was all the notice taken of the discharge. The true reason of thus distinguishing Mackintosh was that he could discover who employed him, whereas the other persons apprehended were such as had collected together without knowing of any previous plan."

Mackintosh was styled the "First Captain-General of Liberty Tree," and had charge of the illuminations, hanging of effigies, etc. Long afterward, in speaking of the tea party, he said, "It was my chickens that did the job." My informant, Mr. Schuler Merrill, then a boy of ten, remarks that it was a mystery to him, at that time, "how chickens could have anything to do with a tea party!" Mackintosh is described by Merrill as "of slight build, sandy complexion, and nervous temperament." He died in extreme poverty, at North Haverhill, N.H., about the year 1812, at the age of seventy. His unmarked grave can be pointed out by Mr. Merrill, who still resides in North Haverhill, at the age of eighty-two.

COLONEL JOHN MAY,

Born in Boston, November 24, 1748, died July 16, 1812. On the afternoon of December 16, 1773, he went in haste to his home, on North Square, and said to his young wife, "Nabby, let me have a beefsteak as quickly as possible." While he was eating it, a rap was heard on the window, and he rose at once from the unfinished meal and departed. He returned late, tired and uncommunicative. In the morning, there was found in his shoes, and scattered upon the floor, a quantity of *tea*. The inevitable inference from these circumstances is strengthened by evidence of a very different character. Near the close of Major Melvill's life, he gave, while dining with a few friends, some anecdotes of the tea party, and turning to Henry Knox May, the son of Colonel May, he said, "Harry, there was one John there." The son, who knew the family tradition, was eager to learn more. "Not now, Harry," said the major, "Come and see me, and I will tell you all about it." Mr. May called repeatedly upon him, but could never obtain any further satisfaction respecting the object of his inquiry. Colonel May was a man of great energy and courage, an ardent patriot, and one not likely to be overlooked in the making-up of a company of picked men for such an enterprise. He was at one time colonel of the Boston regiment, and was for many years a selectman, and a firewarden of the town. He made a journey of exploration to the Ohio region, in 1788 and 1789, an account of which has been published. Two sons, Frederick and George Washington May, were skilful physicians, in Washington, D.C. He has numerous grandchildren living, among them Prof. Edward Tuckerman, of Amherst College, and Samuel P. Tuckerman, Mus. Doc., resident in England.

I am indebted for the above facts to my friend, John Joseph May, Esq., of Mayfield, Dorchester.

MAJOR THOMAS MELVILL

Was born in Boston, January 16, 1751, and died there September 16, 1832. He was the grandson of Thomas, minister of Scoonie Parish, Fifeshire, a cadet of the Scottish family of the Earls of Leven and Melvill. Allan, his father, left Scotland, and established himself in business in Boston, in 1743. Left an orphan at the age of ten, the care of his education devolved upon his maternal grandmother, Mrs. Mary Cargill, a relative of the celebrated surgeon, Dr. Abernethy. Young Melvill was graduated at Princeton College, in 1769, with a view to the ministry, but impaired health led him to make a visit to Scotland, in 1771. Returning to Boston, in 1773, he established himself in business in that town, just at the time when the tea excitement began, and being strongly in sympathy with the "Sons of Liberty," and a member of the Long Room Club, he took an active part in the event of December 16, 1773. Some of the tea taken from his shoes, after his return home, was preserved, and is now in the possession of Mrs. Thomas Melvill, of Galena, Illinois. The picture here given is a fac-simile of the venerable relic itself. In 1773, he received the honorary degree of Master of Arts, from Harvard College. In 1774, Melvill married Priscilla, daughter of John Scollay, a prominent Boston merchant. He had been selected by General Warren as one of his aids, just before the fall of the latter at Bunker's Hill, and was successively captain and major in Colonel Thomas Crafts's regiment of artillery, raised for the defence of the State. When, soon after the evacuation of the town, in March, 1776, the British fleet was driven from Boston harbor, Captain Melvill discharged the first guns at the hostile ships, from his battery, at Nantasket. He afterwards served in the Rhode Island campaigns of 1777 and 1779. After the war, he was naval officer of the port of Boston, in 1786-89, and through the influence of his friend, Samuel Adams, was, in the latter year, appointed inspector under the United States Government, a post which he held until made naval officer, in 1811. President Jackson removed him from this office in 1829, after which period he was a member of the Massachusetts House of Representatives. From 1779 to 1825, he was one of the firewards of Boston, and on retiring from his forty-seven years' service, was made the recipient of a silver pitcher as a testimonial of the appreciation of his services, by his associates. Major Melvill's long and honorable connection with the Boston Fire Department began in the good old times, when the firewards carried staves, tipped at the end with a brass flame, and marshalled the bystanders into lines for passing buckets of water to the scene of conflagration. One of the town engines was named "Melvill," in honor of the major, whose death was finally caused by over-fatigue at a fire near his house. He was a Democrat, and a firm friend of Samuel

The relic of the Tea, destroyed in Boston, Dec. 16th 1773. Found on the following morning, by Thomas Melvill, in his shoes; and put into this phial, for preservation.

INTRODUCTION. cxxxv

Adams, of whom he had a small portrait, by Copley, now at Harvard University. At the time of his death, he was president of the Massachusetts Charitable Society. Major Melvill was a man of sound judgment and strict integrity. He is still remembered by our older citizens as the last to wear, in Boston, a cocked hat and small clothes — the costume of the Revolution. Herman Melville, a grandson, has attained popularity as an author. The front door of Major Melvill's residence, which formerly stood near the easterly corner of Green and Staniford Streets, now does similar duty for the house at the corner of Bartlett and Lambert Streets, Roxbury. The accompanying portrait is from an oil painting in the possession of his grand-daughter, Mrs. Samuel Downer, of Dorchester. The beautiful garden at Downer Landing, Hingham, near which is her summer residence, perpetuates the name of this worthy and patriotic citizen of Boston. Admitted member Mass. Lodge, 1772.

WILLIAM MOLINEUX,

A distinguished and patriotic merchant of Boston, died there October 22, 1774; aged fifty-eight. Like Revere and Johonnot, he was of Huguenot ancestry. About the year 1760, he, with William Phillips and others, established the "Manufactory House," on the east side of what is now Hamilton Place. Here the people were taught spinning and weaving, free of cost, and soon many were clad in garments of their own manufacture. This building was put to other uses, in 1768. Molineux, from the very beginning of the dispute with the mother country, was an active and influential Whig. He was a member of the "Long Room Club," formed in 1762, and of the Sons of Liberty, in 1765; was one of the Boston committee of correspondence, from its origin, in 1772; one of the committee, and its spokesman, appointed by the Liberty Tree meeting, November 4, to request the consignees of the tea to resign, and took an active part in all the public meetings that followed. Molineux and Dr. Young were the only prominent leaders of the people who were known to have been actively present at the destruction of the tea. Molineux was a member of a committee, of which Samuel Adams was the chairman, to demand the removal of the British troops from Boston. John Adams relates that Molineux was obliged to march by the side of the troops, to protect them from the indignation of the people. With the exception of Samuel Adams, no name is oftener found, in connection with the public acts of the day, than that of William Molineux, and his death, a few months before the war broke out, was a great loss to the patriot cause. While the Boston Port Bill was under discussion in the British Cabinet, Governor Hutchinson was told by Lord Mansfield that the Lords of the Council had their pens ready to sign the warrant for the transportation to England and trial of Adams, Molineux and others, for high treason, but were prevented by the doubts of the Attorney and Solicitor-Generals as to the sufficiency of the evidence to convict them. Molineux resided at the corner of Beacon and Mount Vernon Streets, near John Hancock, where in 1760 he built a mansion-house that was considered as "quite splendid" for those days.

THOMAS MOORE,

Son of Hugh Moore, wharfinger, on Fish Street, informs his father's "good customers," in the *Gazette* of November 24, 1773, that he "carries on the business as usual, and solicits their custom." Ben. Russell speaks of seeing Moore and his (Russell's) father blacking each other's faces on the 16th of December, 1773. He died in August, 1813; aged sixty.

ANTHONY MORSE.

"Anthony Morse, my father, afterwards a lieutenant during the Revolutionary war, and Mr. Joseph Roby, now (1819) of Hanover, N. H., were active in the destruction of the tea, December 16, 1773."

— Niles' Acts and Principles of the Revolution, p. 326.

JOSEPH MOUNTFORD,

A cooper, on Prince Street, died in Pepperill, Mass., May 11, 1838; aged eighty-eight.

E[LIPHELET N[EWELL],

Of Charlestown, repeatedly informed Dr. Joseph Bartlett, author of a historical sketch of that town, that he was one of the Indians who destroyed the tea in Boston harbor. He was a member of the Masonic Lodge of St. Andrew, in 1778.

Eliphelet Newell

JOSEPH PEARSE PALMER

Was the only son of General Joseph Palmer, a prominent actor in the Revolutionary drama in Massachusetts, and Mary, the sister of Judge Richard Cranch, who resided in that part of Braintree called Germantown. Before the war he dealt in West India goods and hardware, at the town dock. Of his share in the tea party his widow says: "One evening, about ten o'clock, hearing the gate and door open, I opened the parlor door, and there stood three stout-looking Indians. I screamed, and should have fainted, but recognized my husband's voice saying, 'Don't be frightened, Betty, it is I. We have only been making a little saltwater tea.' His two companions were Foster Condy and Stephen Bruce. Soon after this, Secretary Flucker called upon my husband, and said to him, 'Joe, you are so obnoxious to the British Government, that you had better leave town.' Accordingly we left town, and went to live in part of my father's house, in Watertown." During the war, Mr. Palmer served in Boston and in Rhode Island, first as brigade major, and next as quartermaster-general. Soon after his father's death, in 1788, he went to Vermont, with Colonel Keith, to examine the facilities for establishing themselves in some branch of the iron business. Shortly after he reached Windsor he lost his life, having accidentally fallen from a bridge, then erecting over the Connecticut. He left a numerous family. His daughter, Mary, married Royal Tyler, of Vt. Member Massachusetts Lodge, 1773.

JONATHAN PARKER

Was a Roxbury farmer, a "high Son of Liberty," who safely brought through the British lines on the Neck, and secreted in Muddy Pond Woods, the two cannon which, by a clever stratagem, had been taken from the gun-house, on Boston common, at noon-day. Next day, a party of Red Coats were in Roxbury searching for them in every direction, but in vain. These are supposed to be the same pieces now in the chamber at the top of Bunker Hill Monument. Parker took the guns from the stable of the second house west from the court house, on the south side of Court Street. He brought a load of hay, and took home a load of stable manure, the guns being in the bottom of the wagon.

JOSEPH PAYSON

Was a housewright, on Foster's wharf, in 1789, and at 5 Bennet Street, in 1796. He was a descendant of Edward Payson, one of the first settlers of Roxbury, and his wife, Mary, a sister of the Apostle Eliot, and was born in 1743.

SAMUEL PECK

Was a cooper, and in 1789 did business at Hallowell's shipyard, near the foot of Milk Street. He was a prominent Son of Liberty, also a leading and influential member of the North End Caucus. He was one of the guard on the "Dartmouth," on the night of November 30, 1773, and on the morning following the destruction of the tea, his apprentices noticed traces of red paint behind his ears. He was thought to have been one of the leaders in the affair. He joined the Masonic Lodge of St. Andrew in 1756.

Samuel Peck

JOHN PETERS,

A native of Lisbon, Portugal, died in Philadelphia, April 23, 1832, at the great age of one hundred years, five months and twenty-three days. He was able to attend to his business up to the close of 1831. He came to America soon after the earthquake of 1755, and settled in Boston. He was one of the tea party; was in the battles of Lexington and Bunker Hill, — in which latter he lost a finger, — at Princeton, Monmouth and Trenton. He was also at the capture of Burgoyne and of Cornwallis, was again wounded, and after being discharged, in 1783, resided in Philadelphia, where he reared a numerous family.

WILLIAM PIERCE,

Born in Boston, December 25, 1744, died October 10, 1840.

He served his time with John Adams, a barber, in Dock Square, at the sign of the "Great Boot," and opened a shop for himself in Marshall Street, some years before the Revolution. His shop was a sort of exchange for the gossip current at the North End, and was frequented by many celebrated residents of that locality. He boasted of having shaved Franklin, and he stated that Franklin told him that he was born in the house on the corner of Union and Hanover. Streets, at the sign of the "Blue Ball." Hewes relates that Pierce was one of those that boarded the ships on December 16, 1773. He continued actively engaged in his business until the year 1835, having followed his profession seventy-six years!

LENDALL PITTS,

Youngest son of Hon. James Pitts, a merchant and an active patriot of Boston; born in 1747, died December 31, 1787, and being captain of a volunteer company, was buried with military honors. According to Hewes, Pitts commanded the division of the tea party that boarded the brig "Beaver," and after the affair was over, formed the party in military order, with the aid of Major Barber and Colonel Proctor, and marched them back into town. A solemn pledge, for the protection of those engaged in this affair, was entered into by the committee of correspondence, — of whom Lendall's brother, John Pitts, was one, — about a week afterwards, when it was currently supposed that those who had borne a part in that daring performance would

INTRODUCTION.

be arrested, if discovered, and executed for treason. It was worded as follows:

"The subscribers do engage to exert our utmost influence to support and vindicate each other, and any person or persons who may be likely to suffer for any noble efforts they may have made to save their country, by defeating the operations of the British Parliament, expressly designed to extort a revenue from the Colonies against their consent."

The names of four members of this family are prominently associated with the tea episode at Boston. James Pitts, the father, (H. U., 1731,) an eminent and wealthy merchant, who, as member of the Governor's Council, thwarted the chief-magistrate, Hutchinson, in his efforts to have the tea landed, and who died in Dunstable, Mass., January 25, 1776; aged sixty-four. His sons, — JOHN, born in 1737, (H. U., 1757,) a selectman, and on the committee to urge the consignees to resign; an active member of the committee of correspondence, of the Provincial Congress of 1775; Speaker of the House in 1778, and member of the senate in 1780-84, who died at Tyngsboro', Mass., in 1815; SAMUEL, born in 1745, an officer in the company of cadets, said also to have been one of the tea party, and LENDALL, the leader of the party, noted above, who was clerk of the market in 1775-6, and an officer in Hancock's cadets. The sons all had Huguenot blood in their veins, their mother being a sister of James Bowdoin. All were merchants, and active Sons of Liberty, and prior to the Revolution, were in business together, engaged in extensive commercial transactions. Pitts's wharf was just north of Faneuil Hall Market. Pitts Street perpetuates the name and fame of this noted family; no one of their descendants bearing the name now surviving in Boston. The Pitts mansion, a favorite place of meeting

for the Boston patriots, occupied the ground now covered by the Howard Atheneum. The accompanying portrait of Lendall Pitts is taken from a painting owned by his grandson, Lendall Pitts Cazeau, of Roxbury.

For many of the above facts I am indebted to the Pitts "Memorial," by Daniel Goodwin, Jr., of Chicago.

Lendall Pitts

THOMAS PORTER,

A merchant, formerly of Boston, died in Alexandria, Va., in June, 1800.

Captain HENRY PRENTISS,

Born in Holliston, Mass., March 27, 1749, died in Medfield, Mass., August 31, 1821; son of Rev. Joshua, forty-five years pastor of the Holliston church. Captain Prentiss served during the Revolutionary war, at Cambridge, at Long Island, and at Trenton. He was an Overseer of the Poor, in Boston, in 1784; a member of the Ancient and Honorable Artillery Company in 1786; a sea captain in 1789, and was afterwards a merchant of Boston. He, with his brother Appleton, was one of the first to introduce into New England the art of printing calico, — producing a coarse blue and red article on India cotton. Their place of business was at the corner of Buttolph Street. Captain Prentiss'

INTRODUCTION.

residence was in a stone house, near the head of Hanover Street, the former residence of Benjamin Hallowell, Comptroller of Customs, which was ransacked at the time Gov. Hutchinson's House was mobbed. Member Massachusetts Lodge, 1789.

Henry Prentiss

DR. JOHN PRINCE

Was pastor of the First Church, in Salem, from 1779 to his death, June 3, 1836. He was a native of Boston, and was a witness only of the destruction of the tea, as he informed Colonel Russell, of the "Centinel," long afterward. Admitted member Massachusetts Lodge, 11th January, 1780.

COLONEL EDWARD PROCTOR,

A prominent citizen and military officer of Boston, died there in November, 1811; aged seventy-eight. He was an importer of West India goods, at the sign of the "Schooner," in Fish Street, at the North End, before the war, after which he was in the auction business, at No. 1 Union Street. He was an active patriot, and was placed on the committee to obtain the resignation of the consignees of the tea, and commanded the guard on the "Dartmouth," on the night of November 29, 1773.[1] In 1756, he joined the Ancient and

[1] The proclamation of the "King of the Mohawks," which accompanies this notice, appears to be in Proctor's handwriting. The original is in the possession of Mr. Jeremiah Colburn, of Boston.

Abrant Kanakaratöpkqua

Chief Sachem of the Mohawks,
King of the Six Nations, and
Lord of all their Castles, &c. &c. &c.

To all our liege Subjects — **Health.**

Whereas Tea is an Indian Plant, and of right belongs to the Indians of every Land & Tribe: And **Whereas** our good **Allies** the English, have in lieu of it, given us that per:nicious Liquour **RUM**, which they have pour'd down our Throats, to Steal away our Brains, and **Whereas** the English have learn'd the most expeditious Way, or Method, of drawing an Infusion of said **Tea** without the Expense of Wood, or Trouble of Fire, to the Benefit and Emolument of the East India Trade as vastly greater Quantities may be expended by this Method, than by that heretofore practised in this Country, and therefore helps to support

Support the East India Company under their present Milancholly Circumstances—

We do of our certain Knowledge, Special Grace, and Meer Motion, permit and allow any of our liege Subjects to barter for, buy, or procure of any of our said English Allies, Teas of any kind: Provided always, each Man purchases not less than Ten, nor more than One hundred and fourteen Boxes, at a Time, and those the property of the East India Company, and provided also, that they pour all the said Tea into the Lakes, Rivers and ponds, that while our Subjects in their Hunting instead of Slakening their Thirst with Cold Water, as usual, may do it with Tea.

Of all which our Subjects will take Notice, and govern themselves accordingly—By Command

Toneteroque.

1st Moon
1774

Honorable Artillery Company, of which his grandfather, Edward Proctor, had been a member in 1699; was in the service during the Revolutionary war, and was a member of the committees of correspondence and of safety. He became a member of the Masonic fraternity in 1765, when he joined St. Andrew's Lodge; was master in 1774-76, and was junior grand warden of the Massachusetts Grand Lodge in 1781. For some years previous to his death, he was one of the Overseers of the Poor, and was a fireward in 1784-89. Hannah, his widow, died October 31, 1832, aged 87.

COLONEL HENRY PURKITT,

Born in Boston, March 18, 1755, died March 3, 1846. He was educated at the public schools of Boston; was afterwards apprenticed to Samuel Peck, the cooper, a zealous "Son of Liberty," and member of the tea party, and was himself active on that occasion, in disobedience to his master's orders. His reminiscences of the affair have been related on a previous page. Enlisting as a soldier in the Revolutionary army, he served through the war, and was present at Trenton and Brandywine, and was at one time a sergeant in Pulaski's Cavalry. After the war, he carried on his trade of cooper successfully, in connection with his former fellow-apprentice, Dolbear, in South Street. In 1803, appointed inspector-general of pickled fish, and performed the duty satisfactorily for thirty-five years. Joining a com-

INTRODUCTION.

pany of cavalry after the war, he passed through all the grades, and rose to that of colonel. He was many years a member of the Massachusetts Charitable Mechanic Association; became a member of St. Andrew's Royal Arch Chapter of Freemasons, in 1798, and was master of St. Andrew's Lodge, in 1804-5. "Uprightness and exactness were prominent traits of his character, and universal love and charity for all mankind were sincerely exhibited in his social intercourse. He had troops of friends, but it is not known that he ever had an enemy." In 1834, a number of Polish refugees arrived here, after the final partition of their native country. A collection for their benefit was proposed. The call was nobly responded to, and among others, Purkitt sent his check, as follows:

"Pay to Count Pulaski, my commander at the battle of Brandywine, his brethren, or bearer, one hundred dollars."

There is in possession of the family a full-length silhouette likeness of Purkitt, and a daguerreotype. The accompanying portrait is from an oil painting, in the possession of Mr. Henry P. Kidder, of Boston.

Henry Purkitt

JOHN RANDALL,

Born in Watertown, Mass., October 2, 1750; married Sarah Barnard, 30th December, 1778.

Henry Purkitt

Better known as Colonel Purkitt.

"Uprightness and exactness were prominent attributes of his character, and universal love and charity for all mankind were sincerely exhibited in his social intercourse. He had troops of friends, but it is not known that he ever had an enemy."—*Biographical Sketches St. Andrew's R.A.C.*

INTRODUCTION.

PAUL REVERE,

Born in Boston, January 1, 1735; died at his residence, in Bennet Street, May 10, 1818. He was of Huguenot ancestry, and learned the goldsmith's trade of his father. Articles of silverware, with his engraving, are still extant in Boston. He also engraved on copper, an art in which he was self-instructed, producing a portrait of his friend, the Rev. Jonathan Mayhew; a picture emblematical of the Stamp Act; a caricature of the "Seventeen Rescinders," one of Lord North forcing the tea down the throat of America; a picture of the Massacre in King Street, and another representing the landing of the British troops in Boston, in 1774. There were then but three engravers, besides Revere, in America. In 1775, he engraved the plates, made the press, and printed the bills of the paper money, which was ordered by the Provincial Congress of Massachusetts. He was sent by this Congress to Philadelphia, to obtain information respecting the manufacture of gunpowder, and on his return was able, simply from having seen the process, to construct a mill, which was soon in successful operation. Revere was an active patriot during the whole of the struggle for Independence. He was one of those who executed, as well as planned, the daring scheme of destroying the tea in Boston harbor, and was one of a club of young men, chiefly mechanics, who watched the movements of the British troops in Boston. He acted an important part in rousing the country around Boston on the morning of the memorable nineteenth of April, 1775, an event worthily commemorated in Longfellow's poem, — "Paul Revere's Ride." Revere had

INTRODUCTION.

served at Fort Edward, near Lake George, as a lieutenant of artillery, in 1756, and after the evacuation of Boston, was commissioned major in Crafts' artillery regiment, raised for the defence of the State, in which he attained the rank of lieutenant-colonel, and remained in service until the close of the war, after which he resumed his business as a goldsmith. He was in the unfortunate Penobscot expedition, in 1779. At a later period, he erected an air-furnace, in which he cast brass cannon and church bells. He also erected extensive works at Canton, for rolling copper and casting guns,—a business still carried on there by his successors. In 1795 he assisted in laying the corner stone of the State House, at Boston. At the time of his death he was actively connected with many benevolent and useful institutions, and was the first president of the Massachusetts Charitable Mechanic Association; member of the Masonic Lodge of St. Andrew's, in 1761, and grand master of the Grand Lodge of Massachusetts, in 1794-96.

Paul Revere

JOSEPH ROBY

Resided in Prince Street, Boston, in 1807, but was living in Hanover, N. H., in 1817.

JOHN RUSSELL

Was by trade a mason, and died in Boston, in 1778. His son, the well-known journalist, Colonel Benjamin Russell,

LORD NORTH FORCING THE TEA DOWN THE THROAT OF AMERICA.

"Preserve union, and judge in all causes amicably and mildly, preferring peace." — PAUL REVERE, 1795.

though only a school-boy at the time, remembered seeing, through the window of the wood-house, his father and Mr. Thomas Moore, his neighbor, besmearing each other's faces with lampblack and red ochre.

John Russell

WILLIAM RUSSELL.

William, son of Samuel and Elizabeth Hacker Russell, was born in Boston, 24th May, 1748, and died 7th March, 1784, in Cambridge, Mass. He was sometime usher in Master Griffiths' school, on Hanover Street, below the Orange Tree. On returning to his home, on Temple Street, after the tea party, he took off his shoes, and carefully dusted them over the fire, in order that no tea should remain, and saw every particle consumed. He afterwards taught school in Newton. Joining Crafts' artillery regiment, he served as sergeant-major and adjutant in the Rhode Island campaign. He next joined a privateer, as captain's clerk, was captured, and kept in Mill Prison, Plymouth, England, from August, 1779, until January, 1782. Again in a privateer, he was again taken, and this time suffered confinement in the horrible prison-ship "Jersey," at New York. These privations and sufferings occasioned his early death. His son, Colonel John Russell, was a publisher and journalist in Boston. He joined St. Andrew's Lodge of Freemasons in 1778.

INTRODUCTION.

ROBERT SESSIONS,

Whose interesting account of the tea party appears on page LXXIX, was born in Pomfret, Conn., March 15, 1752, and died in Hampden, Mass., in 1836. His grandfather, Nathaniel, was one of the earliest settlers of Pomfret, in 1704. Darius Sessions, Lieutenant-Governor of Rhode Island at the opening of the Revolution, and an active patriot, was his uncle. Robert Sessions served in the Revolutionary army, attaining the rank of lieutenant. In 1778, he married Anna Ruggles, a descendant of the Roxbury family of that name; settled in Pomfret, and in 1781 removed to South Wilbraham, now Hampden, Mass. The high estimation in which he was held by his fellow citizens, is evident from the number of offices of trust and responsibility in which he was placed. He was for many years a justice of the peace; town clerk and treasurer twelve years; representative in the State Legislature for five years, (1814-19,) and was almost always chosen moderator of the town-meeting. His sons, William V. and Sumner Sessions, are yet living, at an advanced age.

The above facts, as well as the narrative on page LXXIX, were furnished by my friends, Mr. John A. Lewis, of Boston, and Hon. William Robert Sessions, the well-known agriculturist, of Hampden County, and a member of the Massachusetts Senate of 1884, a grandson of Robert.

Robert Sessions

JOSEPH SHED

Was born in Boston, June 17, 1732, and died there October 18, 1812. He was the son of Joseph, (born October 26,

INTRODUCTION.

1698,) who was the son of Zachary, (born June 17, 1656,) who was the son of Daniel, the original settler of that name in Braintree, and afterwards at Billerica, Mass. The subject of this notice was a carpenter by trade, and worked upon Faneuil Hall during its rebuilding, or enlargement. He was associated with Samuel Adams, and other patriots, before and during the Revolutionary war, and later on was an ardent Jeffersonian Democrat,—hating the very name of Federalist. His residence was on Milk Street, on the spot now occupied by the Equitable Life Insurance building. At his residence a party of persons dressed, who were concerned in the destruction of the tea, he being one of the number. His friend, Samuel Adams, was often a visitor at his house, and his grandson has the china punch-bowl from which the old patriot drank, when Independence was declared. During the latter part of his life he kept a grocery store, on the spot where he lived so many years, on Milk Street. He was buried in the Granary burial ground, where many other patriotic citizens of Boston are also interred.

Communicated by his grandson, Mr. Joseph G. Shed, of Roxbury.

Joseph Shed

BENJAMIN SIMPSON,

(Erroneously named Isaac in Thatcher's list of 1835,) whose story of the tea party is told on pages LXXVII–VIII, was a bricklayer's apprentice. He served in the Revolutionary army; removed to Saco, Maine, about 1790, and died at Biddeford, Maine, March 23, 1849.

Captain PETER SLATER

Died in Worcester, Mass., October 13, 1831 ; aged seventy-two. He was apprenticed to a rope-maker, in Boston. His master, apprehensive that something would take place that evening relative to the tea, then in the harbor, shut Peter up in his chamber. He made his escape from the window; went to a blacksmith's shop, where he found a man disguised, who told him to tie a handkerchief round his frock, to black his face with charcoal, and to follow him. The party soon increased to twenty persons. Slater went on board the brig, with five others ; two of them brought the tea upon deck, two broke open the chests, and threw them overboard, while he, with one other, stood with poles to push them under water. Not a word was exchanged between the parties from the time they left Griffins' wharf till the cargo was emptied into the harbor, and they returned to the wharf and dispersed. Slater served five years in the Revolutionary army. A monument in Hope Cemetery, New Worcester, erected by his daughter, Mrs. Howe, bears the names of Slater, and many of his companions of the "tea party."

Samuel Sloper

Was one of the party, of whom we have no further information.

THOMAS SPEAR

Lived on Orange Street, in 1789. He was one of those whom Peter Mackintosh remembered to have seen run into his master's blacksmith's shop, and blacken their faces with soot.

SAMUEL SPRAGUE,

The father of the poet, Charles Sprague, was born in Hingham, Mass., — the home of four generations of his ancestors, — December 22, 1753, and died in Boston, June 20, 1844. He was a mason by trade, and was athletic and tall of stature. His share in the tea party he thus related to his son: " That evening, while on my way to visit the young woman I afterwards married, I met some lads hurrying along towards Griffin's wharf, who told me there was something going on there. I joined them, and on reaching the wharf found the 'Indians' busy with the tea chests. Wishing to have my share of the fun, I looked about for the means of disguising myself. Spying a low building, with a stove-pipe by way of chimney, I climbed the roof and obtained a quantity of soot, with which I blackened my face. Joining the party, I recognized among them Mr. Etheridge, my master. We worked together, but neither of us ever afterwards alluded to each other's share in the proceedings." Sprague married Joanna Thayer, of Braintree, a woman of great decision of character. They lived in a two-story wooden house, at No. 38 Orange (now Washington) Street, directly opposite Pine Street.

Samuel Sprague

COLONEL JOHN SPURR.

Born in Dorchester, Mass., in 1748, died in Providence, R.I., November 1, 1822; after December 16, 1773, he went to Providence; joined the army in 1775; was commissioned a captain in a Rhode Island regiment, in 1776, major in 1777, and served throughout the Revolutionary war.

JAMES STARR,

Born in New London, Conn., died in Jay, Maine, in January, 1831; aged ninety years and six months. He served in the old French war; afterwards settled and married in Boston, and removed thence to Bridgewater. During the Revolutionary war, he was taken prisoner, carried to Halifax, and detained fourteen months. Placed on board a transport for New York, and destined to the horrible Jersey prison-ship; after being two days at sea, the prisoners rose on the ship's company, captured the vessel, and took her into Marblehead.

CAPTAIN PHINEAS STEARNS,

A farmer and blacksmith of Watertown, born February 5, 1736, died March 27, 1798. He was a soldier at Lake

George in 1756, and commanded a company at Dorchester Heights, when the British evacuated Boston. He, with Samuel Barnard and John Randall, all of Watertown, were among the famous Boston tea party. He was offered a colonel's commission in the army, but the care of his young motherless children, and of a family of apprentices and journeymen, prevented his continuing in the public service. He was distinguished for his benevolent and cheerful disposition, and for strong common sense and strict integrity.

GENERAL EBENEZER STEVENS,

A distinguished artillery officer in the Revolutionary war, son of Ebenezer and Elizabeth Weld Stevens, of Roxbury, was born in Boston, 11th August, 1751, and died at his residence, in Rockaway, now Astoria, N.Y., 22d September, 1823. He joined Paddock's artillery company, which was composed almost entirely of mechanics, many of whom were active members of the organization, which, under the name of Sons of Liberty, did effective service in opposing the machinations of the crown. Under its first lieutenant, Jabez Hatch, (Captain Paddock being a Tory,) this company volunteered as a watch on the "Dartmouth." The Boston Port Bill drove the mechanics out of the town, and Stevens went to Providence, where he became a partner with John Crane, in the business of carpentering. Commissioned first lieutenant of Crane's train of Rhode Island artillery, 8th May, 1775, he accompanied it to Boston, and served through the siege; made captain in Knox's artillery regiment, 1st January, 1776; took part in the expedition to Canada; made major 9th November, 1776, and in the campaign ending in the surrender of Burgoyne; appointed lieutenant-colonel 3d April, 1778, and soon after assigned to Colonel Lamb's regiment, with which he took part in Lafayette's operations in Virginia, and at Yorktown commanded the artillery alternately with Lamb and Carrington. After the war, he was a leading merchant of New York; member of the New York assembly in 1800, an alderman in 1802, and major-general of the State militia during the war of 1812. He was a founder of the Tammany and the New England Societies, and a member of the Society of the Cincinnati. General Stevens's connection with the tea party is related on a previous page.

Dr. ELISHA STORY,

Born in Boston, December 3, 1743, died in Marblehead, Mass., August 27, 1805. His father, William Story, was Register of the Court of Admiralty. His office, on the north-westerly corner of State and Devonshire Streets, was broken into at the time of the Stamp Act riots, on the supposition that the stamps had been deposited there for distribution, and all the books and papers carried into King (now State) Street, and burned. Elisha Story, fully sympathizing with the patriots of the day, joined the "Sons of Liberty;" was one of the volunteer guard on the "Dartmouth," on the night of November 29, and on the evening of December 16, convened, with other disguised Sons of Liberty, in an old distillery, preparatory to their "little operation" in tea. He was a pupil of Master Lovell, and studied medicine with Dr. Sprague. He was surgeon of Colonel Little's Essex regiment, and fought as a volunteer at Lexington, and at Bunker's Hill, until obliged to remove a wounded friend to Winter Hill, where he passed the night in caring for the wounded. He was with Washington at Long Island, White Plains and Trenton. In 1774, he removed from Boston to Malden, and in 1777, settled in Marblehead, where he practiced his profession, with success, until his death. In 1767, he married Ruth, daughter of Major John Ruddock, by whom he had ten children. By his second wife, Mehitabel, daughter of Major John Pedrick, he had eleven children, the eldest of whom was Joseph, afterwards Associate-Justice of the United States Supreme Court. Isaac, the second son, was the father of Judge Isaac, of Somerville, Mass. Dr. Story was a skilful physician, and a man of great benevolence. " It is said that he at one time led a party of men to the Boston common, near where is now the Park Street gate, where there was a sentinel guarding two brass field-pieces. While Story overawed the sentinel, by presenting a pistol at his head, and enjoined silence upon him, the others came from behind and dragged away the guns, one of which was afterwards placed in the Bunker Hill Monument."

Communicated by Hon. Isaac Story, of Somerville.

COLONEL JAMES SWAN,

Merchant, politician, soldier and author before the age of twenty-two; born in Fifeshire, Scotland, in 1754, died in Paris, March 18, 1831. He came to Boston when very young, and in 1772, when a clerk in a counting-house, published "A Dissuasion to Great Britain and the Colonies from the Slave-Trade to Africa." At the time of the tea

INTRODUCTION.

party, in which he was an actor, his place of business was next to Ellis Gray's, opposite the east end of Faneuil Hall, and he boarded in Hanover Street, where he and other young apprentices disguised themselves. Next morning, at breakfast, the tea in their shoes, and smooches on their faces, led to some mutual chaffing. He was a volunteer at Bunker's Hill; was a captain in Crafts's artillery regiment; afterwards secretary to the Massachusetts Board of War; member of the Legislature in 1778; Adjutant-General of the State, and at the close of the war was major of a cavalry corps. He acquired a fortune in France through government contracts, but afterwards became deeply involved, through the dishonesty of a partner, and was confined in St. Pelagie, a debtors' prison, in Paris, for many years, keeping up all the while an indefatigable litigation in the French courts. At the age of seventy he was, by French law, released. In 1777, he joined the Masonic Lodge of St. Andrew. He was a man of large enterprise and benevolence, manly in person, and dignified in manner. He owned a fine estate in Dorchester, latterly the residence of his daughter, Mrs. Sargent.

THOMAS URANN,

One of the volunteer guard on the " Dartmouth;" became a member of the Masonic Lodge of St. Andrew, in 1760, and was master of the Lodge, in 1771-72. He was a ship-joiner, in Batterymarch Street, near Hallowell's ship-yard. In 1784, he was surveyor of boards; and was sealer of woods, in 1787-90. By Mary, his wife, whom he married in 1750, he had thirteen children, nine of whom survived him. His will is dated May 7, 1791.

Thomas Uran

CAPTAIN JOSIAH WHEELER

Was a house-wright, who lived in half a double house, on Orange (now Washington) Street, west side, between Pleasant and Warrenton Streets. The other half was occupied by Sprague, also of the tea party. On the afternoon of December 16, 1773, Mrs. Wheeler became aware that there was something unusual on her husband's mind. It was late when he returned home that evening, but she sat up for him, and as he pulled off his long boots, a quantity of tea fell on the floor, revealing the cause of his absence. Seeing the tea, a female neighbor, who had sat up with Mrs. Wheeler to keep her company, in her husband's absence, exclaimed, "Save it; it will make a nice mess." Taking down her broom, this patriotic woman swept it all into the fire, saying, "Don't touch the cursed stuff." Wheeler commanded a company of minute-men at the opening of the Revolution, most of whom were skilled carpenters and joiners, and by Washington's order, he superintended the erection of the forts, on Dorchester Heights. He was also employed in building the State House, in Boston. He died in Boston, in August, 1817; aged seventy-four. His daughter, Mrs. Carney, was living in 1873, at

INTRODUCTION.

Sheepscot, Maine, at the age of eighty-six. George W. Wheeler, a grandson, many years City Treasurer of Worcester, is now (1884) living in that city. Captain Wheeler was one of the volunteer guard on board the "Dartmouth."

JEREMIAH WILLIAMS

Was a blacksmith, who resided in the old mansion, yet standing, near Hog Bridge, in Roxbury, known as the "John Curtis House." He was the brother of Colonel Joseph, a distinguished citizen, and the father of Major Edward Payson Williams, an officer of the Revolutionary army, who died in the service.

THOMAS WILLIAMS,

Also of Roxbury, was one of the minute-men in Captain Moses Whiting's company, at Lexington. He, with his brother-in-law, Thomas Dana, Jr., and other Roxbury men, rendezvoused at the house of his father, John Williams, preparatory to the tea party, and returning home, Williams and Dana refused to join in sacking the house of a Tory, regarding it as no part of their enterprise. In 1812, Williams settled in Cazenovia, N. Y., and died in Utica, N. Y., July 31, 1817; aged sixty-three.

NATHANIEL WILLIS,

Journalist, born in Boston, February 7, 1755, died near Chillicothe, O., April 1, 1831. After serving an apprenticeship in a printing-office, in Boston, he became one of the proprietors and publishers of the "Independent Chronicle," a leading political journal, from 1776 to 1784. He subsequently issued the first newspaper ever published in Ohio, the "Scioto Gazette," and was for several years State printer of Ohio. His son, Nathaniel, also a journalist, was the father of Nathaniel P. Willis, Richard Storrs Willis, and Sarah Payson Willis, ("Fanny Fern,") afterwards Mrs. Parton. Member of St. Andrew's Lodge in 1779.

JOSHUA WYETH,

Whose relation is given on a preceding page, was the son of Ebenezer Wyeth, of Cambridge, and was born there in October, 1758. He served in the Revolutionary army; afterwards removed to the west, and was residing in Cincinnati, in 1827.

Joshua Wyeth

DR. THOMAS YOUNG,

A physician, was a conspicuous figure in the early Revolutionary movements in Boston. He was the first president of the North End Caucus, at which measures of importance to the town were initiated and discussed, and delivered the first oration commemorative of the Boston Massacre, March 5, 1771, at the Manufactory House, on Tremont Street. He was an original member of the Boston committee of correspondence, whose work was so important in uniting the Colonies, and was a talented and vigorous contributor to the papers of the day, and to the Royal American Maga-

INTRODUCTION.

zine, on medical, political and religious topics. He was a popular speaker in the public meetings of the day, and to him is attributed the first public suggestion of throwing the tea overboard. He was John Adams's family physician, and an army surgeon, in 1776, and was afterwards a resident of Philadelphia. Several spirited letters from his pen may be found in the "Life and Times of General John Lamb." "Tea," writes Young in the "Evening Post," "is really a slow poison, and has a corrosive effect upon those who handle it. I have left it off since it became a political poison, and have since gained in firmness of constitution. My substitute is camomile flowers."

It is not long, since an eminent Englishman, visiting Boston, asked the committee of the city government, who attended him, to point out the place where the tea was thrown overboard. He was taken to a distant wharf, known by its form as the T, and popularly associated with that event from the similarity of sound. Boston has appropriately marked many of her historical sites; surely the spot rendered forever memorable by the bold deed of the Sons of Liberty, on December 16, 1773, ought not longer to remain unmarked. No stranger, at all familiar with American history, would leave unvisited the scene of an event at once so unique in its character, and so important in its consequences. The precise locality is definitely known, and a tablet, suitably inscribed, or an enduring monument of some kind, should be placed there without further delay.

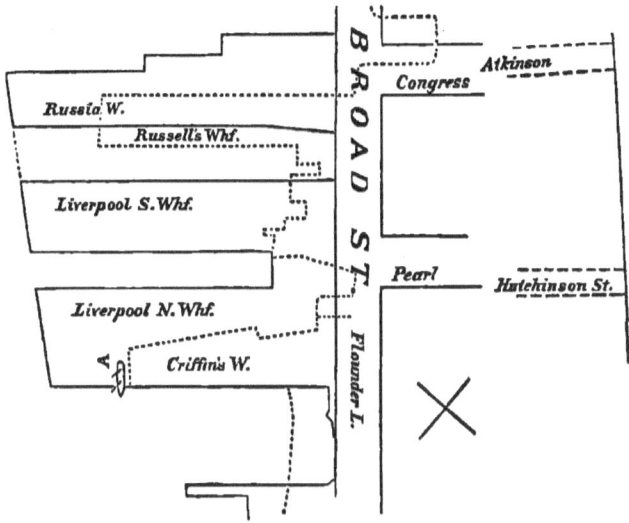

LOCATION OF GRIFFIN'S (NOW LIVERPOOL) WHARF, WHERE THE TEA-SHIPS LAY.

In this diagram the old boundaries are designated by dotted lines. The place where the tea-ships lay, at the foot of Griffin's wharf, is coincident with the lower end of the large coal-sheds of Messrs. Chapin & Co., the present owners of the wharf. They have extended and widened the wharf, and have built a three-story brick block at its head. A mural tablet might be set in the front of the central building, at a small expense. The wharf should be rechristened "Tea Party Wharf."

A BALLAD OF THE BOSTON TEA PARTY.

BY DR. OLIVER WENDELL HOLMES.

No! never such a draught was poured
    Since Hebe served with nectar
The bright Olympians and their Lord,
    Her over-kind protector ;
Since Father Noah squeezed the grape
    And took to such behaving,
As would have shamed our grandsire ape,
    Before the days of shaving;
No! ne'er was mingled such a draught,
    In palace, hall, or arbor,
As freemen brewed, and tyrants quaffed,
    That night in Boston harbor !
It kept King George so long awake,
    His brain at last got addled,
It made the nerves of Britain shake
    With seven score millions saddled :
Before that bitter cup was drained
    Amid the roar of cannon,
The western war-cloud's crimson stained
    The Thames, the Clyde, the Shannon;
Full many a six-foot grenadier
    The flattened grass had measured,
And many a mother many a year
    Her tearful memories treasured.
Fast spread the tempest's darkening pall,
    The mighty realms were troubled,
The storm broke loose, but first of all
    The Boston tea-pot bubbled !

An evening party, — only that,
    No formal invitation,
No gold-laced coat, no stiff cravat,
    No feast in contemplation ;
No silk-robed dames, no fiddling band,
    No flowers, no songs, no dancing !

INTRODUCTION.

A tribe of red men, — axe in hand, —
  Behold the guests advancing!
How fast the stragglers join the throng,
  From stall and work-shop gathered;
The lively barber skips along
  And leaves a chin half-lathered;
The smith has flung his hammer down,
  The horse-shoe still is glowing,
The truant tapster at the Crown
  Has left a beer-cask flowing;
The coopers' boys have dropped the adze,
  And trot behind their master;
Up run the tarry ship-yard lads; —
  The crowd is hurrying faster.
Out from the mill-pond's purlieus gush,
  The streams of white-faced millers,
And down their slippery alleys rush
  The lusty young Fort-Hillers.
The rope-walk lends its 'prentice crew,
  The Tories seize the omen;
"Ay, boys! you'll soon have work to do
  For England's rebel foemen,
'King Hancock,' Adams, and their gang,
  That fire the mob with treason, —
When these we shoot, and those we hang,
  The town will come to reason."
On — on to where the tea-ships ride!
  And now their ranks are forming, —
A rush and up the Dartmouth's side,
  The Mohawk band is swarming!
See the fierce natives! what a glimpse
  Of paint and fur and feather,
As all at once the full-grown imps
  Light on the deck together!
A scarf the pig-tail's secret keeps,
  A blanket hides the breeches, —
And out the cursed cargo leaps,
  And overboard it pitches!

O woman, at the evening board,
  So gracious, sweet and purring,

INTRODUCTION.

So happy while the tea is poured,
   So blest while spoons are stirring,
What martyr can compare with thee?
   The mother, wife, or daughter, —
That night, instead of best Bohea,
   Condemned to milk and water!

Ah, little dreams the quiet dame,
   Who plies with rack and spindle,
The patient flax, how great a flame
   Yon little spark shall kindle!
The lurid morning shall reveal
   A fire no king can smother,
When British flint and Boston steel
   Have clashed against each other!
Old charters shrivel in its track,
   His worship's bench has crumbled,
It climbs and clasps the Union Jack, —
   Its blazoned pomp is humbled.
The flags go down on land and sea,
   Like corn before the reapers;
So burned the fire that brewed the tea
   That Boston served her keepers!

The waves that wrought a country's wreck
   Have rolled o'er Whig and Tory;
The Mohawks on the Dartmouth's deck
   Shall live in song and story.
The waters in the rebel bay
   Have kept the tea-leaf savor;
Our old North-Enders in their spray
   Still taste a Hyson flavor.
And Freedom's tea-cup still o'erflows,
   With ever-fresh libations,
To cheat of slumber all her foes,
   And cheer the wakening nations!"

INTRODUCTION.

COMMEMORATIVE VERSES.

FRAGMENT OF A RALLYING SONG OF THE TEA PARTY AT THE GREEN DRAGON.

Rally Mohawks! bring out your axes,
And tell King George we'll pay no taxes
    On his foreign tea;
His threats are vain, and vain to think
To force our girls and wives to drink
    His vile Bohea!
Then rally boys, and hasten on
To meet our chiefs at the Green Dragon.

Our Warren's there, and bold Revere,
With hands to do, and words to cheer,
    For liberty and laws;
Our country's "braves" and firm defenders
Shall ne'er be left by true North-Enders
    Fighting Freedom's cause!
Then rally boys, and hasten on
To meet our chiefs at the Green Dragon.

A TEA PARTY BALLAD.

Just by beauteous Boston lying
    On the gently swelling flood;
Without Jack or streamers flying,
    Three ill-fated tea-ships rode.

Just as glorious Sol was setting,
    On the wharf, a numerous crew —
Sons of Freedom, fear forgetting,
    Suddenly appeared in view.

INTRODUCTION.

Armed with chisel, axe and hammer, —
  Weapons new for warlike deed;
Towards the herbage-freighted vessels,
  They approached with dauntless speed.

O'er their heads aloft in mid sky,
  Three bright angel forms were seen;
This was Hampden, — that was Sidney,
  With fair Liberty between.

Soon they cried, "Your foes you'll banish,
  Soon the glory shall be won;
Nor shall setting Phœbus vanish,
  Ere the matchless deed be done!"

Quick as thought the ships were boarded,
  Hatches burst and chests displayed;
Axe and hammers help afforded, —
  What a glorious crash they made!

Quick into the deep descended,
  Cursed weed of China's coast;
Thus at once our fears were ended, —
  Freemen's rights shall ne'er be lost!

A FAREWELL TO TEA.

(From Thomas's "Massachusetts Spy.")

Farewell, the tea-board with its equipage
Of cups and saucers, cream-bucket and sugar-tongs,
The pretty tea-chest also lately stored
With Hyson, Congo, and best Double Fine.
Full many a joyous moment have I sat by you
Hearing the girls tattle, the old maids talk scandal,
And the spruce coxcomb laugh — at maybe nothing.
No more shall I dish out the once-loved liquor,
Though now detestable;
Because I'm taught — and I believe it true,
Its use will fasten slavish chains upon my country;
And Liberty's the goddess I would choose
To reign triumphant in America.

INTRODUCTION.

Gen. JOSEPH WARREN

And the memorable Suffolk County Resolves of 1774.

The mansion where the famous Suffolk County Resolves were passed, September 9, 1774, is still standing. It is situated in Milton, Mass., a few doors from the Boston and Milton line, on the Quincy road. It is a low, two-story double house, 20 x 40 feet, with the main door in its centre, and a chimney on each end. In its front there is inserted a marble tablet, 14 x 28 inches, with the following inscription:

"IN THIS MANSION,

On the 9th day of Sept., 1774, at a meeting of the delegates of every town and district in the County of Suffolk, the memorable Suffolk Resolves were adopted.
They were reported by Maj.-Gen. Warren, who fell —— in their defence in the battle of Bunker Hill, June 17, 1775.
They were approved by the members of the Continental Congress at Carpenter's Hall, Phila., on the 17th Sept., 1774.
The Resolves to which the immortal patriot here first gave utterance, and the heroic deeds of that eventful day on which he fell, led the way to American Independence.
'Posterity will acknowledge that virtue which preserved them free and happy.'"

In Warren's oration, March 5, 1772, more than two years before these Resolves were passed, the spirit of liberty burned within his heart. Nine months after these Resolves the battle took place, which finally resulted in the birth of American freedom. *See portrait, page* XLVII.

This print shows the Major in his Continental hat, the last he wore; now carefully preserved and in possession of Mr. John L. D. Wolfe, Tremont Street, Boston, near Brookline and Boston line, who has kindly allowed us to sketch it for this work.

INTRODUCTION.

JOSEPH LOVERING.[1]

Respecting Mr. Lovering's connection with the Tea Party, Mr. George W. Allan, of West Canton Street, Boston, now eighty-two years of age, relates that about the year 1835, he frequently conversed with that gentlemen, who told him that on the evening of December 16, 1773, when he was fifteen years of age, he held the light in Crane's carpenter's shop, while he and others, fifteen in number, disguised themselves preparatory to throwing the tea into Boston harbor. He also said that some two hundred persons joined them on their way to the wharf, where the tea-ships lay. Mr. George H. Allan, the son of George W. Allan, received a similar statement from Mr. Lovering, a short time before the latter's death, which occurred June 13, 1848, at the age of eighty-nine years and nine months.

Mr. Lovering appears to have been the youngest person connected with this affair, of whom we have any knowledge. His boyish curiosity led him to accompany the party to the scene of operations at Griffin's wharf, and on the following morning he was closely questioned and severely reprimanded by his parents, for being out after nine o'clock at night, as they were strict in their requirement that he should be in bed at that hour.

His son, Mr. N. P. Lovering, now seventy-seven years of age, resides in Boston, and is treasurer of the Connecticut and Passumpsic River Railroad Company. To this gentleman, and to his grand-daughter, Mrs. C. D. Bradlee, Boston, we are under obligation for the copy of a photograph from Mr. Lovering's oil-painting of his father.

[1] See ante pp. XLIX., CVI.

INTRODUCTION.

BENJAMIN FRANKLIN

Was born in Boston, 1706; died in Philadelphia, in 1790, and was buried in Christ Churchyard. A small marble slab, level with the ground, marks the spot. "No monumental display for me," was his request as expressed in his will.

Some years before his death he wrote his own epitaph. His usefulness to his country during the Revolutionary period will warrant us in giving it place in our "Tea Leaves:"
A. O. C.

The body of
BENJAMIN FRANKLIN, PRINTER,
Like the cover of an old book,
its contents torn out,
And stript of its lettering and gilding,
Lies here, food for worms.
Yet the work itself shall not be lost,
For it will (as he believed) appear once more
in a new
and a more beautiful edition
corrected and amended
by the Author.

It is believed that Benjamin Franklin was made a Freemason in St. John's Lodge, of Philadelphia, early in the year 1731. In 1734 he printed and published the first Masonic book ever issued in America, being the work known as "Anderson's Constitution of 1723." Copies are now exceedingly rare, and readily sell for fifty dollars each. One is now in the library of the Grand Lodge of Massachusetts, in an excellent state of preservation.

SERENO D. NICKERSON,
Recording Grand Secretary, Grand Lodge of Mass.

"As a philosopher he ranks high. In his speculations he seldom lost sight of common sense, or yielded up his understanding either to enthusiasm or authority." — GOODRICH.

LETTERS AND DOCUMENTS.

LETTERS AND DOCUMENTS.

No. 1.

LETTER FROM MR. WILLIAM PALMER.

To the Directors of the East India Company.[1]

Gentlemen:

As the Act allowing a Drawback of the whole of the cuftoms paid on tea, if exported to America, is now paffed, in which there is a claufe empowering the Lords of the Treafury to grànt licences to the India Company, to export tea, duty free, to foreign States, or America, having at the time of granting fuch licences upwards of ten millions of pounds in their warehoufes, and as the prefent stock of

---

[1] The East India Company was a famous joint stock trading corporation, formed in England early in the seventeenth century, to carry on commerce with the East Indies. They established stations in various places, and in 1702, were newly chartered as "The United Company of Merchants Trading to the East Indies." The executive power of the Company was vested in a court of twenty-four directors, each of whom must own £2000 of stock, and held office four years. This Company became a great territorial power, and laid the foundation of the British Empire in India. Its monopoly of the China trade was abolished in 1833, and the Company was then deprived of its original character as a commercial association. The Sepoy Mutiny, in 1857, combined with other causes, induced Parliament to transfer the dominion of India to the Crown. This change was effected in 1858, after strenuous opposition from the Company. Trading companies to the East Indies were also chartered by Holland, France, Denmark, and Sweden; that of Holland being the oldest.

tea is not only near feventeen million, but the quantity expected to arrive this feafon does alfo confiderably exceed the ordinary demand of twelve months, and the expediency of exporting tea to foreign States having been confidered, I prefume to lay before this Court the following extracts, &c., from letters relative to the confumption in America, and calculation of advantages attending the exportation of tea by licence, and as an affurance the fame are formed upon fome experience of this trade (having not only been concerned in a great part of the tea which has been fhipped to America fince the allowance of the drawback, in 1767; but being now about to repurchafe at your enfuing fale no fmall quantity of Bohea tea for the fame account,) I am defirous, at my own hazard, to include in fuch purchafe, an affortment of all other kinds, viz.: Congou, Souchong and Hyfon, but more particularly the feveral fpecies of Singlo, namely, Hyfon, Skin, Twankay and Firft Sort, from a conviction that, by degrees, the confumption of thefe fpecies, alfo and particularly Singlo tea, might be introduced into America, at leaft so far for the benefit of the Company, as in part to relieve them from the difagreeable neceffity, they will, without fome fuch vend, be fubject to, of forcing that fpecies of tea to market, before it is greatly damaged by age, provided you are of opinion the fame may poffibly tend to the advantage of the Company; or, fhould it be the opinion of this Court, an immediate confignment fhould take place, I am ready to give fuch affiftance towards carrying the fame into execution as may be thought moft conducive to the intereft of the Company, together with fuch fecurity as the nature of the truft may require. In the profecution of thefe confignments, I would propofe to obtain a more exact computation of the actual confumption; what quantity might probably find a sale there, and the moft probable means of fuccefs in fuch fales, whether by waiting for a demand in the ordinary way, or by public fales there; conducted upon the outlines of thofe made in England, by fixing a future day of payment, and by a reftriction in felling any future quantity for a limited time, but particularly (under my mode) in what manner, and within what time affurances can be given by remittances being made on account of fuch fales.

I am, gentlemen, your humble servant,

WM. PALMER.

London, 19th May, 1773.

EXTRACTS FROM LETTERS, &C., TO PROVE THE STATE OF THE TEA TRADE IN AMERICA.

Extract from a Letter from Bofton, dated 29th April, 1771, in Anfwer to a Confignment made in February, 1771, at 3s. 1d., with the whole drawback of £23 18s. 7½d. pr cent.:

"Were it not for the Holland tea, the vent of Englifh would have anfwered your expectation here, but the profit is immenfe upon the Holland tea, which fome fay coft but 18d., and the 3d. duty here is faved. Many hundred chefts have been imported. What is fhipped may go off in time, without lofs, for there muft be buyers of Englifh tea; the tranfportation of the Dutch by water being attended with much trouble and rifk."

Extract from a Letter from Boston, dated 11th July, 1771:

'So much tea has been imported from Holland, that the importers from England have been obliged to fell for little or no profit. The Dutch traders, it is faid, had their firft teas at 18d. pr lb., the last at 2s.; either is much cheaper than from England, and they fave the 3d. duty here. The Company muft keep theirs nearer the prices in Holland. The confumption is prodigious."

Extract from a Letter from Boston, 2d Sepr., 1771:

"The confumption of Bohea tea thro' the Continent increafes every year. It is difficult for us to fay how great it is at prefent. We imagine there may be confumed in this Province, which is perhaps a feventh part of the Continent, 3000 chefts in a year. We are fure nothing can difcourage the running of it but the reducing the price as low, or lower, than it was two or three years paft in England"

Extract from a Letter from Boston, (Messrs. Hutchinson,) dated 10th Sepr., 1771:

"From a more particular eftimate of the confumption we are of opinion, the two towns of Bofton and Charleftown confume a cheft, or about 340 pounds of tea, one day with another. Thefe two towns are not more than one-eighth, perhaps not more than one-tenth, part of the Province.

Suppofe they confume but 300 chefts in a year, and allow they are but one-eighth, it will make 2400 chefts a year for the whole Province. This Province is not one-eighth part of the Colonies, and in the other governments, efpecially New York, they confume tea in much greater proportion than in this Province. In this proportion, the confumption may be eftimated at 19,200 chefts per annum, or upwards of fix millions of pounds. Yet at New York or Penfylvania they import no teas from England, and at Rhode Ifland very little. Here we find the Dutch traders continually gaining ground upon us. If teas do not fall with you before the fpring fhippings, we fear the Dutch will carry away all the trade of the Colonies in this article."

Extract of a Letter from Bofton, dated 11th Sepr., 1772:

"We have delayed anfwering your laft enquiries relative to the tea concern, in hopes of being able to form a better judgment, but to no great purpofe; the great importation from Holland, principally through New York and Philadelphia, keeps down the price here, and confequently the fale of teas from England. We have fet ours fo low we fhall have no profit from this years adventure, yet there are 50 chefts ftill on hand. You afk our opinion whether the difference between the Englifh and Dutch teas, if it did not exceed the 3d. duty and 9 pr cent., would be fufficient encouragement to the illicit trader? If the difference was not greater we think fome of the fmugglers would be difcouraged, but the greater part would not. Nothing will be effectual fhort of reducing the price in England equal to the price in Holland. If no other burthen than the 3d. duty in the

Colonies, to fave that alone would not be fufficient profit, and the New Yorkers, &c., would soon break thro' their folemn engagements not to import from England."

Extract from a Letter from Boston, dated 25th Feb., 1773, in Anfwer to a calculation fent of the fuppofed price at which the illicit trader can now import tea into America from Holland:

"In your calculation of the profits on Dutch teas, 12 pr cent. is too much to deduct for the rifque of illicit trade. We are confident not one cheft in five hundred has been feized in this Province for two or three years paft, and the cuftom houfe officers feem unwilling to run any rifk to make a feifure. At New York, we are told it is carted about at noon day. There is fome expence in landing, which we believe the importers would give five pr cent. to be freed from."

Copy of a Letter from Rotterdam, dated 12th June, 1772:

"I have to acknowledge the receipt of your favor of the 5th inftant, defiring information of the prefent ftate and prices of tea at this market, and alfo what the freight and charges are thereon to North America, to all which I cheerfully give you every elucidation in my power, and with the greateft pleasure, as neither you nor your friends have any thought of engaging in faid trade, which, with every other branch of fmuggling, muft be held in abhorrence by all good men. The present prices of tea are —

			d.		d.
Dutch Bohea's,	in whole chefts,		20	@	22
" "	half	"	. 22		24
" "	quarter	"	. 24		25
Swedifh,	whole	"	. 21		22
Danifh,	"	"	. 21		22½
Congo, . .			. 28		45
Souchon, .			. 36		65
Peco, . .			. 32		55
Imperial, .			. 49		50
Green, . .			. 48		50
Tonkay, .			52		53
Heyfan Skin,			. . 60		62
Heyfan, . .			. . 90		95

The tare on whole chefts is 84 lbs., if they weigh lefs than 400 lbs., and if they weigh 400 lbs. or upwards, then 90 lbs.; for the half chefts, under 200 lbs., tare 54 lbs.; if 200 lbs., or upwards, then 60 lbs.; for the quarter chefts, under 100 lbs., tare, 23 'lbs.; if 100 lbs., or upwards, then 30 lbs. The advantages on the tares are calculated at 7 or 8 pr cent. on the whole chefts, at 12 @ 13 pr cent. on the half chefts, and at 15 @ 16 per cent. on the quarter chefts. The quantity of teas on hand is not confiderable, fo that we do not apprehend a decline; on the contrary, if any orders of the leaft importance were to appear, the prices would go higher. There are now about 400 chefts fhipping for America, from Amfterdam, from which port the teas that go to North America from this country are always fhipped, and not from this city; they are fent to Rhode Ifland, and not to Bofton. Of Green teas there are hardly any left, neither fine Souchong nor Congos, but ordinary, in abundance. The freight of a whole cheft of Bohea to St. Euftatius, one of the Dutch West India Iflands, comes to about 7¼s. pr cheft. It is reckoned by the foot fquare, at 6s. the foot to North America. It is generally £4 pr cheft, New York currency, but the captain is not anfwerable in any cafe of feizure.

Agreeable to your defire, I fend you a pro forma invoice of 6 chefts Dutch Boheas, fo as they come to ftand on board if they were fhipped here; but as the fhipping is at Amfterdam, the charges may be fomewhat higher. In regard to what they eftimate, the rifk that in America for running in the teas I cannot inform you, this you may be better able to learn from fome of your New England houfes, as our underwriters will not fign againft the rifk of feizures; but I fancy the rifk is not very great, as the trade is carried on for so large parcels.

Pro forma invoice of 6 chefts of Dutch Bohea tea:

```
                                    lbs.
    320  Tare of 4 chefts, under   400
    360         at 84 lb. each, 336 ⎫ 2270
    370                              ⎬
    390  do. of 2 chefts above       ⎪  516
    410       400 @ 90 lb. each 180 ⎭ ──1754 @ 24s.  £2104 16
    420                                  off 1 pr cent.,   21  2
                                                        ─────────
                                                         £2083 14
```

CHARGES.

Cuftom and Paffport, ...	£20	4s
Sleding, ...	1	7
½ weigh money, ...	13	0
Brokerage, ...	10	8
Shipping, ...	3	0
Commiffion, 2 per cent. on £2131 13s.	42	12
	90	11

£2174 5[1]

Eftimate of the advantages attending the Tea trade to North America, if carried on from England:

Obferve 1ft. In the following calculation, no more than half the confumption of the Continent, as eftimated by Meffrs. Hutchinfon, in their letter of the 10th Sepr., 1771, is affumed as the whole, as from the mode in which they were under the neceffity of making their eftimate, it was liable to error, and 19,200 chefts is more than has been hitherto annually imported from China by all foreign companies.

2ndly. That this calculation is formed upon Bohea tea only, the fpecies of tea already confumed there ; yet it is probable by degrees other fpecies might be introduced, the vend of which may be more profitable to the Company. 9600 chefts of Bohea tea, each containing 340 lbs., makes 3,264,000 lbs., if fold at 2s. 6d. Bofton currency, (which is 4d. lower than it appears to have been even at the time it

[1] In this sample invoice the amount seems extraordinary. The editor of this volume, however, considers his duty ended when he gives a faithful transcript of the manuscript in his possession, allowing the facts alone to appear.

was purchafed in Holland, at 15 ftivers, or under 18d. pr lb.,
amounts to £408,000
Deduct 25 pr cent. for exchange, . . 102,000
　　　　　　　　　Sterling, . . £306,000
Deduct 6 pr cent. for commiffion and charges, 18,360
Annual net proceeds before the American } £287,640
duty is deducted, ...

Application of thofe Net proceeds to the following purpofes:

To the revenue for the duty on 3,264,000, @ 3d. £40,800
To the fhip owners, for freight from England to
　America, if according to the prefent rate of
　15 pr cheft, ... 7,200
To the fhip owners for freight from China to
　England, according to Sir Richard Hotham's
　plan, of £21 pr ton, of 10 hundred weight, or
　for every 3 chefts of tea, ... 67,200
To the purchafe at Canton, if at 15 tale pr pecul
　would amount thus: say 3,264,000 lb., divided
　by 133⅓ for each pecul, makes peculs 24,480
　@ 15 each, is tales 367,200, which, at 6s. 8d. pr
　tale, is flerling, ... 122,400
Commiffion on the purchafe in China, . . 6,120
Charges of all forts, rated at 10s. pr cheft, . . 4,600
　　　　　　　　　　　　　　　　　　　　248,320
To the Company for Net profit after all de- ⎫
　ductions whatfoever upon the moft reduced ⎬ 39,320
　eftimate, upwards of 30 pr cent. on the pur- ⎪
　chafe, or . . . . ⎭
　　　　　　　　　　　　　　　　　　　　£287,640

No. 2.

LETTER FROM Mr. GILBERT BARKLY.

Gentlemen :
I take the liberty to enclofe for your confideration a memorial, regarding the eftablifhment of a branch from the Eaft India houfe in one of the principal cities in North America. Should the defign meet with your approbation, as I am well acquainted with the teas moft faleable in that country, fhall be extremely happy in giving you every information in my power, I have the honor to be with due efteem, gentlemen,
Your moft obedt. & very humble fervant,
GILB'T BARKLY.
Lombard Street,
26th May, 1773.

To THE HON'BLE THE COURT OF DIRECTORS OF THE EAST INDIA COMPANY.

MEMORIAL.

The Memorial of Gilbert Barkly, merchant, in Philadelphia, in North America, who refided there upwards of fixteen years, and who is well acquainted with the confumption of that country, particularly in the article of Teas, &c.

Humbly propofes.   In order to put a final ftop to that desftructive trade of fmuggling :
That the Company fhould open a chamber in one of the principal, & central cities, of North America, under the

direction of managers, and that an affortment of teas from England fhould be lodged in warehoufes, and fales to commence quarterly upon the same terms & conditions as thofe in London.

By this means the merchants and grocers from the Southern and Northern Provinces will attend the fales and purchafe according to their abilities. The goods thus brought from home to them, and fold cheaper than they can be fmuggled from foreigners, the buyers will be bound by intereft, and think no more of running that rifk, to which may be added that they have them when paid for, immediately, for whereas, when commiffioned from abroad, they generally wait fix months before the receipt of them.

This country is now become an object of the higheft confequence, peopled by about three millions of inhabitants, one third of whom, at a moderate computation, drink tea twice a day, which third part, reckoning to each perfon one fourth part of an ounce pr day, makes the yearly confumption of 5,703,125 lbs. This quantity, at the medium price of 2s. 6d. pr lb., amounts to £712,890 2s. 6d.

The common people in all countries are the greateft body, few of thofe in North Briton or Ireland drink tea, this is not the case in America, all the planters are the real proprietors of the lands they poffefs; by this means they can afford to come at this piece of luxury, which has been greatly introduced among them by the example of the Dutch and German fettlers.

The great object to be confidered is to bring the goods to market in fuch a manner as to afford them as cheap as they can be bought of foreigners. Should this be the cafe the fuccefs of the defign is beyond a doubt.

The duty of 3d. pr lb. fome time ago laid on teas payable in America, gave the colonifts great umbrage, and occafioned their fmuggling that article into the country from Holland, France, Sweden, Lisbon, &c., St. Eustatia, in the Weft Indies, &c., which, from the extent of the coaft, (experience has taught) cannot be prevented by cuftom officers, or the king's cruizers, and as the wifdom of Parliament reckons it impolitical to take off this duty, the colonifts will perfevere in purchafing that article in the ufual manner if the above method is not adopted, and the goods brought into their country and fold as cheap as they can have them abroad.

The freight, &c., of teas to America would not much exceed what they might coft to Holland, or any other foreign company, particularly as the fhips may load back with mafts, and other goods that might nigh pay the whole expence, and fhould the Company think of exporting their overftock of teas to Holland, or any other foreign country, it is not to be expected that the merchants abroad would buy them but with a view of profit. This, with freight, commiffion, duty, &c., would far exceed the expence of fales and freight to America.

If this fcheme fhould be approved of, the fooner it is executed the better, as the fmugglers in America will soon be laying in their fall and winter ftock of teas, unlefs they are prevented by this defign, and as Spanifh dollars are the current coin in that country, the Company can be furnifhed with any quantity they may require towards their payment, fhould they require it.

The managers may be paid by a commiffion on the fales, and at the fame time bound to obey fuch orders and directions as they may receive from time to time from the Hon'ble the Court of Directors, and as your memorialift is univerfally acquainted with the trade, and has refpectable connections in that country, he humbly offers himfelf as a proper perfon to be one of the managers, and if required, will find fecurity for the truft repofed in him. Your memorialift alfo prefumes to mention John Inglis, Esq., of the city of Philadelphia, as another proper perfon, being univerfally efteemed in America, and well known in the city of London, as a man of probity, fortune and refpect.

No. 3.

LETTER FROM Mr. BROOK WATSON, TO DANIEL WIER, Esq.

Dear Sir:

The annual confumption of teas in Nova Scotia is about 20 chefts Bohea, and 3 or 4 of good Common Green. Should the Company determine on fending any to that Province, I pray your intereft in procuring the commiffion to Watfon's & Rafhleigh's agent there, John Butler, a man of long ftanding in the Province and in the Council, and by far the fitteft perfon to be employed, for whom W. & R. will be anfwerable. At Bofton I have two friends equally deferving. You would do the Company fervice, and me an acceptable kindnefs, by recommending them, Benjamin Faneuil, Jun., & Jofhua Winflow. The confumption at

Bofton is large, fay at leaft 400 chefts Bohea & 50 of Green pr annum. The freight to both thefe places I fhould be glad to have if you could procure it without inconvenience to yourfelf.

Yours faithfully.

BROOK WATSON.[1]

4 June, 1773.

No. 4.

A PROPOSAL FOR SENDING TEA TO PHILADELPHIA.

Received from the Hon'ble Mr. Walpole.[2]

As Philadelphia is the capital of one of the moft populous and commercial Provinces in North America, and is fituated in the center of the middle Britifh Colonies, it is propofed:

That the Eaft India Company fhould, by the middle of June at fartheft, fend to Philadelphia at leaft five hundred chefts of black teas, one hundred half chefts of green teas,

[1] Sir Brook Watson, a merchant of London, and Lord Mayor in 1796, born in Plymouth, England, February 7, 1735, died October 2, 1807. Early in life he entered the sea service, but, while bathing in the harbor of Havana, in 1749, a shark bit off his right leg, below the knee, and he was obliged to abandon his chosen profession. A painting, by Copley, represents this scene. Watson then became a merchant, and was a commissary to the British troops in Canada, in 1755 and in 1758. Visiting the American colonies just before the

and feventy five half chefts of Congou and Souchon teas.

That they fhould confign thefe teas to a houfe of character and fortune in Philadelphia, and direct the proceeds thereof to be remitted hither in bills of exchange or fpecie.

That previous, however, to the teas being fhipped, factors fhould be appointed in Philadelphia, and the directors of the Eaft India Company fhould *immediately* advife them of their intended confignation, and direct them to engage *proper* warehoufes for the reception thereof.

That. the factors fhould be authorized to fell the teas at public auction, (giving notice of the times of the fale in all the North American newfpapers, at leaftt one month before hand,) and in fuch fmall lots as will be convenient for the country ftorekeepers to fupply themfelves with fuch fales.

That the factors fhould grant the purchafers the fame allowance of tare, tret, difcount, &c., as are cuftomary at the company's fales in this city.

That in cafe the factor fhould be of opinion, the fales of the tea would be encreafed both in quantity and price, by having occafional auctions in Bofton and New York, in the manner propofed at Philadelphia ; that they fhould be at liberty to fend from time to time to Bofton & New York

Revolution, he professed himself a Whig, but intercepted letters showed his true character to be that of a spy. In 1782, he was commissary-general to his friend, Sir Guy Carleton, in America; held the same office with the Duke of York, in 1793-95, and that of Commissary-General of England, in 1798-1806. He was a member of Parliament from London, in 1784-93; sheriff of London and Middlesex in 1785, and was made a baronet December 5, 1803. As a reward for his services in America, Parliament voted his wife an annuity of £500 for life.

² Hon. Thomas Walpole, merchant, banker, and member of Parliament, second son of Horatio, first Lord Walpole, and nephew of the famous statesman, Sir Robert Walpole, died at Chiswick, March 21, 1803. He was born October 25, 1727.

as many chefts as they may think neceffary for the confumption & *commerce* of thofe places, but that the factors, or one of them, fhould always attend the fales in Bofton and New York.

That the Eaft India Company fhould be at the charge & expence of the warehoufe rent in America, the cartage, and the freight of the teas from Philadelphia to Bofton & New York, and that the factors fhould be allowed for receiving and felling the teas, collecting the payment thereof and remitting the fame, a commiffion of 2½ pr cent. on the amount of the fales.

N.B. — It is fubmitted whether it would not be proper for the directors of the Eaft India Company to fend two perfons to Philadelphia, who have been accuftomed to pack and repack teas at the India Houfe, to the end that they may be employed for that purpofe, and in dividing whole chefts of black teas into half chefts, for the greater accommodation of the country fhopkeepers.

No. 5.

Mr. Palmer's Compliments to Mr. Wheler, encloses the Outlines of a Plan upon which the Exportation of Tea on behalf of the Company to America take place. Mr. P. will attend the Committee whenever he is desired.

PLAN.

Admitting that an exportation of tea to America by licence takes place immediately, in order to prevent the colonifts from becoming purchafers at the fales of foreign companies, usually made from September to November, and confequently at leaft difcourage thofe companies from encreafing their China trade, and alfo to obtain fome information, though imperfect, before the inveftments for the China fhips of the enfuing feafon are ordered. It is propofed that chefts of Bohea tea, chefts of each fpecie of Singlo tea, together with a fmaller affortment of Hyfon, Souchong, & Congou tea be configned to fuch a number of merchants conjointly as may be thought fufficient, (for whom their correfpondents in England fhall give fatisfactory fecurity,) together with fuch perfons as fhall be thought proper for that purpofe to be fent from thence. That upon the arrival of fuch tea in Bofton public notice fhall be given thereof through the Continent, and alfo that it is the intention of the Eaft India Company, if the fales of this cargo fhould be found to anfwer, to repeat fuch confignments, in order to fupply that Continent with teas at leaft equal in price to what they muft pay for the fame if obtained in a way of illicit trade. That in order to conduct these fales in the moft advantageous manner, the parties to whom the cargoes fhall be entrufted fhall act as one body; that the concurrence of the majority fhall be neceffary for any act therein; that each party fhall be anfwerable for himfelf only, but that no credit fhall be given to bills received for paying without the affent of at leaft three of the perfons fo appointed; that it fhall be the object of the perfon who may be appointed to go with the cargo to obtain all poffible information refpecting the actual confumption, mode of fale, fpecies of tea that may be introduced, & opportunity of remittances at Bofton, where it is propofed the firft confignment shall be made, as it is the only confiderable mart, where tea from England is at prefent received without oppofition, and having fo done he shall vifit fuch other places on the Continent as may be thought proper, but particularly New York and Philadelphia, in order to obtain the fame information at thofe feveral places, and learn, from being on the fpot, how far the New Yorkers, &c., will hold their folemn engagements, when they find the advantages they will probably reap by receiving tea from England. They having obtained all fuch neceffary information, he shall return to England & report the fame, from which time it is prefumed there will be full employ for fuch agent without any additional expence to the Company in preparing fuch affortments of tea as may from time to time be required for this market, and can be beft fpared from the neceffary demand of Great Britain & Ireland, and alfo in negotiating the remittances that may from time to time be received on account of this concern.

That fuch an appointment is abfolutely neceffary muft appear to every one at all acquainted with the nature of the tea trade, not only properly to regulate thefe inveftments, but alfo from time to time to preferve proper affortments of tea for the confumption of Great Britain & Ireland, and indeed in this particular alone could the directors for fome years paft have had fuch information, from any perfon in whofe abilities & integrity they could have placed a proper confidence, and who, from the nature of fuch trufts, muft be placed above the temptation to any finifter practices the Company, from the refources of the tea trade alone, would probably never have been involved in their prefent difficulties.

LETTERS AND DOCUMENTS.

LETTER FROM Messrs. GREENWOOD & HIGGINSON.

Gentlemen:

We are informed that you have come to a refolution to fhip tea to America, we therefore beg leave to recommend our friends, Mr. Andrew Lord, and Meffrs. Willm. & George Ancrum,[1] of Charles Town, in South Carolina, merchants, for the confignments of fuch part as you may fhip to that place. Both houfes are of the firft repute, and have been long eftablifhed there, and alfo to tender to you our fhip the London, Alexander Curling, Mafter, to carry the fame out, who fhall be ready to fail whenever you pleafe to account.

We are, your moft humble fervants,

GREENWOOD & HIGGINSON.

London, 4 May, 1773.

To the Hon'ble the Court of Directors
of the United Company of Merchants
of England, trading to the Eaft Indies.

LETTER FROM Mr. FRED'K PIGOU, Jun[r].

Gentlemen:

Being informed you intend to export teas to feveral different fettlements in America, to be fold there under the

---

[1] William Ancrum, was a loyalist, in 1782, and his property was conof Charleston, S.C., He was banished fiscated.

LETTERS AND DOCUMENTS. 209

direction of agents to be appointed. I beg leave to acquaint the Court that I have a houfe eftablifhed in New York, under the firm of Pigou & Booth, and I humbly folicit the favor of that houfe having a fhare of the confignments.

Philadelphia being alfo a port to which the Company will moft likely fend teas, I beg leave to recommend Meffrs. James & Drinker, of that city, to be one of your agents there.

Should I be fo happy to fucceed in my requeft, I am certain the greateft attention will be paid by thofe gentlemen to the Company's orders, and that the Company's intereft will be made their ftudy in the fales and remittances. I alfo beg leave to obferve that if fhips fhould be wanted for this fervice, I have veffels now ready for the ports of Philadelphia and New York.

     I am, gentlemen,
       Your moft obed't & very humble ferv't,
            FRED'K PIGOU, Jun'.:
Mark Lane, 1st June, 1773.
To the Hon'ble the Court of Directors
of the United Eaft India Company.

LETTER FROM MR. JONATHAN CLARKE.

London, 1ft July, 1773.
Gentlemen :
  I intended to have made a purchafe of teas at your prefent fale to have exported to America, but the candid

intimation given by you of an intention to export them to the Colonies on account of the Company, renders it difadvantageous for a fingle houfe to engage in that article.

I now beg leave, gentlemen, to make a tender to you of the fervices of a houfe in which I am a partner, Richard Clarke and Sons,[1] of Bofton, New England, to conduct the fale of fuch teas as you may fend to that part of America, in conjunction with any other houfes you may think proper to entruft with this concern; altho' I have not the honor of being perfonally known to many of you, I flatter myfelf our houfe is known to the principal merchants who deal to our Province, and are known to have always fulfilled our engagements with punctuality & honor, and truft I fhall procure you ample fecurity for our conducting this bufinefs, agreeable to the direction, we may from time to time receive from you.

[1] Richard, son of Francis Clarke, merchant, graduated at Harvard College, in 1729, and died in London, at the residence of his son-in-law, John Singleton Copley, the artist, February 27, 1795. He, with his sons, Richard and Jonathan, constituting the firm of Richard Clarke & Sons, did business in King (now State) Street, and became exceedingly obnoxious to the people, on their refusal to resign their appointment as factors of the East India Company's tea. The residence of the Clarke's, on School Street, (corner of Chapman Place,) was mobbed on the evening of November 17, 1773, but no serious damage was done. (This incident is fully detailed on a previous page.) Jonathan Clarke was in London in the summer of 1773, and received verbal instructions respecting the consignment of tea from the directors of the East India Company. Richard Clarke arrived in London December 24, 1775, after a passage of twenty-one days from Boston. The Clarkes were included in the Act of Proscription, and their estates were confiscated. Richard Clarke was a nephew of Governor Hutchinson. His wife, Elizabeth, was the daughter of Edward Winslow, of Boston. Susan, his daughter, married Copley, the painter, and became the mother of Lord Lyndhurst. Another daughter, Mary, married Judge Samuel Barrett. Copley's portrait of Richard Clarke represents him as a man of commanding presence, with features resembling, in a remarkable degree, those of Washington, in the Stuart portrait.

LETTERS AND DOCUMENTS. 211

In foliciting this favor, I beg leave to avail myfelf further of the circumftance of our having for a long time been concerned in the tea trade, and to greater extent than any houfe in our Province, with one exception. Of the difappointment I have met with in my intended adventure, by which we are deprived of a very valuable branch of our bufinefs, and on my being on the fpot to take fuch inftructions from you as may be requifite in difpofing of what you may fend. And give me leave to add my affurances that the intereft of the Eaft India Company will always be attended to by the houfe of Richard Clarke & Sons, if you think fit to repofe this confidence in them.

I am, very refpectfully, gentlemen,

Your moft obed't & humble fervant,

JONATHAN CLARKE.

To the Hon'ble Directors of the
Eaft India Company.

Mr. Clarke alfo enclofed two letters in his favor; one from Meffrs. Henry & Thos. Bromfield, the other from Mr. Peter Contencin, merchants.

June 5th, 1773.

Sir:

The bearer, Mr. Barkly, is the perfon whom I took the liberty of recommending to you as a perfon able and qualified to give you information touching the quantity of tea that is now confumed in America, and to ferve the Company in that part of the World in cafe the Directors fhall judge it proper to make any eftablifhment there for felling tea on the Company's account, & I am, sir,

   Your moft obedient and moft humble fervant,

            GREY COOPER.[1]

Received from Henry Crabb Boulton, Efq.

Hon'ble Sirs:

  Being informed of your refolution to export a quantity of tea to different parts of America, we take the liberty of recommending our friends, Meffrs. Willing, Morris & Co., to be your agents at Philadelphia, for whom we are ready to be anfwerable.

   We are, very refpectfully,

    Your honors moft obedient, humble fervants,

         ROBERTS, BAYNES & ROBERTS.

8 June, 1773.

To the Hon'ble the Committee of Warehoufes.

---

[1] Grey, afterwards Sir Grey Cooper, studied law at the Temple, London; became an efficient supporter of the Rockingham party, and held the office of Secretary of the Treasury throughout the American troubles, covering the administrations of Chatham, Grafton, and North. He was made a Lord of the Treasury in 1783, a Privy Councillor in 1793, and died at Worlington, Suffolk, July 30, 1801; aged seventy-five. He was an able speaker and parliamentarian.

London, 9th June, 1773.

Gentlemen:

I have underftood that you propofe fixing agents in the different colonies in America, to difpose of certain quantities of tea; if fo, I am a native and merchant of Virginia, and think it will be in my power to execute your commands in that quarter, on terms equal, if not fuperior, to any one in it.

There are fome things refpecting this bufinefs that come within my knowledge, which are too prolix for a letter, but if the Court chufes to notice my petition, I fhall be happy and ready to give any intelligence in my power.

I am, gentlemen,

Your very obed't & hum'ble ferv't,

BENJ. HARRISON, Jun'.

At Webbs, Arundel Street, Strand.

To the Hon'ble Court, &c.

Gentlemen:

Being informed that you have it in contemplation to export tea to the different Provinces in North America, for fale on the Company's account, I beg leave to recommend my brother, Mr. Jonathan Browne, merchant, in Philadelphia, as an agent for any bufinefs you may have to transact at that place, and I flatter myfelf his activity &

knowledge of the trade of that country, acquired by a refidence of upwards of fifteen years, will render him deferving of your notice.

Any fecurity for his conduct I am ready to give, and to any amount you fhall think neceffary for the difcharge of the truft you may be pleafed to repofe in him.

I am, very refpectfully, gent.,

Your moft obed't & humble ferv't,

GEORGE BROWNE.

London, Tower Hill, 11th June, 1773.

To the Committee of Warehoufes.

Gentlemen:

As many difficulties feem at prefent to attend the exportation of tea to America in large quantities, on account of the Company, if the expedient is approved by this Court, of fending about 200 chefts of Bohea tea, and a fmall affortment of other fpecies to Bofton, by way of experiment, and you fhould think proper to entruft fuch cargo to 'the care of Meffrs. Hutchinfon, merchants, there, I am ready, as a fecurity, to advance upon the fame the fum fuch tea fhall amount to, at the prime coft in China & freight from hence, before the fhipping thereof, provided I am permitted to charge intereft upon fuch advance, until remittances for the fame are received from America.

I am, gent.,

Your humble ferv't,

WM. PALMER.

Devonfhire Square, 24th June, 1773.

To the Hon'ble Court of Directors, &c., &c.

Sir:

The Committee of Warehoufes of the Eaft India Company defire you will meet them at this houfe, on Thurfday next, at twelve o'clock at noon, relative to the exportation of tea to America.

I am, fir,

Your moft humble ferv't,

WM. SETTLE.

Eaft India House, 25th June, 1773.

To BROOK WATSON,   ROBERTS, BAYNES & ROBERTS,
JONATHAN CLARKE,   WM. KELLY,
FREDE'K PIGOU, Junr.   GREENWOOD & HIGGINSON,
GILBERT BARKLY.   BENJAMIN HARRISON,
GEORGE BROWNE,   SAMUEL WHARTON,
       GEO. HAYLEY & JOHN BLACKBURN, Esqrs.

Gentlemen :

The enclofed newfpapers contain the fentiments of the Americans with regard to the quantity of teas confumed in that country, and the fatal confequences attending buying it from foreigners, by leading them to purchafe other articles of Eaft India goods at the fame markets which otherwife would not be an object, and which, of courfe, would be commiffioned from the mother-country.

The memorial, which I had the honor to deliver, lately points out an undoubted method for gaining this trade.

The Company being the exporters, pays the American duty of 3d. pr lb., of which they will be amply repaid by the advance on their fales, and as mankind in general are bound by intereft, and as the duty of about a fhill'g pr lb. is now taken off tea when exported, the Company can afford their teas cheaper than the Americans can fmuggle them from foreigners, which puts the fuccefs of the defign beyond a doubt.

It may be fuggefted that the Americans have not money to pay for thofe goods. The Province of Pennfylvania alone fhips yearly to the Weft Indies, Spain, Portugal & France, &c., above 300,000 barrels of flour, large quantities of wheat, Indian corn, iron, pork, beef, lumber, and above 15,000 hhds. of flax feed to Ireland, and the other Provinces are equally induftrious. The principal returns are in filver and gold, with bills of exchange, an incredible part of which will center with the Company fhould the fame be executed agreeable to the plan propofed, and fmuggling will be effectually abolifhed without any additional number of officers and cruizers.

Warehoufe rent, &c., in America, will come as cheap as it is in England, and by the mode • propofed for difpofing of the teas, the grocers and merchants will be quickly ferved without any rifk of lofs by bad debts. I beg your forgivenefs for the freedom I have taken. I have the honor to be, with due refpect, gentlemen,

Your moft obed't & humble fervant,

GILBERT BARKLY.

Lombard Street, 29 June, 1773.
To the chairman & deputy chairman of the Eaft India Comp'y.

(See Mr. Barkly's letter in the mifcellany bundle for the Pennfylvania packet of 17th May, 1773.)

Sir:

Upon my coming to town, I found a letter from the clerk of the Committee of Warehoufes, defiring my attendance at the Eaft India Houfe, relative to the exportation of teas to America.

I fhould have waited on the Committee of Warehoufes at the time defired, if I had been in town, and I will attend them if they wifh to fee me any day next week, which may be convenient to them. I am, fir,

Your moft obedi'. humb. ferv't,

SAMUEL WHARTON.

Argyle Street, June 30th, 1773
Crabb Boulton, Efqr.

SOME THOUGHTS UPON THE EAST INDIA COMPANY'S SENDING OUT TEAS TO AMERICA.

Submitted to the confideration of Henry Crabb Boulton, Esq., Chairman of the Eaft India Company.

The ufual exports to America, confifting of callicoes, muflins, and other produce of India, (tea excepted,) have been feldom lefs than £600,000 pr an., as fuch the confequence of that trade, and the intereft of the merchants concerned therein, ought to be well confidered before this meafure of fending out teas to America fhould be adopted, left it might defeat the one and prejudice the other.

The merchants are much alarmed at this ftep of the Company, fearing it will prevent, in a great degree, the remittances from their correfpondents by fo much or near it as the fales of the teas amount to; for it is beyond a doubt, that the people in America, if they admit the teas, (which I much doubt,) will be tempted to purchafe them with the very money arifing from the fales of muflins, callicoes, Perfians, &c., bought of the Company inftead of fending it to the merchants in England, and thereby tend to encreafe the diftrefs which is already too feverely felt, for want of remittances. And I fhould not be furprized at the merchants forming a refolution fimilar to that of the dealers, viz., not to purchafe anything from a Company who are interfering fo effentially with their trade, and ftriking at the root of their interefts. I am of opinion, if a proper application was made to the miniftry, aided by a petition from the American merchants, it might produce a relaxation of that difagreeable and fatal duty of 3d. pr lb., and in cafe of fuccefs I could almoft promife that in the course of six months there would be exported not lefs than one million of pounds of tea, and further, that the ufual annual export would be upon an average four millions of pounds of teas. This mode would relieve the Company from its prefent load, and place the correfpondence and connection in its ufual and natural channel. But admitting that the miniftry would not comply with such a requeft, is it not too hafty a refolution before anfwers are come from America if they will receive the teas through the channel of the merchants, and particularly when they fee the drawback is encreafed from 14 to 24 pr cent. ad valorem, and thereby they are enabled to introduce that article cheaper from hence than from Holland.

It is well known to every gentleman converfant in trade, that on account of fome difagreeable Acts of Parliament paffed here, the people of America formed a refolution, which was too generally adhered to, not to import any goods from hence. This refolution continued for two years. However, the merchants of New York, (who are men of underftanding and liberal principles,) forefeeing the fatal confequences that attend England & the Provinces by a continuance of dif-union with the mother-country, fummoned a meeting of the principal inhabitants of the town, and then came to a compromife with the people, that in cafe they would agree to admit all other goods, they promifed not to import any teas from England, under very fevere penalties, until the Act impofing a duty of 3d. pr lb. was repealed, and the feveral captains of fhips in the trade were enjoined upon pain of forfeiting the good efteem of the inhabitants to comply therewith. The like refolutions were agreed to in Philadelphia & South Carolina.

There is another difficulty which occurs to me in this bufinefs, and that is, there is not fo much fpecie in the country as would pay for the quantity faid is intended to be exported. The Company fhould be very cautious who they appointed to receive the produce of the fales, for fhould the contractor for money have that power, who are the general drawers of bills, it would enable them to make a monopoly of the ready fpecie, and to make exchange advance 25 pr ct., to the lofs of the remitter.

Thus have I ftated the principal objections to the meafure, and in compliance with my promife, I fhall give you my opinion relative to its introduction, & the proper modes of fale, admitting the Company perfevere in their refolutions of exporting the teas on their own account.

A fhip fhould be hired by the Company, capable of carrying the quantity they intend to export, and at fo much pr month. She fhould call in the firft place at Bofton, and there land 300 chefts, under the care of one of the Company's own clerks; from thence to New York, and there land 300 chefts, in the like manner as at Bofton; from thence to Philadelphia, and there land 300 chefts, as before, and from thence to Carolina, and there land 100 chefts, under the care of the clerk of the Company, all of which may be performed in the courfe of three months from her failing from hence, until her arrival at her laft deftined port, provided the people in the different Provinces don't difturb the voyage upon the arrival of the teas. Public notice fhould be given in the papers of each Province at leaft one month preceding the fale, and the following valuation prices affixed for the buyers to bid upon, subject to the allowances, as limited in your own fales : Bofton, @ 2s., lawful money, pr lb.; New York, 2s. 9d., currency; Philadelphia, 2s. 3d., currency ; Charles Town, South Carolina, 10s. pr lb., currency. Thefe prices are for Boheas. The feveral clerks of the Company can with eafe correfpond with each other, as there is a conftant and regular communication by poft, fo that if there fhould be an over quantity at one place, and a deficiency at another, it may be fupplied. The clerks fhould have directions to pay the proceeds of the fales to fome eminent merchant at each Province, who fhould be a perfon well acquainted with the article, and one who has great weight with the other merchants and people, both as to efteem, rank and property ; this merchant to remit the money by good bills of exchange, which he muft guarantee, and a fecurity given here for such a truft.

Great care fhould be had to regulate the fale by the confumption of each Province, and not to be held at the fame time, but to follow each other by the diftance of a fortnight, fo that in cafe there fhould be more buyers at one Province than the quantity will furnifh, they may have an opportunity of writing or going to the next fale at another Province.

I fear there may be an oppofition made by fome of the Provinces upon a furmife that Government is aiding in this plan, and mean to eftablifh principle and right of taxation, for the purpofe of a revenue, which at prefent is very obnoxious, as fuch great care fhould be had not to employ either paymafter, collector, or any other gentleman under the immediate fervice of the Crown, to receive the money.

Garlick Hill, 1ſt July, 1773.

Gentlemen :

In compliance with your defire, we have reflected on the bufinefs & expence which will attend the fale of and remitting for fuch teas as the Eaſt India Company may ſhip to North America, and confidering that none but gentlemen of known property, integrity and of experience in trade can, with propriety and fafety to the Company, be employed therein, we humbly conceive that five pr cent. commiſſion, and one pr cent. for truckage, warehoufe rent, brokerage, and other incidental charges, making in the whole fix pr cent. on the grofs fales, is as little as the bufinefs can be tranfacted for. And we further beg leave to fuggeſt that no perfon ought to be employed who will not give fecurity to the Company, in London, for faithfully following fuch inſtructions, as they may from time to time receive from them, for remitting to the Company all monies which they may receive on account of teas fold, firſt deducting the above fix pr cent., together with fuch freight and duties as they may have paid on account thereof, and intereſt thereon, till reimburfed, fuch remittances to be made in bills of exchange, within two months after receiving the money, which bills, to be drawn upon their fecurity in London, payable fixty days after fight, or in fpecie, at the Company's riſk and expence ; if in bills of exchange, the fecurity to be obliged to accept and pay them. Should the Company determine to ſhip teas on their own account and riſk to North America, we prefume to recommend to their fervice,

Benjamin Faneuil, Junr., Efqr., & Jofhua Winflow, Efqr.,[1] of Bofton, *jointly*, to tranfaƈt their bufinefs, for whom we are ready to give fecurity to the amount of ten thoufand pounds for their performance of the before mentioned conditions, and in like manner a fecurity of two thoufand pounds for John Butler, Efqr., of Halifax, in Nova Scotia, who we alfo beg leave to recommend to the Company's fervice. We are, with great refpect, gentlemen,

Your obe't, hum^e ferv'ts,

WATSON & RASHLEIGH.

To the Hon'ble the Committee
of Warehoufe, &c., &c., &c.

[1] Joshua Winslow, son of Joshua and Elizabeth Savage Winslow, born in Boston, in 1737, died there in March, 1775, after an illness of only three days. Joshua, his father, (1694-1769,) third in descent from Governor Edward, of Plymouth, was the son of Colonel Edward Winslow, sheriff of Suffolk County. In 1720, he founded a mercantile house in Boston, in which his brother Isaac (the Tory) was a partner, from 1736 to 1757, and in 1760 admitted his son, Joshua, to a share of the business, he himself retiring with an ample fortune, in 1767. This firm carried on an extensive and profitable trade. With the proceeds of consignments from Bristol, England, vessels were built in Boston, and loaded with fish for Leghorn, or some other foreign port, return cargoes being taken for Bristol. They also became considerable shipowners, and had one ship constantly in the London trade. Their place of business was on the corner of King and Broad Streets. Joshua Winslow, who was one of the consignees of the tea, seems to have been present when they were called upon by the Sons of Liberty, at Clarke's warehouse, but does not afterwards appear, except by proxy. He must have absented himself from Boston soon after that occurrence, as he did not go with the other consignees to the castle. He married Hannah, daughter of Commodore Joshua Loring, and left her a widow, with one son and four daughters.

London, July 2, 1773.
Gentlemen :

If it fhould be agreeable to you to confign to the houfe of Richard Clarke & Sons, of Bofton, New England, this fummer or fall, I would beg leave to propofe to you, that I will find fecurity to the amount of two or three hundred chefts, that in eight months after the fale of them in America, the accounts fhall be forwarded you, and the money for the net proceedings paid to your order within that time, you allowing our houfe five pr cent. commiffion on the fales, and one pr cent. for ftorage & other charges, the freight and American duty to be chargeable on the teas befides, & we to be free from the rifk of fire or any other accident that may occur before the delivery of the tea.

I am, with the greateft refpect, gentlemen,

Your moft obed't, hum. fer't,

JONATHAN CLARKE.

To the Hon'ble Directors, &c., &c.

London, July 5, 1773.
Sirs :

The terms which I had the honor to converfe with you upon, relative to the fale of teas in America, I take leave to recapitulate as necefsary, to underftand each other, viz.: You expect that the houfes here who recommend their friends abroad, and are in confequence appointed as your factors to difpofe of that article, fhould ftipulate that it be fold agreeable to fuch orders as you may think proper to give for that purpofe, and that the factors pay the cartage, warehoufe rent, brokerage, and other charges incidental to the fale, and remit the net proceeds in two months from the laft, prompt, in good bills of exchange or bullion, for the whole of which fervice they are to retain a commiffion of 6 pr cent. on the grofs fales, the Company to be at the rifk and expence of fhipping the tea out, to pay duty and entry abroad, and to be alfo at the rifk and expence of fending bullion home, which terms I do agree to in behalf of thofe which I fhall recommend, whofe names are at the foot. And as it feems prudent to guard againft accident by death, as well as that the Company be fecured againft the neglect & mifconduct of its fervants in this bufinefs, I do hereby, for myfelf and my houfe, here guarantee the fafety of the houfes named as above, for the execution of this bufinefs, and alfo that fuch bills of exchange, as they fhall remit on the above account, fhall be good.

The agents in this bufinefs hope to be indulged with giving their fhips in the trade the freight of the tea out, in preference to others.

I am, with the higheft refpect, firs,

Your moft obed't & moft hum. ferv't,

WILLIAM KELLY.

To the Hon'ble the Com^tee of Warehoufes, &c., &c., &c.

For New York:
Meffrs. Abraham Lott & Co.[1]
Meffrs. Hugh & Alex[r] Wallace.

Mr. Lott has been a merchant of reputation there about 18 years, and Public Treafurer of the Province about 7 years. The latter is a houfe of long ftanding and of great credit, and is well known to many gentlemen here, particularly Meffrs. Bourdieu & Chollet.

For Bofton:
John Erving, Jun[r].[2]
Henry Lloyd.[3]

Both men of fortune and eftablifhed charaƈters as merchants.

For Philadelphia:
Meffrs. Francis Tilghman.
Meffrs. Reefe Meredith & Son.

Both houfes of great credit & eftablifhed reputation.

P. S. — Mr. Kelly, on confideration, thinks that one month from the laft prompt, will be too fhort a time for limiting the remittances to be made, and therefore has taken the liberty to put down two.

[1] Abraham Lott, of New York, was treasurer of that colony, and died in New York, 1794; aged sixty-eight. In September, 1776, he was ordered by the Whig Convention to settle his accounts as treasurer, and pay over the balance to his successor. In August, 1781, some Whigs went in a whale boat to his residence, robbed him cf six hundred pounds, and carried off two slaves. In 1786, the Legislature of New York passed an Act, "more effectually to compel Abraham Lott to account for money received while he was treasurer of the colony, and for which he has not accounted."

[2] Colonel John Erving, Jr., a flour merchant, on Kilby Street, Boston, and a

London, 6 July, 1773.

Sir:

Mr. Kelly will give the Committee my propofals for doing the Company's bufinefs in Virginia, and if they require further knowledge of me, Meffrs. Harris & Co., and Mr. John Blackburn, will give them it. I am, fir,

Your hum. ferv't,

BENJ. HARRISON.

Mr. Wm. Settle, Clerk,
to the Committee of Warehoufes.

Hon'ble Gentlemen:

Purfuant to your requeft, I beg leave to lay before you the propofal of my friend, Henry White, Esqr., of New

graduate of Harvard College, (1747,) was in 1778, proscribed and banished, and in 1779 his property was confiscated under the Conspiracy Act. His mansion, on the west corner of Milk and Federal Streets, was afterwards the residence of Robert Treat Paine, a signer of the Declaration of Independence. Prior to the Revolution Irving was colonel of the Boston regiment. In 1760, he signed the Boston memorial against the acts of the revenue officials, and was thus one of the fifty-eight merchants who were the first men in America to array themselves against the officers of the Crown. But, in 1774, he was an addresser of Hutchinson, and was appointed a mandamus coun-

cillor. In 1776, he fled to Halifax, afterwards went to England, and died at Bath, in 1816; aged eighty-nine years. His wife, Maria Catherina, youngest daughter of Governor Shirley, died a few months before him. George Erving, his brother, also a loyalist, died in London, in 1806; aged seventy.

*Henry Lloyd, a merchant of Boston, agent of the contractors for supplying the royal army, was an addresser of Gage, in 1775. In 1776, he went to Halifax, and was proscribed and banished in 1778. He died in London, late in 1795, or early in 1796; aged eighty-six. His place of business was at No. 5 Long Wharf.

York, for the fale of what teas you may think proper to commit to his charge, and in juftice to my friend, I think it my duty to declare that there is no gentleman more capable of tranfacting this bufinefs, feeing from his long experience in that branch, that his confequence as a merchant of fortune he will be capable of advancing the intereft of the Company in the fale thereof, as well as filencing any prejudices that may arife from the mode of its introduction, viz.:

That the money arifing from the fale of fuch teas fhall be paid into the hands of your treafurer in three months immediately following the receit thereof, firft deducting 6 pr cent. in lieu of all charges confequent to their landing, fave the duty of 3d. pr lb. and freight, and I hereby engage to join myfelf with one or two more gentlemen of fortune in a bond for the faithful performance of the above covenant.

.I am, with all due refpect, hon'ble gentlemen,

Your moft obedient, &c., &c., &c., &c.,

JOHN BLACKBURN.

Scots Yard,
Tuesday, 6 July, 1773.

N.B.— The firm of Mr. White's houfe is the Hon'ble Henry White, Efqr., at New York.

To the Hon'ble Directors, &c., &c., &c.

Sir:

Your letter of the 30th ultimo, addreffed to the chairman of the Eaft India Comp^y, having been read in a

LETTERS AND DOCUMENTS. 229

Committee of Warehoufes, they defire you will pleafe to meet them at this houfe tomorrow, at twelve of the clock at noon, relative to the exportation of tea to America.

I am, fir,

Your moft ob. serv't,

WM. SETTLE.

Eaft India Houfe,
7th July, 1773.

Samuel Wharton, Efqr.

TO THE WORSHIPFUL COMMITTEE OF WAREHOUSES FOR THE HON'BLE THE EAST INDIA COMPANY.

The Petition of Walter Manfell,[1] *of the City of London, Merchant, refpectfully fheweth:*

That your petitioner, having received certain information of the Hon'ble Eaft India Company's intention to export large quantities of teas to His Majefty's American Colonies, your petitioner therefore humbly begs leave to acquaint this Committee, that he and his partner, Thos. Corbett, now refident there have long carried on confiderable bufinefs as merchants, in Charles Town, South Carolina, where your petitioner has been refident himfelf for near 20 y^{rs} and flatters himfelf that he is well acquainted with the

[1] Mansell was a South Carolina loyalist, whose estate was confiscated, in 1782.

trade of that and the neighbouring Provinces. That your petitioner has at a very confiderable expence erected and built large and commodious brick warehoufes, for the reception of all kind of merchandize, in Charles Town, and has a fhip of his own, of the burthen of two hundred tons, conftantly employed in the Carolina trade only; that your petitioner humbly hopes and doubts not, but that this Hon'ble Com^{tee} will upon the ftrictest enquiry into his character and circumftances, being poffeffed of houfes and lands, in Charles Town, of upwards of £500 fterling pr an., and from his American connections find him not unworthy of their countenance and favor.

Your petitioner therefore humbly prefumes to offer his fervices to this Hon'ble Comm^{tee} to tranfact as their agent any bufinefs relative to the exportation to and fale of their teas in South Carolina, or elfewhere in the Colonies of America, as they fhall think fitting to commit to his care and management.

WALTER MANSELL.

Hon'ble Sirs:

We take the liberty of recommending Meffrs. Willing, Morris & Co.,[1] of Philadelphia, to be your agents there

---

[1] The firm of Willing, Morris & Co., established in 1754, was the most extensive importing house in Philadelphia. They worked actively and zealously for the non-importation articles of agreement, after the Stamp Act and the Tea Act were inflicted on this country. Robert Morris (1733-1806,) was the well-known financier of the Revolution. Thomas Willing, (1741-1821,) from 1754 to 1807, held successively the offices of Secretary to the Congress of Delegates, at Albany; mayor of the city of Philadelphia; Representative in the General Assembly; President of the Provincial Congress; delegate to the Congress of the Confederation; President of the first chartered Bank in America,

for any quantity of tea you may pleafe to confign them for fale, and which they will difpofe of in the beft manner they can for the benefit of the Com^y. on the following terms:

The tea to be fold at two months prompt, to be paid for on delivery, and the money to be paid at the exchange, which fhall be current at that time, into the Company's treafury within three months after it is received from Philadelphia. Willing, Morris & Co. to be allowed 5 pr cent. for commiffion, and 1 pr cent. for warehoufe room and all other charges, except freight & duty.

Meffrs. Peter & John Berthon are ready to become joint fecurities with us for Meffrs. Willing, Morris & Co.

We are, very refpectfully,
   Your honors moft obed^t humble fervants,
      ROBERTS, BAYNES & ROBERTS.

King's Arms Yard, July 8th, 1773.
To the Hon'ble the Com^{tee} &c., &c.

London, 8 July, 1773.
To the Hon'ble Committee of Warehoufes.
Gentlemen:

We beg leave to recommend Meffrs. James & Drinker, of Philadelphia, to be one of your agents at the

and President of the first bank of the United States. He was a man whose integrity and patriotism gained him the esteem and praise of his countrymen. From the beginning of the Revolutionary war, Willing & Morris were the agents of Congress for supplying their naval and military stores. To the great credit and well-known patriotism of this house, the country owed its extrication from those trying pecuniary embarrassments, so familiar to the readers of our Revolutionary history.

difpofal of teas, which you may think proper to fend to Philadelphia, undertaking that they fhall difpofe of fuch teas in no other manner than as you direct, on condition of your allowing them 5 pr cent. for commiffion, for felling and making remittance, and 1 pr cent. for truckage, warehoufe rent or any charge whatever; fhould any teas get damaged on board of fhips, any expence arifing on them to be allowed by the Company. We do alfo engage, that in two months after the prompt day, remittance in bills or fpecie, fhall be made to the Company, provided the teas are cleared, the fpecie to be at the rifk of the Company, they paying the charges attending it. We further agree, that in cafe any bills are protefted, we will pay the Company the amount of them in two months after they become due. And we are willing to enter into bond for the performance of the agreements, provided the Directors think proper to allow the teas to be fent to any other port, if the Penfilvanians refufe to admit the duty to be paid, or to confume them in that country, in the latter cafe, our bond to be void.

We are, &c., &c.,

PIGOU & BOOTH.

We beg leave to folicit the freight to Penfilvania.

Gentlemen:

Having been informed that the Directors of the Eaft India Company propofe fhipping teas to fome of the American Colonies, to be there fold by agents on the Company's account, and as I apprehend South Carolina may be fixed upon as one of them, I beg leave to propofe Mr. Roger Smith, of South Carolina, for whofe folidity I am willing to become refponfible.

If the intended plan takes effect, and you do *give* me the honor to admit of my application, I fhall be ready to attend you on the bufinefs whenever you may be pleafed to give me notice thereof. I have the honor to be, gentlemen,

Your moft obd' h'ble ferv'

JOHN NUTT.

New Broad Street Buildings,
14th July, 1773.

To the chairman and deputy chairman
of the Hon'ble Eaft India Company.

Sirs:

We beg leave to tender you the fervices of Mr. Samuel Chollet, merchant, in Charleftown, South Carolina, and Meffrs. Hugh and Alexander Wallace,[1] merchants, in

[1] Hugh and Alexander Wallace, brothers, were merchants, of New York, and partners in business. Hugh was a member of the Council, and second President of the Chamber of Commerce. He was arrested as a loyalist, and confined to the limits of Middletown, Conn., and his estate was confiscated. At the peace he went to England, and died at Waterford, Ireland, in 1788.

Alexander, his brother, also a loyalist, whose property was confiscated, had originally been a member of the committee of correspondence, and undoubtedly sympathized with the Whigs, but like many others, ultimately fell off from the great body of his countrymen, and clung to the royal cause. In August, 1776, he was arrested and confined at Fishkill. At the peace he went to England, with his brother, and died at Waterford, Ireland, in the year 1800.

New York, for the fale of fuch teas as you may think proper to fend there, being perfons in every refpect well qualified to difpofe of them to the beft advantage.

We are willing to enter into fuch covenants as may be required for the fecurity of the confignments & the remittances of the fales, on the fame terms as are to be granted to other houfes on the Continent of America, provided we are allowed a proper confideration for fuch guarantee.

We have the honor to be, firs,

Your moft obed' hble. ferv^{ts.}

BOURDIEU & CHOLLET.

Lime Street, July 15, 1773.

London, 15th July, 1773.

Gentlemen:

Hearing that you are going to appoint agents in America for the fale of your teas, permit us to propofe our partner, Mr. Daniel Stephenfon, of Blandensburgh, Maryland, as one (fhould you adopt this meafure,) and we flatter ourfelves, that from his long refidence & connexions in Virginia & Maryland, in bufinefs, that he will be thought an eligible perfon, & for his refponfibility, we are ready to give the fecurity of our houfe, fhould he be appointed on the fame terms as the other gentlemen. We apprehend his prefent fituation is well calculated for this meafure, being at a proper diftance between New York & James River, & near the centre of the Maryland bufiness.

We are, refpectfully, gentm^{n.} your moft odb' fervants,

GALE, FEARON & CO.

To the Committee of Warehoufes.

Sir:

Upon confidering the exportation of teas by the Company, having no direction or power from our correfpondents at Bofton or New York, to make terms, we decline offering any recommendation in the prefent ftate of the affair, at the fame time think our thanks are due to you, for your readinefs in attending to any propofitions we might make. We are, refpectfully,

Your moft ob^t ferv^{ts}

DAVISON & NEWMAN.

Fenchurch Street, July 15, 1773.

Edwd Wheeler, Efq^r deputy chairman.

Sir:

The Committee of Warehoufes of the Eaft India Company defire you will meet them at this houfe, on Thurfday next, at twelve o'clock at noon, relative to the exportation of tea to America. I am, fir,

Your moft obd^t ferv^t

WM. SETTLE.

Eaft India Houfe, 17th July, 1773.

To BROOK WATSON,
JONATHAN CLARKE,
FREDE'K PIGOU, Junr.,
GILBERT BARKLEY,
GEORGE BROWNE,
ROBERTS, BAYNES & ROBERTS,
MR. BERTHON,
WILLIAM KELLY,
GREENWOOD & HIGGINSON,

SAMUEL WHARTON,
JNO. BLACKBURN,
BENJN. HARRISON,
WALTER MANSELL,
JOHN NUTT,
DAVISON & NEWMAN,
BORDIEU & CHOLLETT,
GALE, FEARON & CO.

Gentlemen :

In confequence of my converfation this day, with the gentlemen of the Committee of Warehoufes, relative to the rate of exchange from Bofton, I beg leave to confirm the offer I made, of abiding by the ftandard exchange of £133 6s. 8d. currency for £100 fterling, upon an allowance of 2½ pr cent., with the provifo of the intended exportation being made by way of experiment, that is not exceeding 500 chefts to Bofton, before the fuccefs thereof is known.

I am, gentlemen,

Your h'ble ferv't,

WM. PALMER.

Devonfhire Square, 22 July, 1773.

To the Hon'ble the Court of Directors, &c.

Sirs :

It is fo perfectly contrary to all mercantile ufage, to fix a certain rate of exchange for commiffion bufinefs, that we muft beg leave to decline making any further propofals for your intended confignments to New York and Carolina, becaufe the revolutions in all exchanges cannot be forefeen. We have known the New York exchange at 168 & 190, at prefent it is 177½, the par between Philadelphia and New York is, as 160 at the former, to 170⅔ at the latter.

LETTERS AND DOCUMENTS. 237

If you fhould hereafter adopt the regular and ufual mercantile form — of receiving your remittances at the current exchange of the place at the time of remitting, we fhall be obliged to you for your confignments to Mefsrs. Hugh and Alexander Wallace, of New York, and Samuel Chollett, of Charleftown, South Carolina, for whom we will become fecurity for the ufual commiffion of guarantee of 2½ pr cent.

We are, firs,

Your moft obd' h'ble ferv.^{ts}

BOURDIEU & CHOLLET.

Lime Street, July 23rd 1773.

Sir:

The Committee of Warehoufes of the Eaft India Company defire you will meet them at this houfe tomorrow morning, at eleven o'clock, relative to the exportation of tea to America.

I am, fir,

Your moft obd' fervant,

WM. SETTLE.

Eaft India Houfe, 29th July, 1773.

To WALTER MANSELL,	FREDERICK PIGOU, Junr.,
WILLIAM PALMER,	WILLIAM KELLY,
BROOK WATSON,	SAMUEL WHARTON,
JONATHAN CLARKE,	GILBERT BARKLEY,
JOHN BLACKBURN,	GEORGE BROWNE.

238   LETTERS AND DOCUMENTS.

Sir:
I am directed by the Comm'ᵗᵉᵉ to acquaint you that the Court of Directors of the E. I. C. have agreed to ſhip for *Boſton* three hundred cheſts of tea, and conſign to your correſpondents an equal proportion thereof, of which pleaſe to inform them.
Shall be obliged to you to acquaint me the firm of your correſpondents at *Boſton*.   I am, ſir,
Your moſt hum. ſervᵗ
Wᴍ. Sᴇᴛᴛʟᴇ.
Eaſt India Houſe, 4ᵗʰ Augᵗ 1773.

To Jᴏɴᴀᴛʜᴀɴ Cʟᴀʀᴋᴇ, ⎫   Jᴏʜɴ Bʟᴀᴄᴋʙᴜʀɴ,   ⎫
    Wᴍ. Pᴀʟᴍᴇʀ,   ⎬ Esqʳˢ· Boston. Wᴍ. Kᴇʟʟʏ,   ⎬ Esqʳˢ· New York.
    Bʀᴏᴏᴋᴇ Wᴀᴛsᴏɴ,   ⎭   Fʀᴇᴅ'ᴋ Pɪɢᴏᴜ, Junʳ·⎭

                  Gᴇᴏ. Bʀᴏᴡɴᴇ,   ⎫
                  Gɪʟʙᴇʀᴛ Bᴀʀᴋʟʏ,   ⎬ Esqʳˢ· Philadelphia.
                  Fʀᴇᴅ'ᴋ Pɪɢᴏᴜ,   ⎪
                  Sᴀᴍ'ʟ Wʜᴀʀᴛᴏɴ,   ⎭

Sir:
At foot you have the firm of our correſpondents at Boſton, which we gave into the Comᵗᵉᵉ of Warehouſes for partaking of the India Comʸˢ· Tea conſignments, and for whom we are ready to give ſecurity.
Benjⁿ Faneuil, Junʳ,   ⎱ Eſqʳˢ of Boſton,
Joſhua Winſlow, late of Nova Scotia, ⎰   jointly.
        Security — Brook Watſon, Robᵗ Raſhleigh,
                              Watſon & Raſhleigh.
London, 4ᵗʰ Augᵗ 1773.
Mr. Wm. Settle.

LETTERS AND DOCUMENTS. 239

Security offered for Mr. Gilbert Barkly, — Wm. Rofs, Esq[r.] No. 24 Auftin Fryars.

Securities offered for Walter Manfell, — Henry Laurens, Fludyer Street, Carolina Merchants; William Barrett, Old Palace Yard.

Sir:
The firm of the houfe I have recommended to the Court of Directors for New York, is Pigou & Booth, and at Philadelphia, Mefsrs. James & Drinker, as agents for the difpofal of teas. I am, sir,
Your moft hum. fer[t]
FRED'K PIGOU, Jun[r.]
Mark Lane, 4 Aug[t]
Mr. Wm. Settle.

Sir:
I was favored with your letter of yefterday, *laſt* night *after* ten o'clock, acquainting me that the Court of Directors of the E. I. C. had agreed to fhip for Philadelphia fix hundred chefts of tea, and confign to my correfpondents an equal proportion thereof, you will be pleafed to inform the Directors that I gave notice to my brothers, Thomas & Ifaac Wharton, (the perfons whom I recommended,) by the

240   LETTERS AND DOCUMENTS.

laſt night's New York mail, of the refolution of the Court of Directors to ſhip the above quantity of teas to Philadelphia. I am, ſir,

Your moſt hum. ferv't,

SAM'L WHARTON.

Argyle Street, Augt 5, 1773.
Mr. Wm. Settle.

Mr. Browne's compliments to Mr. Settle, and begs leave to inform him that the addrefs of the houfe at Philadelphia, whom he recommends for an agent for the fale of tea, is Jonathan Browne, merchant, at Philadelphia.

Augst 5, 1773.

Sir:

Laſt evening I had the pleafure to receive yours of yeſterday, mentioning the refolution of the Court of Directors of the Hon'ble Eaſt India Company relative to the exportation of tea to New York, and defiring me to acquaint you with the firm of my correfpondent there, which is Abraham Lott & Co. I am, ſir,

Yours, &c.,

WILLIAM KELLY.

Crefcent, 5th Augt 1773.
Mr. Wm. Settle.

LETTERS AND DOCUMENTS. 241

MR. PALMER'S OPINION IN WHAT MODE TO SHIP TEA TO AMERICA.

The Bohea tea to be taken out of what was refufed by the buyers laft fale; but particular care to be taken that none under the degree of middling, or good middling, nor any damaged chefts are fent, to be marked & invoiced, not according to the King's numbers, but the Company's, to be reweighed, by thus marking them, each bed will be kept feparate, and there will not only be no pretence abroad for finding fault, as from No. to No., will be exactly of the fame quantity, having been packed from the faid heap or pile at Canton, and fince examined in England. But the tafte of the Americans will alfo be better known, that is, whether they prefer a frefh middling tea, provided it is not abfolutely faint, or a ftrong, rough tea. A certain quantity of each of thefe kinds to be fent to each place, that either may not have the advantage over the other, by having teas of a fuperior quality, their refpective qualities to be remarked in the invoices. A fmall affortment of about a dozen or twenty fmall chefts of Hyfon, Souchong, Congou, and each fpecie of Singlo tea, viz.: Twankey, Skin and Firft Sort, to be fent to each place, with proper remarks thereon in the refpective invoices, each of thefe fpecies to be taken out of fome bed or break of teas now laid down, or intended fo to be, for next September fale, regard being had to their refpective qualities, and to be taken out of fuch beds or breaks, which fhall be fufficiently large, not only to fupply each Colony with its quantity, but alfo to leave a confiderable part thereof to be fold at the enfuing fale, by which means the Company may hereafter compare the prices to the fame parcel of tea fells for, not only at each Colony, but alfo at their own fales, which can no otherwife be done, as each of thefe fpecies, going under the fame general denomination of Hyfon, Souchong, Congo and Singlo, vary almoft 100 pr cent. in the price they fell for, according to quality, & not 10 pr cent. in the purchafe.

As it would be a great object with the Company to introduce, if poffible, the confumption of Singlo tea into America, that being a kind of tea which fpoils by age, much more than Bohea, and alfo that of which they are much more confiderably overloaded with, and further, fuch an introduction would have this advantage alfo, that the foreign countries could not foon rival us, not being themfelves importers of any confiderable quantity of this fpecie of tea. It fhould be recommended to the agents, to endeavour all they can, at fuch introduction, which it is conceived may be brought about, at leaft in fome degree, from the experience of the confumption here in England, which will appear to have conftantly gained ground proportionally, as its price at the Company's fales has approached nearer to Bohea tea, and in the prefent fituation of this branch of the Company's trade, it might eafily be made appear, it would be for their advantage, even to fell it in America, at the quoted price of Bohea, by which means they might be relieved from the difagreeable alternative of felling it here under prime coft, or keeping a greater quantity unfold in their warehoufes, until it is fpoiled by age.

London, Augt 5th 1773.
St. Paul's Churchyard, N° 55.

Sir:

I am favored with yours of yefterday's date, and agreeable to your requeft, I fhall immediately communicate the information therein contained, to Richard Clarke, Efqr., & Sons, Merchants, in Bofton, New England, which is the houfe with which I am connected, and who I flatter myfelf will acquit themfelves of the truft the Hon'ble the Court of Directors have been pleafed to repofe in them.

I would alfo beg leave to folicit part of the freight of the tea for a veffel which I fhall poffibly have ready in ten days, provided it will agree with the time you propofe to fhip them.

I am, fir,

Your moft hum. ferv^t

JONATHAN CLARKE.

Mr. Wm. Settle, 17th Aug^t

Wm., Capt Jofeph Royal
Loring, will be ready in 5 days.

Sir:

The Committee of Warehoufes defire you will inform them whether you have a conftant trader to Bofton or South Carolina ready to fail, as the Eaft India Com^y intend

LETTERS AND DOCUMENTS.

to export teas to both thofe Colonies, and are defirous of giving you the preference of the freight.

I am, fir,

Your moft obedi* fer*

WM. SETTLE.

Eaft India Houfe, 5th Augt 1773.
To George Hayley, Efqr
Thos. Lane, Efqr.
Alex. Champion, Efqr.

———

Sir:

The deputy chairman of the Eaft India Com' defires you would point out to the Com"." of Warehoufes what forts of tea and quantity of each are, in your opinion, proper to be fent to Bofton & South Carolina, to make up to the former of thofe places, an export equal to 300 large chefts of Bohea tea, and the latter a quantity equal to 200 large chefts Bohea.

Mr. Holbrook fays if you can be with him this morning, you will expedite his bufinefs very much, as the Com"" have directed him to make ready for fhipping immediately.

I am, fir,

Your moft hum. ferv*

WM. SETTLE.

Eaft India Houfe, 6th Augt 1773.
Mr. Wm. Settle.

MR. PALMER'S ASSORTMENT OF TEAS FOR AMERICA.

		Boston.	So. Carolina.	New York.	Philadelphia.	Total.
Bohea,	l. ch^{ts.}	268	182	568	568	1586
Congo,	fm^l d^{o.}	20	10	20	20	70
Singlo,	d^{o.}	80	50	80	80	290
Hyfon,	d^{o.}	20	10	20	20	70
Souchong,	d^{o.}	10	5	10	10	35

WEIGHT OF TEA EXPORTED TO AMERICA.

	lbs.
Bohea,	562,421
Singlo,	22,546
Hyfon,	5,285
Souchong,	2,392
Congou,	6,015
Total lbs.,	598,659

The Hayley, James Scott, is now ready to fail, & I mean to difpatch her 15.th Augt. The Dartmouth, James Hall,[1] will be here about 14 days longer. These two are conftant traders to Bofton.

I have no connection with the Carolina trade, but I underftand the London, Curling, belonging to Greenwood &

[1] James Hall, captain of the "Dartmouth," the first tea-ship to arrive in America, was a Boston loyalist, and was consequently proscribed and banished in 1778.

246   LETTERS AND DOCUMENTS.

Higginfon, is now ready for failing, and is a conftant trader. Mr. Settle will pleafe to inform the Com.ᵗᵉᵉ of the above & thereby oblige,

His humble fervant,

GEORGE HAYLEY.

Eaft India H? 10 Augᵗ 1773.

To GREY COOPER, Efqʳ· or Jɴº· ROBINSON, Efqʳ·

Sir:

By order of the Court of Directors of the United Eaft India Compʸ, I tranfmit you the enclofed petition, with their requeft that you will be pleafed to lay the fame before the Right Hon'ble the Lords Commiffioners of the Treafury.

I am, very refpectfully, fir,

Your moft obedᵗ & hum. ferᵗ

PETER MITCHELL, Secʳ·

To THE RIGHT HON'BLE THE LORDS COMMISSIONERS OF HIS MAJESTY'S TREASURY.

The humble Petition of the United Company of Merchants of England trading to the Eaft Indies.

Sheweth :

That by an Act paffed in the laft feffion of Parliament, it is among other things enacted, " That it fhall and may be lawful for the Commiffioners of his Majefty's treafury, or any three or more of them, or the High Treaſurer for the time being, to grant a licence or licences to the ſaid United Company, to take out of their warehouſes ſuch quantity or quantities of tea as the ſaid Commiſſioners of the Treaſury, or any three or more of them, or the High Treaſurer for the time being, ſhall think fit, without the ſame having been expoſed to ſale in this kingdom, and to export ſuch tea to any of the Britiſh colonies or plantations in America, or to foreign parts diſcharged from the payment of any of the cuſtoms or duties whatſoever."

That the ſaid United Com[ny] have agreed to export to the Britiſh colonies or plantations in America a quantity of teas, equal in weight to 1700 large cheſts of Bohea tea, which quantity will not in the whole exceed ſix hundred thouſand pounds weight. And your petitioner having in the affidavit hereunto annexed ſhewed unto your lordsps that after the taking out of their warehouſes the ſaid quantities of teas ſo intended to be exported, that there will be left remaining in the warehouſes of the ſaid United Company a quantity of tea not leſs than ten millions of pounds weight, as by the ſaid Act is directed.

Your petitioners therefore pray your lordſhips to grant them a licence to take out of their warehouſes the quantities of teas above mentioned, not exceeding in the whole ſix hundred thouſand pounds weight, without the ſame having been expoſed to ſale in this kingdom, and to export ſuch tea diſcharged from the payment of any cuſtoms or duties whatſoever.

By order of the Court of Directors of the ſaid Company.

P. MITCHELL, Secy.

Eaſt India Ho. 19th April, 1773.

LICENCE TO EXPORT TEA.

After our hearty commendations. Whereas, the united company of merchants of England trading to the Eaſt Indies, have, by the annexed petition, humbly prayed us to grant them, in purſuance of an Act paſſed the laſt ſeſſion of Parliament, a licence to take out of their warehouſes a quantity of teas, equal in weight to one thouſand ſeven hundred large cheſts of Bohea tea, which quantity will not in the whole exceed ſix hundred thouſand pounds weight, without the ſame having been expoſed to ſale in this kingdom, and to export ſuch tea diſcharged from the payment of any cuſtoms or duties whatſoever, to the Britiſh colonies or plantations in America. And it appearing to us by the annexed affidavit, that there will be left remaining in their warehouſes a quantity of tea not leſs than ten millions of pounds weight, as by the ſaid Act is provided and directed. Now we, having taken the ſaid application and the ſeveral matters and things therein ſet forth into our conſideration, do think fit to comply with the requeſt of the ſaid petitioners. And in purſuance of the powers given unto us by the ſaid Act, we do hereby authoriſe, permit and grant licence to the ſaid Company to take out of their warehouſes the ſaid quantity of tea, not exceeding in the whole ſix hundred thouſand pounds weight, without* the ſame having been expoſed to ſale in this kingdom, and to export ſuch teas diſcharged from the payment of any cuſtoms or duties whatſoever, to any of the Britiſh colonies or plantations in America. Neverthelefs, you are therein to take eſpecial care, that all and every the rules, regulations & reſtrictions and orders directed by the ſaid recited Act, relating to the

LORD NORTH.

exportation of fuch teas, or any ways concerning the fame, be in all and every refpect fully obeyed and obferved. And for fo doing, this fhall be as well to you as to the faid Company, and to all other officers & perfons whatfoever herein concerned, a fufficient warrant.

Given under our hands and feals at the Treafury Chambers, Whitehall, the 20th day of Auguft, one thoufand feven hundred and feventy three; in the thirteenth year of the reign of our fovereign lord, George the Third, King of Great Britain, France and Ireland, and fo forth.

            NORTH.
            C. TOWNSHEND.
            C. J. FOX.

To our very loving friends the Commiffioners, for managing His Majefty's Revenues of Cuftoms and Excife, now and for the time being, and to all other officers and perfons herein concerned.

Eaft India Company, Licence to Export Teas

Hon'ble Sirs:

We have the fhip Eleanor, James Bruce, about 250 tons, (a conftant trader,) which we intend for Bofton, and fhould be much obliged for the freight of the teas you intend exporting to that place.

We have no fhip bound to South Carolina, but are much obliged for the preference given us. We are, firs,

      Your moft h'ble fert$^{s.}$

         LANE, SON & FRASER.

Nicholas Lane, 6th Augst 1773.

The Hon'ble the Court of Directors, &c., &c.

John Dorrien, Efq[r.] recommends for Bofton, the Beaver, Capt[n] Coffin.

Sir:
I wrote you under date of the 5th inft[t] that you would be pleafed to inform the Committee of Warehoufes, whether you had a conftant trader ready to fail for Bofton or South Carolina, but fhould have faid to Bofton only. I am therefore to defire the favor of an anfwer whether you have a conftant trader ready for that colony.

I am, &c., &c.,

WM. SETTLE.

Eaft India H[o.] Aug[t] 10, 1773.
Alex. Champion, Efq[r.]

Sir:
In anfwer to your efteemed of the 5th and 10th current, am obliged by the favor intended, but at prefent have only one fhip under my care bound to Bofton, who will depart in a very few days, but fhe is not a conftant trader. It is not, therefore, in my power to accept of the offer.

I am, fir,

Your moft hum. ferv[t.]

ALEXANDER CHAMPION.

Bifhopgate Street, Aug[t] 10, 1773.
Mr. Wm. Settle.

Hon'ble Sir:

Being informed you have fome teas to fhip to America, I have now a veffel, Britifh built, burthen about 160 tons, which fhould be glad to lett to your honors for the above purpofe.

I am, with due regard, hon'ble firs,

Your moft obed^t fervt^t,

THOS. WALTERS.

Carolina Coffee Houfe,
Birchen Lane, 17th Augt 1773.

The Elizabeth, John Scott, for any part of America.

To the Hon'ble Directors of
the Eaft India Company.

Mr. Abraham Dupies, in Gracechurch Street, will become obligated for Richard Clarke & Sons, of Bofton.

Gentlemen:

I have a veffel in this port, which will be ready to return to America in a few days, therefore take the opportunity to acquaint you that I am willing to take on board her 600 chefts of tea, either for New York or Philadelphia, at the a cuftomary freight given from hence to thofe places.

I am, gentl^n your moft hum. fervant,

JOSEPH CABOT.

Threadneedle Street, 24 Augt 1773.
To the Hon'ble Committee of Warehoufes.

London, Augt 26, 1773.

Sir:

We pray you to inform the Com^{tee} of Warehoufes for the Hon'ble the Eaft India Company that we have a fhip, *river built*, called the Nancy, commanded by Captain Colville, compleately fitted and ready to receive the tea for New York, which we beg leave to recommend to the Committee. We are, fir,

   Your moft obedient and humble fervants,

        JOHN BLACKBURN.
        PIGOU & BOOTH.
        W^M. KELLY & CO.

Mr. Wm. Settle.

Sir:

Pleafe to acquaint the Hon'ble Committee of Warehoufes, that we have taken up the Polly, Capt Ayres, for Philadelphia, to carry the Company's tea to that port, which veffel lays at Princes Stairs, Rotherhith, and was built at Ipfwich, in the year 1765. She is now ready to take in.

  We are, firs,

    Your moft h'ble ferv^{ts}

        PIGOU & BOOTH,
      For selves & GEORGE BROWNE,
        SAMUEL WHARTON & GILBERT BARKLEY.

Mark Lane, 31ft Augt 1773.

Mr. Wm. Settle.

Sir:

Your remarks to the bond offered you, relative to the 600 chefts of tea, which are to be exported to New York, have been laid before the Committee of Warehoufes, and they are of opinion that the faid bond is according to the agreement made with the feveral gentlemen for the different Colonies, and the merchants who are concerned for the tea to Bofton, have executed their bonds agreeable thereto, and Meffrs. Wharton, Pigou & Barkley have agreed alfo to execute on Thurfday morning. Therefore, I am to defire you to inform me whether you will pleafe likewife to execute the faid bond.

I am, fir,

Your moft h'ble ferv^t

WM. SETTLE.

Eaft India Houfe, 31st Augt 1773.
To John Blackburn, Efq^r·
William Kelly, Efq^r·

Sir:

As the feveral gentlemen mentioned in your polite note of this day have executed the bond, I fhall with pleafure follow their example, and on Thurfday next I propofe waiting on you for that purpofe. I am fir,

Your moft h'ble ferv^t

JOHN BLACKBURN.

Scot's Yard, 31ft Augt 1773.
Mr. Wm. Settle.

Sir:

Laſt evening I had the pleaſure to receive your favor of yeſterday, relative to the bond which I am to ſign for New York, and the objections made to its draught by Mr. Blackburn, Pigou and myſelf, which at the time appeared reſonable to us, but as others have ſigned in the form ſhewn to me, I don't mean to be particular, and therefore ſhall conform, relying on the honor of the Com^{tee} in all future matters.

Tomorrow I am indiſpenſably obliged to go out of town ſhall return on Saturday next, wait on you, & execute the bond. I am, ſir,

Your moſt obedi^t & moſt hum. ſerv^t

WM. KELLY.

Creſcent, Sep. 1^{ſt} 1773.

Mr. Wm. Settle.

Freight of 568 whole, & 130 half cheſts of Tea, ſhipped on the Polly, Capt Saml Ayres, for Philadelphia:

                                                        feet.

568 cheſts con^{g} for freight, ... 8748.6

130 quarter d$^{o.}$ d$^{o.}$ 656.9

                                                      9405.3

9405.3 at 1s. 6d. pr foot, Philadelphia currency, is £705 7 10½

              tons.

Primage on 235⅙ at 2s. ſterl^g pr ton, is £23 10 3

LETTERS AND DOCUMENTS. 257

Freight of Tea on the London, to South Carolina:
feet.
182 chefts meafure 2644.3 at 1s. pr foot, £132 4 3
  75 d⁰·   d⁰·   345.9 d⁰· 17 5 9
257   149 10 0
              Primage, 5 pr cent, . . .   7 10 0
                                                £157 0 0

Freight of Tea fhipped on the William, for Bofton:
feet.
58 chefts meafure 585.11, at 1s. 4d. pr foot, £39 1 3 L.M.
                            Primage, ... 1 9 6 fterlg·

Freight of 698 chefts Tea on the Nancy, for New York:
feet.
698 chefts meafure 9264.8, at 2s. 3d. pr foot, is
Currency, ... £1042 5 4
Sterling, £30 8 2   Primage, 5 pr ct. .   52 2 3
                                                £1094 7 7

Freight of 114 chefts Tea on the Eleanor, for Bofton:
feet.
114 chefts meafure 1383.4, at 1s. 4d. . . £92 4 5 L.M.
                Primage, ... £3 9 0

Freight of 112 chefts Tea on the Beaver, for Bofton:
feet.
112 chefts meafure 1375, at 1s. 4d., is . £91 13 10 L.M.
34½ tons at 2s. pr ton primage, . £3 17 0
29

Whitehall, Dec' 17th 1773.

Lord Dartmouth prefents his compliments to Mr. Wheler, and requefts the favor to fee him at his office, at Whitehall, on Monday morning next, at eleven o'clock, on the fubject of fome advices Lord Dartmouth has lately received from America, refpecting the importation of tea from England.

LETTER TO SUNDRY AMERICAN MERCHANTS.

Sir:

The Com^tee of Warehoufes of the E. I. Com^y defire you would pleafe to inform them whether you have receiv'd any advices from *Bofton* relative to the faid Com^rs exportation of tea to that colony, and if you have, to communicate the purport thereof to the Committee. I am, fir,

Your moft obe. fer^t

WM. SETTLE.

Eaft India Houfe, 20th Dec' 1773.

To Mr. Wm. Palmer,⎱ *Bofton.*
   Brook Watfon, ⎰

Wm. Greenwood,⎱ *South Carolina.*
J^o. Nutt, ⎰

J^no. Blackburn, ⎱ *New York.*
Wm. Kelly, ⎰

Fred^k Pigou, Junr *New York & Philadelphia.*

Geo. Browne, ⎱ *Philadelphia.*
Saml Wharton, ⎰

LETTER TO SUNDRY AMERICAN MERCHANTS.[1]

Sir:

The Comm.ʳˢ of Warehoufes defire the favor of an anfwer under your hand to my letter of yefterday, relative to the exportation of tea to *Bofton*. I am, fir,

Your moft obdᵗ fervant,

WM. SETTLE.

Eaft India Houfe, 21ˢᵗ Decʳ 1773.

Brook Watfon, Esqʳ *Bofton*.
Wm. Greenwood, Esqʳ ⎫
John Nutt, Esqʳ ⎭ *South Carolina*.
John Blackburn, Esqʳ *New York*.
Geo. Browne, Esqʳ *Philadelphia*.

LETTERS FROM SUNDRY AMERICAN MERCHANTS,

WITH ENCLOSURES OF ADVICES FROM THE SEVERAL COLONIES.

BOSTON.

From Mr. Palmer.

Mr. Palmer has received no material advices from Bofton fince the confignment has taken place, but has letters of as late a date from thence as the 3ᵈ of Novemʳ, one of which mentions there was no tea then to be bought.

Eaft India Houfe, 21ft Decʳ 1773

---

[1] These two letters following each other so closely, plainly manifest the anxiety of the Company, in reference to their shipments of tea to Boston.

Garlick Hill, 22d Decem' 1773.

To the Hon'ble the Committee of Warehoufes, Eaft India Houfe.

Gent^m:

In compliance with your requeft, we fend you enclofed extracts from the letters which we have lately received from Bofton relative to the Com^rs teas fent there.

We are, gent^n

Your moft hum. ferv^ts

WATSON & RASHLEIGH.

Extract of a Letter dated Bofton, 18th Octo^r. 1773:

"But what difficulties may arife from the difaffection of the merchants and importers of tea to this meafure of the India Company, I am not yet able to fay. It feems at prefent to be a matter of much fpeculation, and if one is to credit the prints, no fmall oppofition will be made thereto. However, I am in hopes it will be otherwife, and taking it for granted that the tea fhould arrive, and no obftacle happen to prevent its being landed and difpofed of, agreeably to the inftructions of the Company, then I am to add that you may be affured I fhall ftrictly conform to the inftructions which I may jointly receive refpecting it, paying all due regard to the contents of your letter.

"I know not how to write more fully hereon until the tea arrives, and what may poffibly be the confequences attending it. My friends feem to think it will fubfide; others are of a contrary opinion."

Extract of a Letter dated Boston, 30 Oct[r.] *1773:*

"I omitted a letter to you in particular when I wrote to your houſe the 10th inſt., becauſe I thought it was probable, both from the contents of your letter then received, as well as from the public reports, that the tea you mention as coming from the India Com[y] might every day be expected to arrive, as you ſay 4 Aug[t.] they intended ſhipping 300 cheſts immediately, but by my letter, this day received by a veſſel from London, it is not to be ſent.

"I perceive by the prints, that the clamour is ſtill continued againſt this meaſure of the India Company, and ſeems to be purſued with rather more warmth in ſome of the Southern Colonies than in this. For my own part I am not ſufficiently ſkilled in politicks to ſee the pernicious conſequences which 'tis ſaid muſt ariſe therefrom. If they would prevent the Tea Act being enforced, or the payment of the revenue ariſing therefrom to Government, methinks they ſhould either not import any tea, or rather not conſume any, and then the end would be anſwered at once. But while there is ſuch a vaſt quantity exported every year by ſo conſiderable a number of perſons, who all pay the duty thereof on its arrival, I do not ſee why every importer, nay, every conſumer thereof, do not as much contribute to inforce the Tea Act as the India Comp[y] themſelves, or the perſons to whom they may think proper to conſign their tea for ſale. Nor can I but be of opinion that the uneaſineſs is fomented, if not originated, principally by thoſe perſons concerned in the Holland trade, and thereby introduce large quantities of tea, which, paying no duty, by that means they can afford to underſell thoſe who do pay it, and this trade, I am informed, is much more practifed in the Southern Governments than this way.

"To what lengths the oppofition to this tea's being brought or landed, or difpofed of, may be carried, muft be left to time to determine."

Extract of a Letter dated Bofton, 4 Nov.r 1773:

"Thus far I had wrote you with intentions to forward by firft conveyance, when I found there was to be a mufter of the people, to demand that the perfons who are to be employed as agents for difpofing of the tea which may come from the India Company, would refign their commiffions & fwear (under Liberty Tree) to return the tea by the fame or firft veffels for London, &c. You will be fully acquainted of their unreafonable proceedings. After the time had elapfed which was fixed upon for the gentlemen to appear and refign, on their not complying with the order, they marched down in a body to Mr. Clarke's ftore, where we were, and not receiving fuch an anfwer as they demanded, they began an attack upon the ftore and thofe within, breaking down doors, flinging about mud, &c., for about an hour, when they began to difperfe, and a number of gentlⁿ, friends of thofe agents coming to their affiftance, they left the ftore and went upon change, but met with no further infult, tho' there is much threatening. As the tea is not arrived, and it is uncertain when it may, I purpofe to write you again fpeedily.

"In the interim, I am, &c."

Attack on BUNKERS-HILL, or the STORMING of CHARLESTOWN, the 17th. of June 1775.

Printed for I. Bowles, Carington Bowles, now York.

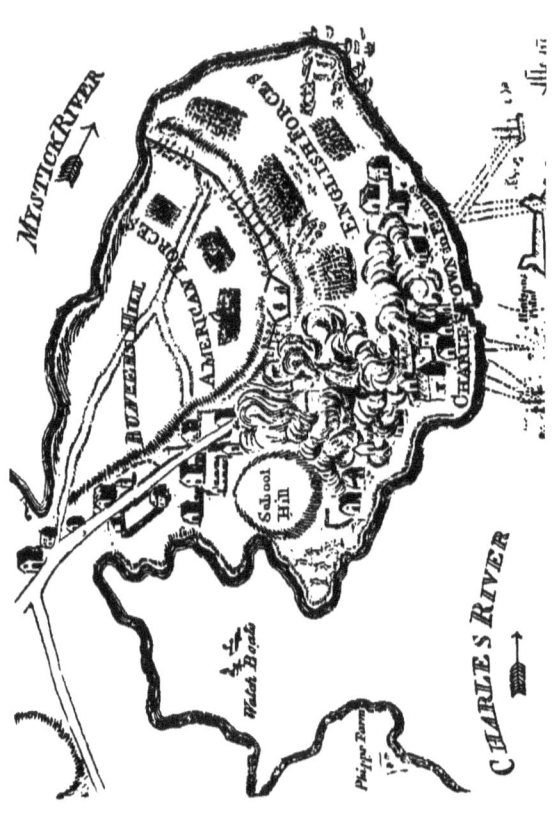

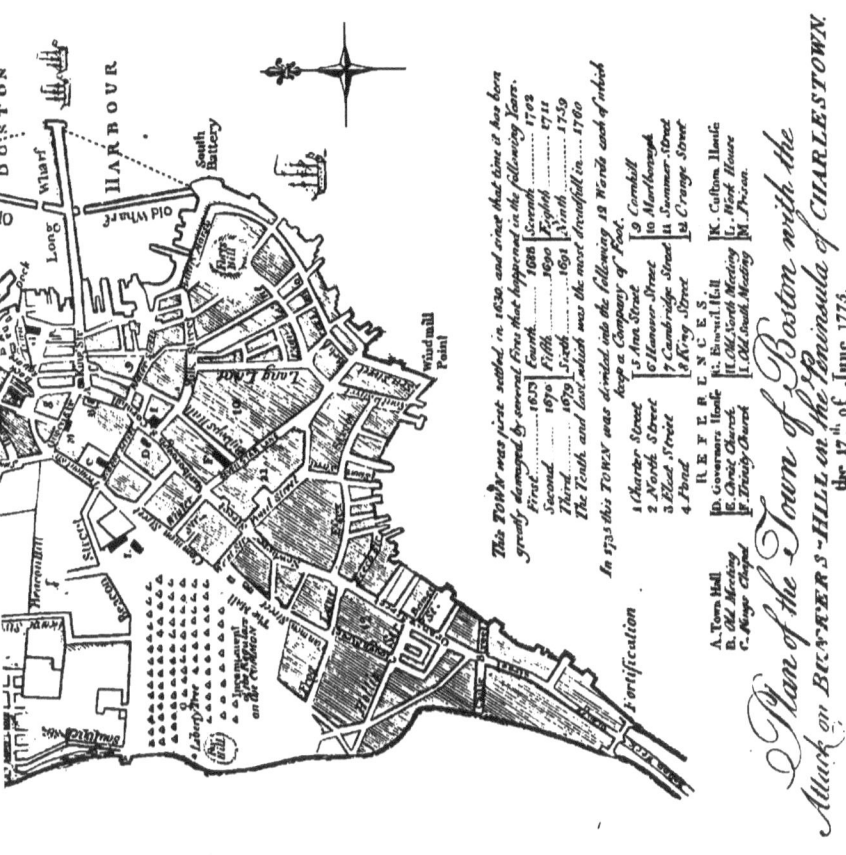

SOUTH CAROLINA.

Letter from Mr. Greenwood.

Sir:

In anfwer to your letter of the 20th inft., I beg you would be pleafed to inform the Com.rs of Warehoufes that I have yet received no advices from South Carolina, relative to the Comp.y's exportation of tea. When I do, they may depend I will take the earlieft opportunity to communicate the fame to them.

I am, fir,

Your moft obe.t ferv.t

WM. GREENWOOD

Queen Street, 22.d Dec.r. 1773.

Mr. Settle.

From Mr. Nutt.

Gentlemen:

In compliance with your defire, intimated to me by Mr. Settle, refpecting any information received from South Carolina, concerning the teas exported by the Eaft I. Com.y to that Colony, I have the honor to acquaint you that the veffel in which they were fhipped did not fail from England before the 18th October, and the lateft dates from thence are only the 1st Nov[r.] fo that we cannot expect for fome time to hear of her arrival. I have the honor to be, gent[n.]

Your moft obed[t] hum. ferv[t.]

JOHN NUTT.

Broad Street, 22nd Decem[r.] 1773.
To the Com[rs.] of Warehoufes, &c., &c., &c.

NEW YORK.

Letter from Mr. Blackburn.

Sir:

I am honored with your two letters of the 20th & 21ft curr[t], defiring me to inform the Com[rs.] of Warehoufes if I have received any advices from New York relative to the Com['s] exportation of tea to that Colony.

The veffel wherein the tea was fhipped was not arrived when the laft letters were difpatched from thence, confequently no precife judgment can be formed whether or not it would be permitted to be landed; but I flatter myfelf from the difpofition of the principal gentle[n] of New York, who are men of moderation, candour and prudence, and as firmly attached to the Government and laws of this Kingdom as any of his Majefty's fubjects; that they will, by their example and influence, be able to fupprefs every riot and difturbance occafioned by the oppofers of this meafure.

I expect a ship from New York, which was to depart about the 26th Novemr. by which I shall receive some fresh intelligence relative to this business, and if I should be furnished with any advices that regard the interest of the Company, I shall not fail to wait on the Directors immediately. I have the honor to be, sir,

Your most obedt & hum. serv.
JOHN BLACKBURN.

Scots Yard, 22nd Decr. 1773.
Mr. Wm. Settle.

Extract of a Letter from a merchant in New York, to Wm. Kelly, of London, dated 5th Novr. 1773 :

"The introduction of the East India Comyany's tea is violently opposed here, by a set of men who shamefully live by monopolizing tea in the smuggling way."

Extract of a Letter from Abraham Lott, Esqr. of New York, to Wm. Kelly,[1] of London, dated New York, 5th Novr. 1773, & received with the above mentioned Extract of Mr. Kelly, 22d Decr. 1773:

"Herewith you will receive several papers relating to the importation of the India Comy.s tea. If it comes out free of a *duty here* on importation, things I believe may go

---

[1] William Kelly is, I suppose, the person referred to in the following paragraph in Leake's "Life of John Lamb," pp. 75, 76. "A certain Mr. Kelly, former resident of the city, (New York,) then in London, and canvassing some one of

quiet enough, tho' you will obferve much is faid againft it even on that fuppofition. But if it fhould be fubject to a duty here, I am much in doubt whether it will be fafe, as almoft every body in that cafe fpeaks againft the admiffion of it, fo that, altho' I am well affured that the Governor will not fuffer the laws to be trampled on, yet there will be no fuch thing as felling it, as the people would rather buy fo much poifon, than the tea with the duty thereon, calculated (they fay) to enflave them and their pofterity, and therefore are determined not to take what they call the naufeous draft. A little time will determine how matters will terminate, that is, if the tea comes out. If it does, I hope it may come free of duty, as by that means much trouble and anxiety will be faved by the agents. I. do affure you they have all been very uneafy, tho' at the fame time determined to do their duty, but in the moft prudent & quiet manner. It is now two o'clock, P.M., when I received the paper figned Caffius, in which you will find Mr. L——R——de handfomely complimented, and yourfelf feverely handled, on a fuppofition that you fhould have fpoken words to the import, as afferted in the paper. Mr.

the Ministerial Boroughs for an election to Parliament, ridiculed the apprehensions of those who refused to insure the cargoes of tea from destruction, and declared that if animosities should rise as high as during the time of the Stamp Act, the tea might safely be shipped and securely landed. That then the Colony had an old man to deal with (Colden); but now they would have to contend with a vigorous military governor, (Tryon,) one who had shown his energy in putting down insurrectionary movements in North Carolina. The Committee of Vigilance took note of these offensive declarations, and on November 5, called a meeting at the Coffee House. The people assembled, denounced Kelly, and burnt his effigy, and after the representative was consumed, a gentleman observed that it was matter of regret that the principal could not be dealt with in the same summary and exemplary manner."

R——e's name is not mentioned, but there is no doubt but he is the perfon alluded to, as upon the arrival of the London fhips, who refufed to bring the tea. It was currently reported that he had wrote his partner nearly in the fame words as mentioned in the paper. You are the beft judge of the truth of the affertion, but whether true or not, his conduct is ungenerous and mean. If the paper fpeaks truth, that he was offered part of the confignment of tea, he muft be a man of great influence to have fo great an offer made him, when fo many other people of weight were applying for it and could not obtain it."

From Mr. Fred^k Pigou, Junr.

Sir:
   Pleafe to acquaint the Com^{tee} of Warehoufes of the Hon'ble the Eaft India Company, that from the advices I have received from *Philadelphia*, I fhould be of opinion the tea fent to that place will, if landed, meet with much difficulty in being difpofed of.

At New York, I am of opinion it will meet with lefs oppofition, and may poffibly be fold in that city. It would have been fortunate if the New York veffel could have arrived as foon or before the Philadelphia fhip.

   I am, fir, your moft hum. ferv^t
            Fred'k Pigou, Junr.
Mark Lane, 21ft Decr. 1773.
To Mr. Settle.

PHILADELPHIA.

Letter from Mr. Geo. Browne.

Sir:

The advice I have from my brother at Philadelphia, relative to the Com$^{r\underline{s}}$ confignment of tea, is, that it was very doubtful how it would be received there, the meafure being looked upon in an unfavorable view in general. He had only juft received an account (from another hand) of his being nominated one of the agents, and refers me to the public prints for an account of the refolutions entered into by the people in oppofition to it. I am, fir,

Your moft obedi^t fer^t

GEO. BROWNE.

Mr. Settle.

From Mr. Saml Wharton.

Sir:

I underftand that Mr. Walpole, of Lincolns Inn Fields, had received fome advices from my brother, refpecting the teas fent to Philadelphia. I applied to him for them, and he requefted that I would fend them to you, with what intelligence I had myfelf received. I am, fir,

Your very hum. ferv^t

SAMUEL WHARTON.

Argyle Street, Decem^r 23, 1773.

Mr. Settle.

LETTERS AND DOCUMENTS. 273

Extract of a Letter from Thomas Wharton,[1] *Esqr· of Philadelphia, dated Oct. 5, 1773, to Saml Wharton, in London:*

"I have closely attended to the course of your arguments, and think they are of great weight, but you know it is impossible always to form a true judgment from what real motives an opposition springs, as the smugglers and London importers may both declare that this duty is stamping the Americans with the badge of slavery, and notwithstanding the Directors of the East India Company have a just right to send their teas where they think proper, yet the Americans allege they may and ought to refuse to purchase and use it.

"A little time after the ship's arrival we shall know what is to be done, and I expect we shall before that time have a conference with the agents from New York, *which I proposed,* that our conduct might be uniform, and as much as possible answer the end of *our appointment.*"

---

[1] Thomas Wharton was a wealthy and influential merchant of Philadelphia, and of the sect called Quakers. In the enterprise of Galloway and Goddard to establish the "Chronicle," a leading newspaper, he was their partner, and the parties supposed that Franklin, who was a correspondent of Wharton's, on his return from England, would join them. In 1777, he was apprehended, and sent prisoner to Virginia, and at a later period was proscribed as an enemy to his coun.ry, and lost his estate, under the Confiscation Acts of Pennsylvania. His son, Thomas Wharton, Jr., was a distinguished Whig, and President of Pennsylania. In the early part of the Revolution, and indeed until the time when blood was shed, father and son acted together, and were members of the same deliberative assemblies and committees.

Extracts of two Letters from Tho[s.] *Warton, Esq*[r.] *of Philadelphia, dated Oct. 5 and Oct. 30, 1773, to the Hon'ble Tho*[s.] *Walpole, of London:*

"About a week before the arrival of the September mail, a letter reached this city, informing us that particular perfons (tho' not all of them the proper ones) were nominated agents for the Eaft India Directors. This gave the inhabitants a knowledge of the intention of the Directors, and fome perfons immediately declared, that as the duty was ftill retained, that, tho' fmall, yet it as implicitly fixed the power and eftablifhed the badge of flavery, as if it had been greater. The fame fentiments, I am told, are expreffed in letters from New York. At prefent, therefore. it is impoffible to fay what meafures the people will take on this occafion, but I fhould expect they will not hinder the tea being landed, if they infift on its not being fold, till the duty is taken off by Act of Parliament, or the Eaft India Directors fatisfy the Commiffioners of the Cuftoms in London. For, notwithftanding, it may juftly be urged that the Directors of the Eaft India Comp[y] have a right to export their teas to North America, yet, as it is faid, the inhabitants have alfo a right of judgment refpecting the purchafe and confumption. I fhould expect, that if the oppofition takes place, it will reft with *their* adherence to an engagement of this kind.

"I can have no doubt that the India Com[y] would find their fales lucrative, and that an extenfion of trade would certainly take place, by comprehending the articles of pepper, fpices, and filks in their exports; great quantities of the two firft articles have certainly been introduced in the Continent from Holland and thro' the Weft Indies, and therefore it is that I apprehend the London merchants are miftaken when they fay they already fhip as much as the Continent can confume, for through them are imported only fuch quantities of fpices, &c., as the merchant here can vend, after the run goods are fold, they being imported cheaper than thofe from England, are naturally firft fold. But if the Eaft India Company fhould think proper to extend their trade, I cannot doubt it would in a great meafure put a ftop to the importation from Holland and the Dutch Iflands, and large fums would annually pafs from America to London for thofe commodities. But perhaps little more fhould be faid until it is known in what manner our fellow countrymen fhall view this fcheme of trade."

"Philadelphia, Oct. 30, 1773.

"I fhall endeavor to communicate a more full ftate of the fentiments of my fellow citizens than I could in my laft letter. I could then only conjecture what might be the refult of their judgments refpecting the Hon'ble the Directors of the Eaft I. Com^y fending their teas to this Continent. A communication of fentiments, taking place between the New Yorkers & the Philadelphians, foon produced a number of pieces in the public prints and otherwife, moft abfolutely afferting the rights of the Americans, and denying the power of Parliament refpecting the internal taxation of the Colonies, which led into many comparifons, endeavoring to fhew that the agency of the tea was equally odious & dangerous as the execution of the Stamp Act would have been. I may fay with great truth, that I do not believe one man in a hundred was to be met with who approved of the fending the tea, while the duty was to be paid here. Yet a great number of people acknowledged the right of the Eaft India Directors to export their teas to America, and declared that nothing lefs than a confirmed belief that the admitting this mode of taxation would render the affemblies of the people mere cyphers, could have induced them to proceed in the manner they have done; for when it was mentioned to them that by refufing to admit the tea to be landed, they did as much deprive the India Company of the natural rights of Englifh merchants, as the fubjecting us to the payment of duty poffibly could affect us, they replyed that the Act of Parliament hindered the tea from being landed *until* the duty was firft paid or fecured, and confequently as the Directors knew this, and the oppofition heretofore given by the Americans, they muft take what followed.

"You will perceive by the refolution formed and entered into on the 18th. into what a fituation the agents were driven, there being no poffibility of perfuading the people to wait till we knew the real ftate of facts. The meeting at the State Houfe confifted, (it is faid) of 6 or 700, and be affured, they were as refpectable a body of inhabitants as has been together on any occafion ; many of the *firft* rank. The whole of their proceedings were conducted with the greateft decency and firmnefs, and without one diffenting voice. After the refolution had paffed, they appointed a Com.ee of 12 perfons, who, on the 18th. inft., about 12 o'clock, called on James and Drinker, and then came down to my houfe, where they conducted themfelves with great decency, read the refolution, and informed me they were appointed by their fellow citizens to demand of Thos & Ifaac Wharton, whether we would execute the truft *if* the duty was to be paid here? We told them it involved us in a difficulty which we could not folve, *becaufe we had not received the leaft intimation from the Directors*, and therefore it was impoffible to know the exact ftate the tea was to be fhipped in, but that we would, on being acquainted with the fituation under which it came, openly communicate the fame, and that we would do nothing to injure the property of the India Com.^y or enflave America. This anfwer they received with great fatisfaction, and in the evening they reported to a unanimous body of citizens the anfwers they had received, who gave Thos and Ifaac Wharton very evident marks of their approbation for the candid anfwer they gave.

"Should the tea be fent fubject to the payment of the duty, I am fatisfied it will not be fuffered to be landed, and that it muft return to London, (unlefs the India Directors have in fuch cafe directed the captain where to proceed with it,) which intimation may be in time to fecure the property by infurance fhould they incline."

Copies of the above advices were, by order of the Com.^{tee} of Warehoufes, fent to Lord Dartmouth in the manner directed by their minute of the ———

BOSTON.

LETTER FROM Mr. JONATHAN CLARKE TO EDWARD WHELER, Esqr.

Bofton, New England, 17th Novr. 1773.

Sir:

After a long detention in the Englifh channel, and a pretty long paffage, I arrived here this morning from England, and there being a veffel to fail for London within a few hours, gives me an opportunity of writing you a few lines on the fubject of the confignment of tea, made to our houfe by the Hon'ble Eaft India Company, in which I had your friendly affiftance, and of which I fhall always retain a grateful fenfe.

I find that this meafure is an unpopular one, and before my arrival fome meafures have been taken to oblige my friends to make a refignation of the truft, which they have not thought fit to comply with. They have wrote to our friend, Mr. Abraham Dupuis, very particularly, refpecting the meafures that have been adopted, and to that account I muft beg leave to refer you, as I have not time to repeat it by this opportunity, but I fhall keep the Company fully advifed in future.

I fully fee that we fhall meet with difficulty in executing this truft, but our utmoft endeavors fhall be exerted to fulfill the orders we may receive from the Company.

I am, very refpectfully fir, your moft obliged h'ble fervt

Edward Wheler, Efqr.   Jonª. Clarke.

Received from the Deputy Chairman, 5th Jany. 1774.

LETTERS AND DOCUMENTS.   279

LETTER TO Mr. ABRAHAM DUPUIS.

Sir.

Mr. Wheler, chairman of the Eaſt India Company, having received a letter from Jonathan Clarke, Eſq[r.] dated Boſton, 17th November laſt, wherein he begs leave to refer him to you for the meaſures that have been adopted at Boſton, relative to the Company's exportation of tea to that Colony, I am directed by the chairman to defire you would be pleaſed to communicate to him the advices you have received from Meſſrs. Clarke & Sons, for the information of the Court of Directors of the Eaſt India Company, which will be a favor conferred on him.   I am, ſir,

Your moſt obd[t] ſerv[t.]

WM. SETTLE.

Eaſt India Houſe, 5th Jan[y.] 1774.

Abraham Dupuis, Eſq[r.] Gracechurch Street.

LETTER FROM Messrs. CLARKE & SONS, AT BOSTON TO Mr. ABR[M] DUPUIS,

Referred to in Mr. Clarke's Letter to the chairman, of the 17th Nov[r.] 1773.

Boſton, Nov[r.] 1773.

Mr. ABRAHAM DUPUIS.

Sir:

We now embrace the firſt leiſure we have, to give you an account of the proceedings of ſome of the inhabitants of this town, relative to the expected importation of teas into this port from the Hon'ble Eaſt India Company. As foon as it was known here that the Company had determined on this meaſure, and that certain gentlemen of this town were fixed upon as factors, there appeared a diſſatiſfaction in many perſons. But at firſt there did not appear any reſentment againſt the ſuppoſed factors, nor was there, as far as we ever heard, any mention made of a deſign to bring them under any obligations not to execute their truſt, but the general voice among the oppoſers of the Company's plan was, that the teas muſt not be landed, or, if landed, not ſold. About three or four weeks ago, a printed anonymous addreſs to the Company's factors was brought to this place by the poſt, either from New York or Philadelphia, but whether it was fabricated at either of thoſe places, or this, we cannot determine. The deſign of it was, to repreſent a number of gentlemen, who cannot juſtly be conſidered in any other light than commercial factors, as Crown officers, and they, in the ſaid paper, are expreſſly put on the ſame footing with the late ſtamp officers, doubtleſs with a deſign to render them odious to the people, and much is ſaid in it to diſſuade or intimidate them from executing their expected truſt. Soon after this, a ſecond anonymous addreſs, but much more inflammatory, appeared here in one of the newſpapers from New York. Both theſe were printed in one or more of the newſpapers of this town, and ſeveral other pieces were alſo publiſhed here, to rouſe the people to an oppoſition to the Company's deſign, and their rage againſt us and the other gentlemen, factors for the Company in this place. As things were then circumſtanced in this place, we judged it might tend to undeceive many perſons that were miſled, to publish some obfervations on the Company's plan, to anfwer the objections that were made againft it, and to point out fome of the beneficial confequences attending the execution of it. Accordingly we, by the affiftance of a friend, got printed in Meffrs. Fleet's Evening Poft, of the 24th October, a piece figned Z[1], in which this affair is canvaffed with as much freedom as the temper of the times would bear, and altho' this was penned in hafte, and under the reftriction of the afore-hinted fhackle, we have the fatisfaction to find, that in the opinion of the moft judicious amongft us here, every objection that has been ftarted againft the Company's plan is fully anfwered, and altho' this publifh-

---

[1] A portion of this article, which fairly represents the views of the consignees on the vexed tea question, is as follows: "The objectors say the tea duty will be a means of supporting the Parliament of Great Britain in raising money from us. How it can affect this matter I am utterly at a loss to comprehend. Have not large quantities of tea for some years past been imported into this Province from England, both on account of the dealers in tea there and the merchants here, all which have paid the American duty? How in the name of common sense does it differ, unless it be in favor of America, for a New England merchant to have his tea shipped from Great Britain, on his own account, or receive it on commission from the grocers there, and on its arrival, paying the customary duty, than if it had been shipped by the East India Company, who were the original importers? What consistency is there in making a clamour about this small branch of the revenue, whilst we silently pass over the articles of sugar, molasses and rum, from which more than three-fourths of the American revenue has and always will arise, and when the Act of Parliament imposing duties on these articles stands on the same footing as that respecting tea, and the moneys collected from them are applied to the same purposes? Many of us complain of the Tea Act, not only as it affects our liberties, but as it affects our purses, by draining us annually of a large sum of money. But if it be considered that by this step the East India Company have taken of sending their tea to market themselves at their own cost, and the saving that is thereby made to the merchants here of commissions, freight and charges of importing it, which will be equal to the whole annual tax that has yet been paid, it must silence that complaint." "Z."

ment does not feem to have had its defigned effect as yet, it is to be hoped, when the *people's* temper is become more cool, that the aforefaid piece, with what has fince, and may hereafter be publifhed on this fubject, may not entirely fail of the defign propofed.

Befides thefe paper fkirmifhes, we would inform you that we were told that there were about two or three weeks fince, feveral nightly meetings, held in various parts of the town, of a large number of perfons, to confult and conclude on fome method to prevent the execution of the Company's plan, but what was fixed at thefe meetings we could not learn. But we were not loft in this uncertainty long, for in the morning of the 2nd inftant, about one o'clock, we were roufed out of our fleep by a violent knocking at the door of our houfe, and on looking out of the window we faw (for the moon fhone very bright) two men in the courtyard. One of them faid he had brought us a letter from the country. A fervant took the letter of him at the door, the contents of which were as follows:

"Bofton, 1ft Nov., 1773.

Richard Clarke & Son:

The Freemen of this Province underftand, from good authority, that there is a quantity of tea configned to your houfe by the Eaft India Company, which is deftructive to the happinefs of every well-wifher to his country. It is therefore expected that you perfonally appear at Liberty Tree, on Wednefday next, at twelve o'clock at noon day, to make a public refignation of your commiffion, agreeable to a notification of this day for that purpofe.

Fail not upon your peril. O. C."

LETTERS AND DOCUMENTS. 283

Two letters of the fame tenor were fent in the fame manner to the other factors. On going abroad we found a number of printed notifications pofted up in various parts of the town, of which the following is a copy:

"*To the Freemen of this and the other Towns in the Province.*

Gentlemen:

You are defired to meet at Liberty Tree, next Wednefday, at twelve o'clock at noon day, then and there to hear the perfons to whom the tea, fhipped by the Eaft India Company, is configned, make a public refignation of their office as confignees, upon oath. And alfo fwear that they will refhip any teas that may be configned to them by the faid Company, by the firft veffel failing for London.

Bofton, Nov$^r.$ 1st, 1773. O. C., Secre$^y.$ "

In this you may obferve a delufory defign to create a public belief that the factors had confented to refign their truft on Wednefday, the 3^d inft., on which day we were fummoned by the above-mentioned letter to appear at Liberty Tree, at 11 o'clock, A.M. All the bells of the meeting-houfes for public worfhip were fet a-ringing and continued ringing till twelve; the town cryer went thro' the town fummoning the people to affemble at Liberty Tree. By thefe methods, and fome more fecret ones made ufe of by the authors of this defign, a number of people, fuppofed by fome to be abont 500, and by others more, were collected at the time and place mentioned in the printed notification. They confifted chiefly of people of the loweft rank, very few reputable tradesmen, as we are informed, appeared amongſt them. There were indeed two merchants, reputed rich, and the felectmen of the town, but thefe laſt fay they went to prevent diforder. The gentlemen who are fup; pofed the defigned factors for the Eaſt India Comp^y, viz: Mr. Thos. Hutchinfon, Mr. Faneuil, Mr. Winſlow & Meſſrs. Clarke, met in the forenoon of the 3rd inſtant, at the latter's warehoufe, the lower end of King Street. Mr. Eliſha Hutchinfon was not prefent, owing to a mifunder-ſtanding of our intended plan of conduct, but his brother engaged to act in his behalf. You may well judge that none of us ever entertained the leaſt thoughts of obeying the fummons fent us to attend at Liberty Tree. After a confultation amongſt ourfelves and friends, we judged it beſt to continue together, and to endeavour, with the af-fiſtance of a few friends, to oppofe the defigns of the mob, if they ſhould come to offer us any infult or injury. And on this occafion, we were fo happy as to be fupported by a number of gentlemen of the firſt rank. About one o'clock, a large body of people appeared at the head of King Street, and came down to the end, and halted oppofite to our ware-houfe. Nine perfons came from them up into our counting-room, viz: Mr. Molineux, Mr. Wm. Dennie, Doctor Warren, Dr. Church, Major Barber, Mr. Henderfon, Mr. Gabriel Johonnot, Mr. Proctor, and Mr. Ezekiel Cheever. Mr. Molin-eux, as fpeaker of the above Com^{tee}, addreſſed himfelf to us, and the other gentlemen prefent, the fuppofed factors to the Eaſt India Com$^{y.}$ and told us that we had committed an high infult on the people, in refufing to give them that moſt reafonable fatisfaction which had been demanded in the summons or notice which had been fent us, then read a paper propofed by him, to be fubfcribed by the factors, importing that they folemnly promife that they would not land or pay any duty on any tea that fhould be fent by the Eaft I. Com⁽ʸ⁾ but that they would fend back the tea to England in the fame bottom, which extravagant demand being firmly refufed, and treated with a proper contempt by all of us, Mr. Molineux then faid that fince we had refufed their moft reafonable demands, we muft expect to feel, on our firft appearance, the utmoft weight of the people's refentment, upon which he and the reft of the Com⁽ᵗᵉ⁾ left our counting-room and warehoufe, and went to and mixed with the multitude that continued before our warehoufe. Soon after this, the mob having made one or two reverfe motions to fome diftance, we perceived them haftening their pace towards the ftore, on which we ordered our fervant to fhut the outward door; but this he could not effect, although affifted by fome other perfons, amongft whom was Nathaniel Hatch,[1] Efq⁽ʳ⁾ one of the Juftices of the inferior Court for this country, and a Juftice of the Peace for the county. This gen⁽ᵐ⁾ made all poffible exertions to ftem the current of the mob, not only by declaring repeatedly, and with a loud voice, that he was a magiftrate, and commanded the people, by virtue of his office, and in his Majefty's name, to defift from all riotous proceedings, and to difperfe, but alfo by affifting in perfon; but the people not only made him a return of infulting & reproachful words, but prevented his endeav-

---

[1] Nathaniel Hatch, of Dorchester, graduated at Harvard University, in 1742, and subsequently held the office of Clerk of the Courts. He accompanied the British troops to Halifax, in 1776; was proscribed and banished in 1778, and in 1779 was included in the Conspiracy Act, by which his estate was confiscated. He died in 1780.

ors, by force and blows, to get our doors fhut, upon which Mr. Hatch, with fome other of our friends, retreated to our counting-room. Soon after this, the outward doors of the ftore were taken off their hinges by the mob, and carried to fome diftance; immediately a number of the mob rufhed into the warehoufe, and endeavored to force into the counting-room, but as this was in another ftory, and the ftair-case leading to it narrow, we, with our friends — about twenty in number — by fome vigorous efforts, prevented their accomplifhing their defign. The mob appeared in a fhort time to be difperfed, and after a few more faint attacks, they contented themfelves with blocking us up in the ftore for the fpace of about an hour and a half, at which time, perceiving that much the greateft part of them were drawn off, and thofe that remained not formidable, we, with our friends, left the warehoufe, walked up the length of King Street together, and then went to our refpective houfes, without any moleftation, faving fome infulting behavior from a few defpicable perfons. The night following, a menacing letter was thruft under Mr. Faneuil's door, to be communicated to the other confignees, with a defign to intimidate them from executing their truft, and other methods have fince been made ufe of in the public papers and otherwife, for the fame purpofe. The next day, being the 4th inft., a notification was fent thro' the town, by order of the felectmen, for the inhabitants of the town to meet on this affair the next day, a tranfcript of which, and the proceedings of the town thereon, at their meetings on the 5th and 6th inft., you have a full account of in the enclofed newfpapers, which, being long, we fhall only copy the meffage of the town to us, and our anfwer, which are as follows:—

JOHN HANCOCK'S REPLY TO WASHINGTON'S LETTER TO CONGRESS, RECOMMENDING THE BOMBARDMENT OF THE TOWN OF BOSTON.

"It is true, sir, nearly all the property I have in the world is in houses and other real estate in Boston; but if the expulsion of the British army from it and the liberties of our country require their being burnt to ashes, issue the order for that purpose immediately."

LETTERS AND DOCUMENTS.   289

" *Voted*, That a Com^{tee} be immediately chofen to wait on thofe gentleⁿ who, it is reported, are appointed by the Eaft India Com^y to receive and fell faid tea, and requeft them, from a regard to their own character, and the good order and peace of the town and province, immediately to refign their appointments. And the following gent^m, viz.: the Moderator of the Meeting, Mr. Henderfon Inches, Benj^a Auftin, Efq^{r.,} and Mr. John Mafon, & the felect men of the town, were appointed a com^{tee} accordingly."

Thefe gent^{n,} all except Mr. Mafon, came to our houfe about one o'clock, P. M., but not having an authenticated copy of the Town's vote, we defired to be favored with one, which was accordingly fent us, in a fhort time, from the moderator, John Hancock, Efq^{r.,} to which we returned the following anfwer, viz.: —

"Bofton, Novr 5, 1773.

Sir:

It is impoffible for us to comply with the requeft of the Town, fignified to us this day by their Com^{tee}, as we know not on what terms the tea, if any of it fhould be fent to our care, will come out, nor what obligations, either of a moral or pecuniary nature, we may be under to fulfil the truft that may be devolved on us. When we are acquainted with thefe circumftances, we fhall be better qualified to give a definite anfwer to the requeft of the Town.

We are, fir, your moft humble fervants,

RICH^D CLARKE & SONS,
BENJ^N FANEUIL, for felf & JOSHUA WINSLOW, Efq^{r.}

Hon'ble John Hancock, Efq^{r.,}
Moderator of a Town Meeting
at Faneuil Hall."

This anfwer, you'll fee by the enclofed news paper, was unanimoufly voted to be not fatisfactory to the Town, and the next day, on Mr. Hutchinfon's fending into the Town Meeting an anfwer of the fame purport, both his and ours were voted to be daringly affrontive to the Town, but upon what reafons this vote was founded they have not been pleafed to declare. You may obferve that the Town has refolved that they will, by all means in their power, prevent the fale of the teas exported by the Eaft India Company, and in the preamble to this vote it is afferted that the quantities of teas imported into this place fince a certain agreement, which we prefume they defigned fhould be underftood to commence in the fall of 1770, at which time the non-importation agreement ceafed, had been very fmall in proportion to what had been ufual before faid agreement, and that by a few perfons only. In order to fet thofe facts in a clear light, we obtained from the cuftom houfe an account of teas imported into this place from the beginning of the year 1768, at which time the firft teas that paid the American duty arrived to this time, and got the fame printed in the enclofed news paper, by which it appears that the fact has been groffly mifreprefented, efpecially confidering that this year's importation would probably be encreafed at the end of the year two or three hundred chefts, if the expected exportation on account of the Eaft India Company had not prevented it. Befides the public tranfactions relative to this affair, before recited, we have repeated accounts of the continual nocturnal meetings of the leaders of the mob, and we are informed that they are determined to make the utmoft efforts to prevent the fale of the teas; that their prefent fcheme, or part of it, is to endeavor, by all methods, even the moſt brutal, to force the conſignees to give up their truſt, and if they ſhould fail in this, it is by ſome perſons publickly aſſerted that the tea ſhall not be landed, or if it ſhould be, that it ſhall be burnt.[1]

In our preſent unexpected and difficult ſituation, we have only to deſire you to aſſure the gentlemen, who may have conſigned any part of the Company's teas to our houſe, whom we cannot at preſent write to, as we have not been adviſed who the gentlemen are, that we ſhall make uſe of the beſt advice, and exert our utmoſt endeavors to carry into execution the Company's deſign, which, as far as we are acquainted with it, we judge to be beneficial to the Colonies, and to this Town and Province eſpecially, but whether it will finally be in our power to accompliſh our deſign, we are not at preſent certain. We beg the favor of you, ſir, to communicate the foregoing to the gentlemen who may have had the direction of this affair. We are, with the greateſt eſteem and higheſt ſenſe of our obligations to them and you, ſir,

Your moſt obedient & moſt humble ſervants,

RICHARD CLARKE & SONS.

P. S. — Mr. Faneuil writes to his friend, Mr. Brook Watſon, by this opportunity, adviſing him of the tranſ-actions relating to this affair. In caſe of miſcarriage of his letter, we deſire you to communicate this letter to Mr. Watſon.

[1] The proposition to burn the tea is referred to by Wyeth. See ante p. LXXI.

EXTRACT OF Mr. FANEUIL'S LETTER TO BROOK WATSON, Esqr.

MENTIONED IN MR. CLARKE'S POSTSCRIPT.

Mr. Faneuil, after giving an account of the proceedings of the inhabitants of the 3rd inftant, entirely agreeing in fubftance with Mr. Clarke's relation, goes on —
" By comparing this account with what Mr. Clarke writes his friend, Mr. Dupuis, of London, you will come at the exact ftate of the affair. The Governor has given my Lord Dartmouth an account of the conduct of his Council. I will only fay that next day they voted that the Attorney-General be ordered to profecute the perfons concerned in this riot. The confequence, I fuppofe, will be, the grand jury will not find a bill againft them, and there the affair will end."

On Thurfday, a letter, of which the following is a copy, was found in my entry:

" Gentlemen: It is currently reported that you are in the extremeft anxiety refpecting your ftanding with the good people of this Town and Province, as commiffioners of the fale of the monopolized and dutied tea. We do not wonder in the leaft that your apprehenfions are terrible, when the moft enlightened humane & confcientious community on the earth view you in the light of tigers or mad dogs, whom the public fafety obliges them to deftroy. Long have this people been irreconcilable to the idea of fpilling human blood, on almoft any occafion whatever; but they have lately feen a penitential thief fuffer death for pilfering a few pounds from fcattering individuals. You boldly avow a refolution to bear a principal part in the robbery of every inhabitant of this country, in the prefent and future ages, of every thing dear and interefting to them. Are there no laws in the Book of God and nature that enjoin fuch mifcreants to be cut off from among the people, as troublers of the whole congregation. Yea, verily, there are laws and officers to put them into execution, which you can neither corrupt, intimidate, nor efcape, and whofe refolution to bring you to condign punifhment you can only avoid by a fpeedy imitation of your brethren in Philadelphia. This people are ftill averfe to precipitate your fate, but in cafe of much longer delay in complying with their indifpenfable demands, you will not fail to meet the juft rewards of your avarice & infolence. Remember, gent^{n,} this is the laft warning you are ever to expect from the infulted, abufed, and moft indignant vindicators of violated liberty in the Town of Bofton.

Thurfday evening, 9 o'clock.
Nov. 4, 1773.   O. C., Sec^{y,} pr order.[1]
To Meffrs. the Tea Commiffioners.
    Directed to B——F——Efq^{r.}"

On Friday we had a Town Meeting. What was done there, together with our anfwers and their refolves, you'll

[1] This letter, with all its extravagance and exaggeration, undoubtedly expresses the popular feeling, the public sentiment of the time. It is easy to see from its style, as well as from the sentiments it contains, that it could have emanated from none of the popular leaders. These, however strongly they felt in relation to ministerial aggression, were, though direct and forcible in their utterances, invariably discreet and temperate in their tone and language.

fee in the enclofed news paper. Juft before the meeting broke up, feveral gent⁸· on my telling the purport of our anfwer, advifed me to leave the town for that night; but I have not yet flept out of my own houfe, nor do I propofe to do it, till I find it abfolutely neceffary. I thought it beft, however, to conceal myfelf for two or three hours. But nothing took place more that evening than is ufual on the 5ᵗʰ Novʳ· On Friday, we received an information, which was repeated yefterday, that a number of picked men are determined to break into our houfe one night this week. I can hardly believe it, but thefe continued alarms are very difagreeable. I am, gentlemen,

Your moſt obedᵗ fervᵗ,

BENJⁿ FANEUIL, Junʳ·[1]

---

[1] Benjamin Faneuil, Jr., was the son of Benjamin, a merchant of Boston, (born, 1701; died, 1785,) and a nephew of Peter Faneuil, to whom Boston is indebted for her "Cradle of Liberty." His place of business was in Butler's Row, and he resided in the Faneuil mansion, on Tremont Street. Before the building of Quincy Market and South Market Street, Butler's Row entered Merchants Row, between Chatham and State Streets. With the other tea consignees, Faneuil fled to the Castle, in Boston harbor, November 30, 1773, and being a loyalist, went to Halifax, when Boston was evacuated, in March, 1776. In the following spring he was in London, and subsequently resided in Bristol, Eng., where he died. His wife was Jane, daughter of Addington Davenport. While in London, in lodgings in the Strand, almost opposite Somerset House, he wrote as follows to a friend: "As soon as the Xmas holidays were over, the tea consignees presented a petition to the Lords of the Treasury, praying a support until the affairs in America were settled. We are told we

PROCEEDINGS OF THE INHABITANTS OF THE TOWN OF BOSTON, ON THE 5TH & 6TH NOVEMBER, 1773,

Referred to by Meſſrs. Richard Clarke & Sons, & Benjn Faneuil, Junr., in their above mentioned Letters, from the news papers encloſed.

[From the Massachusetts Gazette of Thursday, Nov. 11, 1773.].

The following notification was iſſued on Thurſday laſt:
The freeholders and other inhabitants of the Town of Boſton, qualified as the law directs, are hereby notified to meet at Faneuil Hall, on Friday, the 5th day of November inſtant, at ten o'clock in the forenoon, then and there to conſider the petition of a number of the inhabitants, ſetting forth, "that they are juſtly alarmed at the report that the Eaſt India Company, in London, are about ſhipping a cargo or cargoes of tea into this and the other Colonies, and that they eſteem it a political plan of the Britiſh adminiſtration, whereby they have reaſon to fear, not only the trade upon which they depend for ſubſiſtence, is threatened to be totally deſtroyed, but what is much more than any thing in life to be dreaded, the tribute laid on the foundation of that article will be fixed and eſtabliſhed, and our liberties, for which we have long ſtruggled, will be loſt to them and their poſterity,

shall be allowed £150 a year. This is a fine affair, and we can by no means live upon it, but there are such a confounded parcel of us to be provided for, that I am told no more will be allowed. . . .

When we shall be able to return to Boston I cannot say, but hope and believe it will not exceed one year, for sooner or later America will be conquered, that you may depend on."

and therefore praying that a meeting of the freeholders and other inhabitants, may be immediately called, that fo the fenfe of the matter may be taken, and fuch fteps be purfued as to their fafety and well being fhall appertain."

By order of the Select men,

WILLIAM COOPER, Town Clerk.

Bofton, Nov.ʳ 4.ᵗʰ 1773.

On Friday laft there was a very full meeting of the freeholders, and other inhabitants of this town, in Faneuil Hall, agreeable to a notification iffued by the Select men, when the Hon'ble John Hancock, Efqʳ, was chofen moderator, and the Town, after due deliberation, came into the following refolutions, viz.:

Whereas, it appears by an Act of the Britifh Parliament, paffed in the laft feffion, that the Eaft India Company, in London, are by the faid Act allowed to export their teas into America in fuch quantities as the Lords of the Treafury fhall think proper. And fome perfons, with an evil intent to amufe the people, and others thro' inattention to the true defign of the Act, have fo conftrued the fame as that the tribute of three pence on every pound of tea is to be exacted by the deteftable tafk mafters here. Upon the due confideration thereof, —

Refolved, That the fense of this Town cannot be better expreffed than in the words of certain judicious refolves, lately entered into by our worthy brethren of Philadelphia. Wherefore,

Refolved, That the difpofal of their own property is the inherent right of freemen; that there can be no property in that which another can, of right, take from us without our confent; that the claim of Parliament to tax America is, in other words, to claim a right to levy contributions on us at pleafure.

2$^{d.}$ That the duty impofed by Parliament upon tea landed in America, is a tax upon the Americans, or levying contributions on them without their confent.

3$^{d.}$ That the exprefs purpofe for which the tax is levied on the Americans, namely, for the fupport of government, adminiftration of juftice, and the defence of His Majefty's dominions in America, has a direct tendency to render affemblies ufelefs, and to introduce arbitrary government and flavery.

4$^{th.}$ That a virtuous and fteady oppofition to this minifterial plan of governing America is abfolutely neceffary to preferve even the fhadow of liberty, and it is a duty which every free man in America owes to his country, to himfelf and to his pofterity.

5$^{th.}$ That the refolution lately agreed to by the Eaft India Company, to fend out their tea to America, fubjected to payment of duties on its being landed here, is an open attempt to enforce the minifterial plan, and a violent attack upon the liberties of America.

6$^{th.}$ That it is the duty of every American to oppofe this attempt.

7$^{th.}$ That whoever fhall, directly or indirectly, countenance this attempt, or in any wife aid or abet in unloading, receiving or vending the tea fent or to be fent out by the Eaft India Company, while it remains fubject to the payment of a duty here, is an enemy to America.

8$^{th.}$ That a committee be immediately chofen to wait on

thofe gentlemen, who, it is reported, are appointed by the Eaſt India Company to receive and fell faid tea, and requeſt them, from a regard to their own characters, and the peace and good order of this Town and Province, immediately to refign their appointments.

And the following gentlemen, viz., the Moderator, Mr. Henderfon Inches, Benjamin Auſtin, Efq^{rs} and the Select men of the Town, were appointed a committee accordingly.

At the fame time, the Town paffed the following refolves, viz.:

Whereas, the merchants of this Continent, did enter into an agreement to withhold the importation of teas until the duty laid thereon fhould be repealed, which agreement, as we are informed, has been punctually obferved by the refpectable merchants in the Southern Colonies, while, by reafon of the peculiar circumſtances attending the trade of this place, some quantities, tho' very fmall in proportion to what had been ufual before faid agreement, have been imported by fome of the merchants here. And whereas, it now appears probable to this Town, that the Britifh adminiſtration have taken encouragement, even from fuch fmall importations, to grant licenfes to the Eaſt India Company, as aforefaid, therefore, —

Refolved, That it is the determination of this Town, by all means in their power, to prevent the fale of teas exported by the Eaſt India Company, and as the merchants here have generally oppofed this meafure, it is the juſt expectation of the inhabitants of this town that no one of them will, upon any pretence whatever, import any tea that fhall be liable to pay the duty from this time, and until the Act impofing the fame fhall be repealed.

GOVERNOR GAGE, THROUGH COL. FENTON, TO SAMUEL ADAMS, 1773.

"Mr. Adams, you have displeased His Majesty, made yourself liable to be sent to England, and tried for treason. Change your political course, you will receive personal advantages, and also make your peace with the King."

Mr. Adams' Reply: "I have long since made my peace with the King of Kings. No personal consideration shall induce me to abandon the righteous cause of my country. Tell Gov. Gage it is the advice of Samuel Adams, to him, no longer to insult the feelings of an already exasperated people."

And then the Town adjourned till three o'clock in the afternoon.

At 3 o'clock, there was again a very full affembly, and the committee reported to the Town that they had waited on Richard Clarke, Efq{r.} and Son, and Benjamin Faneuil, Efq{r.} faid to be factors of the Eaft India Company, and communicated to them the refolve of the Town, whereby they were requefted, immediately, to refign their appointment, and that faid gentlemen informed the committee, that as Meffrs. Thomas & Elifha Hutchinfon, (who are alfo reported to be factors of the faid Company,) were at Milton, and not expected in town 'till Saturday evening, and as they chofe to confult them, they could not return an anfwer to the Town 'till Monday morning.

Then another committee was chofen viz., Mr. Samuel Adams, Mr. Wm. Molineux and Dr. Jofeph Warren, to acquaint Meffrs. Clarke & Faneuil, that as they were not joint factors for the Eaft India Company with the Hutchinfon's, it was fuppofed they could determine for themfelves, and therefore it was the expectation of the Town that they return an immediate anfwer to the meffage, and this committee reported to the Town that an anfwer might be expected in half an hour.

A motion was then made that a committee be appointed to repair to Milton, and acquaint Meffrs. Thomas and Elifha Hutchinfon, with the requeft of the Town, that they immediately refign their appointment, and John Hancock, Efq{r.} Mr. John Pitts, Mr. Samuel Adams, Mr. Samuel Abbott, Dr. Jofeph Warren, Mr. Wm. Powell, and Mr. Nathl Appleton, were appointed for that purpofe.

A letter was brought into the hall, figned by Richard Clarke & Son, & Benjamin Faneuil, for himfelf & Jofhua Winflow, Efq^{rs} and directed to the Moderator, to be communicated to the Town, viz:

"Bofton, 5th Novm$^{r.}$ 1773.

Sir:

It is impoffible for us to comply with the requeft of the Town, fignified to us this day by the committee, as we know not what terms the tea, if any part of it fhould be fent to our care, will come out on, and what obligations, either of a moral or pecuniary nature, we may be under, to fulfil the truft that may be devolved on us. When we are acquainted with thefe circumftances, we fhall be better qualified to give a definitive anfwer to the requeft of the Town. We are, fir,

Your moft h'ble ferv^{ts}.

RICHARD CLARKE & SON,
BENJAMIN FANEUIL, for felf & JOSHUA WINSLOW, Efq$^{r.}$

Hon'ble John Hancock, Efq$^{r.}$
Moderator of a Town Meeting, affembled at Faneuil Hall."

This letter was read, and unanimoufly voted to be not fatisfactory to the Town, and then the meeting adjourned 'till the next day, at eleven o'clock, to receive the report of the committee appointed to wait on the Hutchinfons.

The Town met by adjournment, on Saturday, (the meeting ftill continuing very full,) and the committee reported, that they had feen Mr. Thomas Hutchinfon only, (his brother being neither at Milton or Bofton,) and that the Town might expect an anfwer from him immediately.

The following letter was foon after fent in to the Moderator, figned Thomas Hutchinfon, which was read, and unanimoufly voted to be an unfatisfactory anfwer, viz.:

"Sir:
I know nothing relative to the teas referred to in the requeft or vote of the Town, except that one of my friends has fignified to me by letter, that part of it, he had reafon to believe, would be configned to me and my brother jointly. Under thefe circumftances, I can give no other anfwer to the Town at prefent, than that if the teas fhould arrive, and we fhould be appointed factors, we fhall then be fufficiently informed to anfwer the requeft of the Town. I am, for my brother and felf, fir,
Your h'ble ferv[t]
Thos. Hutchinson, Jun[r]

Hon'ble John Hancock, Efq[r]
Moderator of a Town Meeting, now affembled.

It was then voted, that the letter, figned Richard Clarke & Son, Benjamin Faneuil, for felf and Jofhua Winflow, Efq[r] and alfo the letter figned Thomas Hutchinfon, which had been read, were daringly affrontive to the Town, and the meeting was immediately diffolved.

AN ACCOUNT OF TEA IMPORTED AT BOSTON,

Referred to above, in Mr. Clarke's Letter, from the fame.

Mr. Draper:
Pleafe to publifh the following account of the importation of teas from Great Britain, from the commence-

ment of the year 1768, to the prefent time, for the information of fuch of your readers as defire to be acquainted therewith:

	Chests.		
In 1768, . . , . .	942	by 82	diff' perfons.
1769, ...	340	33	d⁰·
1770, ...	167	22	d⁰·
1771, ...	890	103	d⁰·
1772, ...	375	70	d⁰·
1773, ...	378	61	d⁰·

N. B. — The merchants in London, not having executed the orders for tea this fall, on account of the expected exportation from the Eaft India Company, greatly leffens the quantity of the prefent year.

Q.

HALIFAX.

Mr. Michell prefents his compliments to Mr. Watfon, and by order acquaints him, that the Court of Directors of the Eaft India Company have agreed that the Company's teas, which may be rejected at Bofton, and other places in America, fhould be fent to Halifax, in the manner with which Mr. Watfon was acquainted by the Committee, with whom he this day conferred, and Mr. Michell is to defire Mr. Watfon will, as foon as may be, name to him the other houfe here, which is to join in that bufinefs, and the other gentleman at Halifax, to be concerned in the agency there with Mr. John Butler, that the neceffary difpatch may be given to the advices, to go from hence tomorrow, at 10 in the forenoon, to the plantation office, and be there forwarded to America. He is alfo to requeft Mr. Watfon, will by that time, convey hither fuch letters as he intends fhould go under the Company's cover, by the fame difpatch to Halifax, relating to this bufinefs

Eaft India Houfe,
Friday evening, 7th Jan*y* 1774.

Jofhua Mauger, Efq*r* Member of Poole, in £10,000.
Brook Watfon, } of London, merchants, and in £10,000.
Rob*t* Rafhleigh, }
Joint fecurity for the due execution of the commiffion for the difpofal of the Company's teas by John Butler, Efq*r* and Tho*s* Cochran, of Halifax.

NEW YORK.

THE AGENTS OF NEW YORK, THEIR PETITION TO THE GOVERNOR,

Referred to in their Letter of the 1st Decr.

TO HIS EXCELLENCY WILLIAM TRYON, ESQ*r* CAPTAIN-GENERAL AND GOVERNOR IN CHIEF IN AND OVER THE PROVINCE OF NEW YORK, AND TERRITORIES DEPENDING THEREON, IN AMERICA, CHANCELLOR AND VICE-ADMIRAL OF THE SAME.

The Memorial of Henry White, Abram Lott, & Benjm Booth, of the City of New York, merchants.

Humbly fheweth:

That your memorialifts have, by the laft packet, received advices of their being appointed agents by the Eaft

India Com[y.] for the fale of certain teas by them fhipped and daily expected to arrive in this port.

That your memorialifts are informed by letter from the Directors of the faid Company, that they have given fecurity in double the value of the tea, that a certificate of its being duly landed fhall be returned to the cuftom houfe, in London.

That as the faid tea, on its importation, will be fubject to the American duty, and as there is on that account a general and fpirited oppofition to its being fold, and being well convinced from the nature of the oppofition, that fo confiderable a property of the Company will not be fafe unlefs Government takes it under protection, your memorialifts therefore humbly pray that your Excellency will be pleafed to direct fuch steps to be taken for the prefervation of the faid tea, as your Excellency in your wifdom fhall think moft conducive to that end.

          HENRY WHITE.[1]
         ABR[m] LOTT.
         BENJ[n] BOOTH.

New York, 1ft Dec[r.] 1773.

---

[1] Henry White was an eminent and wealthy merchant of New York, a member of the Council, and an original member and finally president, of the New York Chamber of Commerce. He acted for a time as commissary, while the royal army occupied that city, and being a pronounced loyalist, his estate was confiscated. After the peace he went to England, and died in London, December 23, 1786. Eve, his widow, died in New York, in 1836, at the great age of ninety-eight. Of his sons, John Chambers White, became a vice-admiral in the British navy, and Frederick Van Cortland, became a general in the army

BOSTON.

Proceedings of the inhabitants of the town of Bofton, on the 18th Nov[r.] 1773, referred to by the agents in their letter of the 2d Dec[r.] are miffing, fuppofed to be tranfmitted to Lord Dartmouth.[1]

PETITION OF THE AGENTS, & PROCEEDINGS OF THE COUNCIL OF BOSTON THEREON,

Referred to by the Agents in their Letter of the 2d Decem[r.]

To His Excellency the Governor and the Hon'ble His Majesty's Council.

The Petition of Rich[d] Clarke & Sons, of Benj[n] Faneuil, & Tho[s.] & Elifha Hutchinfon.

That the Hon'ble Eaft India Company, in London, have fhipped a confiderable quantity of tea for the port of Bofton, and as your petitioners are *made* to underftand, will be configned to their addrefs for fale.

That fome of your petitioners have in confequence of this been cruelly infulted in their perfons and property; that they have had infulting and incendiary letters left and thrown into their houfes in the night; that they have been repeatedly attacked by a large body of men; that one of the houfes of your petitioners was affaulted in the night by a

[1] See p. xxxv., ante.

tumultuous and riotous affembly of people, and violent attempts made to force the houfe for the fpace of two hours, that have greatly damaged the fame; that they are threatened in their perfons and property, and further with the deftruction of the faid tea on its arrival into the port; and that the refolves and proceedings of the Town, in their meetings on the 5th and 18th inft., are intended to be expreffive of the general fenfe of the Town, to which we beg leave to refer your Excellency and the Honorable Board.

Your petitioners therefore beg leave to refign themfelves, and the property committed to their care, to your Excellency and Honors, as the guardians and protectors of the people, humbly praying that meafures may be directed to, for the landing and fecuring the teas, until your petitioners can be at liberty, openly and fafely, to difpofe of the fame, or until they can receive directions from their conftituents.

     Signed,   RICH[D] CLARKE,
           BENJ[N] FANEUIL, Jun[r.]
           THO[s.] & ELISHA HUTCHINSON.
A true copy from the original.
  Petition on file.   Atteft:
     Signed,   THO[s.] FLUCKER, Sec[y.]

PROCEEDINGS OF THE COUNCIL THEREON.

At a Council held at the Council Chamber, in Bofton, upon Friday, Nov[r] 19, 1773.
Prefent:
His Excellency Thomas Hutchinfon, Efq[r.] Governor.

LETTERS AND DOCUMENTS. 311

Ifaac Royal,[1] ⎫   James Bowdoin, ⎫   James Pitts,
John Erving,   ⎬ Efq[m.] James Ruffell, ⎬ Efq[n.]
Wm. Brattle,[2] ⎭   James Otis,   ⎭   Sam[l] Dexter, Efq[m.]

His Excellency reprefented to the Council the tumults and diforders prevailing in the town of Bofton, and required their advice upon meafures proper for preferving the peace, and for fupporting the authority of Government. Whilft the Council were debating on the fubject, a petition from Rich[d] Clarke, Benj[n] Faneuil, and Meffrs. Tho[s.] and Elifha Hutchinfon, to the Governor and Council was prefented, fetting forth that the Hon'ble Eaft India Com[y.] in London, have fhip'd a confiderable quantity of tea for the port of Bofton, which they are made to underftand, will be configned to their addrefs, for fale, and that fome of them have, in confequence of this, been cruelly infulted in their perfons and

---

[1] Isaac Royal, of Medford, died in England, in October, 1781. He was a representative from Medford to the General Court, and for twenty-two years a member of the Council. In 1774, he was appointed a Councillor under the writ of mandamus, but was never sworn into office. Appointed a brigadier-general in 1761, and the first who bore that title here. He left the country April 16, 1775; was proscribed in 1778, and his estate was confiscated. He bequeathed upwards of two thousand acres of land in Worcester County, Mass., to found the first law professorship of Harvard University, and his bequests for other purposes were numerous and liberal.

[2] William Brattle, F. R. S., lawyer, preacher, physician, soldier and legislator, son of Rev. William, minister, of Cambridge, died in Halifax, N. S., in October, 1776; aged seventy-four. He was graduated at Harvard University, in 1722; was distinguished both for his talents and eccentricities; was a representative from Cambridge, and many years a member of the Council; a member of the Stamp Act Congress in 1765; a major-general of militia, and was a member of every profession, and eminent in all. For many years he pleased both the Government and the people, but finally forfeited the good will of the Whigs, and accompanied the British soldiers to Halifax on the evacuation of Boston, and died there a few months after his arrival.

property. They therefore beg leave to refign themfelves, and the property committed to their care, to the Governor and Council, as the guardians and protectors of the people, and pray that meafures may be directed to, for the landing and fecuring the teas, until they can be at liberty, openly and fafely, to difpofe of the fame, or until they can receive directions from their conftituents. After long debate, it was propofed and agreed that his Excellency be defired to appoint a future day for the Council to fit, and he appointed the 23^d inft., and the Council adjourned the further confideration to that time accordingly.

November 23^{d,} 1773. Prefent in Council: His Excellency Thos Hutchinfon, Efq^{r,} Governor.

Ifaac Royal, } Efq$^{rs.}$ James Bowdoin, } Efq$^{rs.}$ James Pitts,
John Erving, James Ruffell, John Winthrop,
James Otis, Efq$^{rs.}$

His Excellency directed the Council to proceed in the confideration of the petition of Richd Clarke, Efq^{r,} and others, as entered the 19th inft., for which purpofe he had ordered them to fit at this time, and a debate being had thereupon, it was moved to his Excellency that the Council might fit on a further day, there being only a bare quorum prefent, to which his Excellency agreed ; advifed that all thofe members of the Council who live within 40 miles of the town of Bofton be fummoned then to attend, which was done accordingly, to meet on Saturday, the 27th inft.

Novem^r 27$^{th.}$ Prefent in Council: His Excellency Thos Hutchinfon, Efq^{r,} Governor.

THOMAS GAGE, THE LAST ROYAL GOVERNOR.

LETTERS AND DOCUMENTS. 315

Samuel Danforth,[1] James Ruffel, James Humphrey,
Ifaac Royal, James Pitts, Artemas Ward,
John Erving, Samuel Dexter, John Winthrop, Efq$^{rs\cdot}$
James Bowdoin. George Leonard.

His Excellency, after reprefenting to the Council the diforders prevailing in the town of Bofton, recommended to them to proceed on the petition of Richd Clarke, and others, relative to thofe diforders, and required their advice. After a long debate, it was moved to his Excellency that a Com^{tee} of the Council be appointed to prepare the refult of the faid debate, to be laid before his Excellency, to which he confented, and James Bowdoin, Saml Dexter, and John Winthrop, Efq$^{rs\cdot}$ were appointed accordingly. Mr. Bowdoin made a report, which was confidered and debated by the Council, and it was moved to his Excellency that he would adjourn the Council to a future day for further confideration, and he appointed Monday, the 29$^{th\cdot}$ for that purpofe.

Novem^r 29$^{th\cdot}$ 1773. Prefent in Council: His Excellency Tho$^{s\cdot}$ Hutchinfon, Efq$^{r\cdot}$ Governor.

Samuel Danforth, Efq^r James Bowdoin, Geo. Leonard,
Ifaac Royal, James Ruffell, Artemas Ward,
John Erving. James Pitts, John Winthrop,
Samuel Dexter, Efq$^{rs\cdot}$

[1] Samuel Danforth, son of Rev. John, of Dorchester, died in Boston, at the house of his son, Dr. Samuel Danforth, 27th October, 1777; aged about eighty-one. He was graduated at Harvard University, in 1715; taught school; was a Selectman in 1733-39; representative 1734-38; member of the Council 1739-1774, and several years its president; Register of Probate, 1731-45; Judge of Probate, 1745-75; and Judge of the Court of Common Pleas, 1741-75. At the Revolution he passed out of office, but was so quiet in his deportment that, though understood to be a loyalist, he was not disturbed in the possession of his property. He was distinguished for his love of the natural sciences.

His Excellency directed that the Council proceed upon the bufinefs for which it ftands adjourned. After debate upon the report of the Com:tee: the queftion whether it fhould be accepted was put, which paffed unanimoufly in the affirmative as the advice of the Council to his Excellency, in the words following, viz.:

Previous to the confideration of the petition before the Board, they would make a few obfervations occafioned by the fubject of it. The fituation of things between Great Britain and the Colonies has been for fome years paft very unhappy. Parliament, on the one hand, has been taxing the Colonies, and they, on the other hand, have been petitioning and remonftrating againft it, apprehending they have conftitutionally an exclufive right of taxing themfelves, and that without fuch a right, their condition would be but little better than flavery.

Poffeffed of thefe fentiments, every new meafure of Parliament tending to eftablifh and confirm a tax on them renews and increafes their diftrefs, and it is particularly encreafed by the Act lately made, empowering the Eaft India Company to fhip their tea to America. This Act, in a commercial view, they think introductive of monopolies, and tending to bring on them the extenfive evils thence arifing. But their great objection to it is from its being manifeftly intended (tho' that intention is not expreffed therein,) more effectually to fecure the payment of the duty on tea, laid by an Act of Parliament paffed in the 7th year of his prefent Majefty, entitled, "An Act for granting certain duties in the Britifh colonies and plantations in America," which Act in its operation deprives the colonifts of the right above mentioned (the exclufive right of taxing themfelves), which they hold to be fo effential a one that it cannot be taken away or given up, without their being degraded, or degrading themfelves below the character of men.

It not only deprives them of that right, but enacts that the monies arifing from the duties granted by it may be applied "as his Majefty or his fucceffors fhall think proper or neceffary for defraying the charges of the adminiftration of juftice and the fupport of the civil government, in all or any of the faid colonies or plantations."

This claufe of the Act has already operated in fome of the colonies, and in this colony in particular, with regard to the fupport of civil government, and thereby has operated in diminution of its charter rights to the great grief of the good people of it, who have been and ftill are greatly alarmed by repeated reports, that it is to have a further operation with refpect to the defraying the charge of the adminiftration of juftice, which would not only be a further diminution of thofe rights, but tend in all conftitutional queftions, and in many other cafes of importance to bias the judges againft the fubject. They humbly rely on the juftice and goodnefs of his Majefty for the reftitution and prefervation of thofe rights.

This fhort ftatement of facts the board thought it neceffary to be given to fhew the caufe of the prefent great uneafinefs which is not confined to this neighbourhood, but is general and extenfive. The people think their exclufive right of taxing themfelves by their reprefentatives, infringed and violated by the Act above mentioned. That the new Act empowering the Eaft India Company to import their tea into America confirms that violation, and is a new effort, not only more effectually to fecure the payment of the tea duty, but lay a foundation for enhancing it, and in a like way, if this fhould fucceed, to lay other taxes on America. That it is in its attendants and confequences ruinous to the liberties and properties of themfelves and their pofterity; that as their numerous petitions for relief have been rejected, the faid New Act demonftrates an indifpofition in miniftry that Parliament fhould grant them relief; that this is the fource of their diftrefs, a diftrefs that borders upon difpair, and that they know not where to apply for relief.

Thefe being the fentiments of the people, it is become the indifpenfible duty of this Board to mention them that the occafion of the late demands on Mr. Clarke and others, the agents of the Eaft India Company, and of the confequent difturbances, the authors of which we have advifed fhould be profecuted, but to give a juft idea of the rife of them.

On this occafion, juftice impels us to declare that the people of this Town and Province, tho' they have a high fenfe of liberty derived from the manners, the example and conftitution of the mother country, have, 'till the late parliamentary taxation of the Colonies, been as free from difturbances as any people whatever.

This reprefentation the Board thought neceffary to be made prior to their taking notice of the petition of the agents above mentioned, to the confideration of which they now proceed.

The petitioners beg leave "to refign themfelves, and the property committed to their care, to his Excellency and the Board, as guardians and protectors of the people, praying that meafures may be directed to for the landing and fecuring the tea," &c.

With regard to the perfonal protection of the petitioners, the Board have not been informed that they have applied for it to any of the juftices of the peace, they being vefted by law with all the authority neceffary for the protection of his Majefty's fubjects. In the principal inftance of abufe of which they complain, the Board have already advifed that the authors of it fhould be profecuted according to law, and they do advife the fame in the other inftances mentioned in their petition.

With regard to the tea committed to the care of the petitioners, the Board have no authority to take either that or any other merchandize out of their care, and fhould they do it, or give any order or advice concerning it, and a lofs enfue, they apprehend they fhould make themfelves refponfible for it. With refpect to the prayer of the petition, that meafures may be directed to "for the landing and fecuring the tea," the Board would obferve on it, that the duty on the tea becomes payable, and muft be paid or fecured to be paid on its being landed, and fhould they direct or advife to any meafure for landing it, that would of courfe advife to a meafure for procuring the payment of the duty, and therefore by advifing to a meafure inconfiftent with the declared fentiment of both houfes in the laft winter feffion of the General Court, which they apprehend to be altogether inexpedient and improper.

The Board, however, on this occafion affure your Excellency that as they have feen, with regret, fome late difturbances, and have advifed to the profecuting the authors of them, fo they will in all legal methods endeavor to the utmoft of their power to prevent them in future.

Whereupon advifed that his Excellency renew his orders

to his majefty's juftices of the peace, fheriffs, and other peace officers, to exert themfelves to the utmoft for the fecurity of his Majefty's fubjects, the prefervation of peace and good order, and for preventing all offences againft the laws.

His Excellency thereupon demanded of the Council whether they would give him no advife upon the diforders then prevailing in the town of Bofton, and it was anfwered in general that the advife already given was intended for that purpofe.

A true copy from the minutes of the Council.

Atteft:

Thos· Flucker, Sec^y·

PROCEEDINGS OF THE TOWN OF BOSTON ON THE 29TH & 30TH NOVEMB^R· 1773,

Referred to by the Agents there, in their Letter of the 2^d December, 1773.

At a meeting of the people of Bofton and the neighbouring towns, in Faneuil Hall, in faid Bofton, on Monday, 29th Novem^r· 1773, nine o'clock, A.M., and continued by adjournment to the next day, for the purpofe of confulting, advifing, and determining upon the moft proper and effectual method to prevent the unloading, receiving or vending the deteftable tea fent out by the Eaft India Company, part of which being juft arrived in this harbour, in order to proceed with due regularity, it was moved that a moderator be chofen, and Jonathan Williams, Efq[r.] was then chofen moderator of the meeting.

A motion was made, that as the Town of Bofton had determined, at a late meeting, legally affembled, that they would, to the utmoft of their power, prevent the landing of the tea, the queftion being put whether this body be abfolutely determined that the tea now arrived, in Cap[t.] Hall's fhip, fhall be returned to the place from whence it came, at all events, and the queftion being accordingly put, it paffed in the affirmative, *nem. con.*

It appearing that the hall could not contain the people affembled, it was voted that the meeting be immediately adjourned to the Old South meeting-houfe, leave having been obtained for this purpofe.

The people met at the Old South, according to adjournment.

A motion was made, and the queftion put, viz.: Whether it is the firm refolution of this body, that the tea fhall not only be fent back, but that no duty fhall be paid thereon, and paffed in the affirmative, *nem. con.*

It was moved, that in order to give time to the confignees to confider and deliberate before they fent in propofals to this body, as they had given reafon to expect would have been done at the opening of the meeting, there might be an adjournment to 3 o'clock, P.M., and the meeting was accordingly adjourned for that purpofe.

Three o'clock, P.M. Met according to adjournment.

A motion was made whether the tea non arrived in Cap[t.]

Hall's fhip, fhall be fent back in the fame bottom. Paffed in the affirmative, *nem. con.*

Mr. Rotch, the owner of the veffel, being prefent, informed that body that he fhould enter his proteft againft their proceedings.

It was then moved and voted, *nem. con.*, that Mr. Rotch be directed not to enter this tea, and that the doing of it will be at his peril.

Alfo voted, that Capt. Hall, the mafter of the fhip, be informed that, at his peril, he is not to fuffer any of the tea brought by him, to be landed.

A motion was made, that in order for the fecurity of Capt. Hall's fhip and cargo, a watch may be appointed, and it was voted that a watch be accordingly appointed, to confift of 25 men.

Capt. Edward Proctor was appointed by the body to be cap^{t.} of the watch for this night, and the names were given in to the moderator of the townfmen who were volunteers upon the occafion.

It having been obferved to the body that Governor Hutchinfon had required the juftices of the peace in this town to meet and ufe their endeavours to fupprefs any routs, or riots, &c., of the people, that might happen, it was moved and the queftion put, whether it be not the fenfe of this meeting that the Governor's conduct herein carries a defigned reflection upon the people here met, and is folely calculated to ferve the views of adminiftration. Paffed in the affirmative, *nem. con.*

The people being informed by Colonel Hancock that Mr. Copley, fon-in-law to Mr. Clarke, fen^{r.} had acquainted him that the tea confignees did not receive their letters from

London 'till laſt evening, and were ſo diſperſed that they could not have a joint meeting early enough to make their propoſals at the time intended, and therefore are defirous of a further ſpace for that purpoſe.

[It is neceſſary to note that Mr. Copley, and ſome others, our friends informing us, that to prevent immediate outrage, it was neceſſary for us to ſend ſomething in writing to the Select men, which we then did, abſolutely refuſing to do what they had before informed us the people expected; but Mr. Copley, on his return to town, fearing the moſt dreadful conſequences, thought beſt not to deliver our letter to the Select men, he returned to us at night repreſenting this. We then wrote the letter you ſee printed in this paper.]

The meeting, out of great tenderneſs to theſe perſons, and from a ſtrong deſire to bring this matter to a concluſion, notwithſtanding the time they had hitherto expended upon them, to no purpoſe, were prevailed upon to adjourn to the next morning, 9 o'clock.

Thurſday morning, nine o'clock.

Met according to adjournment.

The long-expected propoſals were at length brought into this meeting, not directed to the moderator, but to John Scollay, Eſqr, one of the Select men. It was, however, voted that the ſame ſhould be read, and they were, as follows, viz.:

"Monday, Novr 29th, 1773.

Sir:

We are ſorry that we could not return to the Town ſatisfactory anſwers to their two late meſſages to us reſpect-

324 LETTERS AND DOCUMENTS.

ing the teas. We beg leave to acquaint the gentlemen, Select men, that we have since received our orders from the Hon'ble East India Com^y.

We still retain a disposition to do all in our power to give satisfaction to the Town; but, as we understood from you and the other gentlemen, Select men, at Messrs. Clarke's interview with you last Saturday, that this can be effected by nothing less than our sending back the teas, we beg leave to say that this is utterly out of our power to do, but we do now declare to you our readiness to store the teas until we shall have an opportunity of writing to our constituents, and shall receive their further orders respecting them, and we do most sincerely wish that the Town, considering the unexpected difficulties devolved upon us, will be satisfied with what we now offer. We are, sir,

Your most humble servants,

    Thos. & Elisha Hutchinson.[1]
    Benjn Faneuil, Junr. for self and
    Joshua Winslow, Esqr.
    Richard Clarke & Sons.

To John Scollay, Esqr."

---

[1] Thomas and Elisha Hutchinson, sons of Governor Hutchinson, were merchants and partners in business, and consignees of one-third of the tea shipped to Boston. I have seen no evidence of a pecuniary interest in this shipment on the part of the Governor, as is asserted by the historian Bancroft. Their names were given to the East India Company by a London correspondent, who solicits the consignment for them, without mentioning their connection with the Governor. Thomas, jr., born in Boston, in 1740, was a mandamus Councillor and Judge of Probate, and was proscribed and banished. When the condition of the country became unpleasantly hostile, he left the mansion house at Milton, and took shelter in Boston, but left all the furniture, silver

Mr. Sheriff Greenleaf came into the meeting, and begged leave of the moderator that a letter, he had received from the Governor, requiring him to read a proclamation to the people here affembled, might be read, and it was accordingly read.

Whereupon it was moved, and the queftion put, whether the fheriff fhould be permitted to read the proclamation, which paffed in the affirmative, *nem. con.*

The proclamation is as follows, viz.:

"Maffachufetts Bay.   By the Governor.

To Jonathan Williams, Efq^{r}" acting as Moderator of an affembly of people, in the Town of Bofton, and to the people fo affembled:

Whereas, printed notifications were on Monday, the 29th inft., pofted in divers places in the town of Bofton, and publifhed in the news papers of this day, calling upon the people to affemble together for certain unlawful purpofes, in fuch notifications mentioned; and whereas, great numbers of perfons belonging to the town of Bofton, and divers others belonging to feveral other towns in the Province, did

---

plate, &c., expecting to be able to pass and repass at pleasure. When Boston was evacuated, he and his family, and Peter Oliver and family, embarked for London, in the "Lord Hyde" packet. He settled at Heavitree, near Exeter, in Devonshire, and died there in 1811. His wife was Sarah Oliver.

Elisha, his brother, born in 1745, graduated at Harvard University, in 1762; was proscribed and banished, and died at Blurton Parsonage, Trentham, Staffordshire, England, in November, 1824. His wife, Mary, daughter of Col. George Watson, of Plymouth, Mass., died at Birmingham, England, in 1803. "Neither of my sons," wrote the Governor, in March, 1774, "have dared to appear in Boston since the latter part of November, to the total neglect and ruin of their business."

affemble in the faid town of Bofton, on the faid day, and did then and there proceed to chufe a moderator, and to confult, debate, and refolve upon ways and means for carrying fuch unlawful purpofes into execution, openly violating, defying and fetting at naught the good and wholefome laws of the Province, and the conftitution of government under which they live; and whereas, the people thus affembled, did vote or agree to adjourn, or continue their meeting to this the 30th inft., and great numbers of them are again met or affembled together for the like purpofe, in the faid town of Bofton:

In faithfulnefs to my truft, and as his Majefty's reprefentative within the Province, I am bound to bear teftimony againft this violation of the laws, and I warn and exhort you and require you, and each of you thus unlawfully affembled forthwith, to difperfe and to furceafe all further unlawful proceedings at your utmoft peril.

Given under my hand, at Milton, in the Province aforefaid, the 30th day of Nov.r· 1773, and in the fourteenth year of his Majefty's reign.

T. HUTCHINSON.

By his Excellency's command.

THOS FLUCKER, Secy."

And the fame being read by the fheriff,[1] there was, immediately after, a loud and very general hifs.

A motion was then made, and the queftion put whether the affembly would difperfe and furceafe all further proceed-

---

[1] Stephen Greenleaf, sheriff of Suffolk County, was arrested by the Council of Massachusetts as a loyalist, in April, 1776. He died in Boston, in 1795; aged ninety-one.

ings, according to the Governor's requirement. It paffed in the neg⁶' *nem. con.*

A propofal of Mr. Copley was made, that in cafe he could prevail with the Meffrs. Clarkes to come into this meeting, the queftion might now be put, whether they fhould be treated with civility while in the meeting, though they might be of different fentiments with this body, and their perfons be fafe, until their return to the place from whence they fhould come. And the queftion being accordingly put, paffed in the affirmative, *nem. con.*

Another motion of Mr. Copley's was put, whether two hours fhall be given him, which alfo paffed in the affirmative.

Adjourned 'till two o'clock, P.M.

Two o'clock, P.M. Met according to adjournment. A motion was made and paffed, that Mr. Rotch and Capt" Hall be defired to give their attendance. Mr. Rotch appeared, and upon a motion made, the queftion was put, whether it is the firm refolution of this body, that the tea brought by Capt" Hall fhall be returned by Mr. Rotch to England, in the bottom in which it came, and whether they accordingly now require the fame, which paffed in the affirmative, *nem. con.*

Mr. Rotch then informed the meeting, that he fhould proteft againft the whole proceedings, as he had done againft the proceedings on yefterday, but that, tho' the returning the tea is an act in him, he yet confiders himfeif as under a neceffity to do it, and fhall therefore comply with the requirement of this body.

Captain Hall being prefent, was forbid to aid or affift in unloading the teas at his peril, and ordered, that if he continues mafter of the veffel, he carry the fame back to London, who replied, he fhould comply with thefe requirements.

Upon a motion, refolved, that John Rowe, Efq[r.] owner of part of Cap[t.] Bruce's fhip, expected with tea, as alfo Mr. Timmins, factor for Cap[t.] Coffin's brig, be defired to attend.

Mr. Ezekiel Cheever was appointed captain of the watch for this night, and a fufficient number of volunteers gave in their names for that fervice.

Voted, that the captain of this watch be defired to make out a lift of the watch for the next night, and fo each captain of the watch for the following nights, until the veffels leave the harbour.

Upon a motion made, voted, that in cafe it fhould happen that the watch fhould be any ways molefted in the night, while on duty, they give the alarm to the inhabitants by the tolling of the bells, and that if any thing happens in the day time, the alarm be by ringing of the bells.

Voted, that fix perfons be appointed, to be in readinefs, to give due notice to the country towns, when they fhall be required fo to do, upon any important occafion, and fix perfons were accordingly chofen for that purpofe.

John Rowe, Efq[r.] attended, and was informed that Mr. Rotch had engaged, that his veffel fhould carry back the tea fhe brought, in the fame bottom, and that it was the expectation of this body that he does the fame by the tea, expected in Cap[t.] Bruce, whereupon he replied, that the fhip was under the care of the faid mafter, but that he would ufe his utmoft endeavor, that it fhould go back as required by this body, and that he would give immediate advice of the arrival of faid fhip.

Voted, that it is the fenfe of this body, that Cap[t.] Bruce shall, on his arrival, strictly conform to the votes passed respecting Capt· Hall's vessel, as they had all been passed in reference to Capt· Bruce's ship.

Mr. Timmins appeared and informed, that Capt· Coffin's brig, expected with tea, was owned in Nantucket. He gave his word of honor that no tea should be landed while she was under his care, nor touched by any one, until the owner's arrival.

It was then voted, that what Mr. Rowe and Mr. Timmins had offered, was satisfactory to the body.

Mr. Copley[1] returned, and acquainted the body, that as he had been obliged to go to the castle, he hoped that if he had exceeded the time allowed him, they would consider the difficulty of a passage by water at this season, as an apology. He then further acquainted the body, that he had seen all the consignees, and though he had convinced them that they might attend this meeting with safety, and had used his utmost endeavors to prevail on them to give satisfaction to the body, they acquainted him, that believing nothing would be satisfactory short of reshipping the tea, which was out of their power, they thought it best not to appear, but would renew their proposal of storing the tea, and submitting the same to the inspection of a committee, and that they could go no further without incurring their own ruin; but as they had not been active in introducing the tea, they should do nothing to obstruct the people in their procedure with the same.

---

[1] John Singleton Copley, a famous painter, son-in-law of Richard Clarke, and father of Lord Lyndhurst, was born in Boston, July 3, 1737, and died in London, September 9, 1813. He was a self-taught artist, and after painting many portraits in Boston, settled in London in 1775, and acquired a high reputation.

It was then moved, and the queftion put whether the return made by Mr. Copley from the confignees be in the leaft degree fatisfactory to this body. It paffed in the negative, *nem. con.*

Whereas, a number of merchants in this Province have inadvertently imported tea from Great Britain, while it is fubject to the payment of a duty, impofed upon it by an Act of Parliament, for the purpofe of raifing a revenue in America, and appropriating the fame, without the confent of thofe who are required to pay it, Refolved, that in thus importing faid tea, they have juftly incurred the difpleafure of our brethren in the other Colonies.

And refolved further, that if any perfon or perfons fhall hereafter import tea from Great Britain, fhall take the fame on board, to be imported to this place, until the faid unrighteous Act fhall be repealed, he or they fhall be deemed by this body an enemy to his country, and we will prevent the landing and fale of the fame, and the payment of any duty thereon, and we will effect the return thereof to the place from whence it fhall come.

Refolved, that the foregoing vote be printed and fent to England, and all the fea ports in this Province.

Upon a motion made, voted that fair copies be taken of the whole proceedings of this meeting, and tranfmitted to New York and Philadelphia, and that Mr. Samuel Adams, Hon'ble John Hancock, Efq^{r.} William Phillips, Efq^{r.} John Rowe, Efq^{r.} Jonathan Williams, Efq^{r.} be a committee to tranfmit the fame.

Voted, That it is the determination of this body to carry their votes and refolutions into execution, at the rifque of their lives and property.

Voted, That the committee of correfpondence for this town be defired to take care, that every other veffel with tea that arrives in this harbour, have a proper watch appointed for her; alfo,

Voted, That thofe perfons who are defirous of making a part of thefe nightly watches, be defired to give in their names at Meffrs. Edes & Gill's printing office.

Voted, That our brethren in the country be defired to afford their affiftance upon the firft notice given, efpecially if fuch notice be given upon the arrival of Captn Loring, in Mr. Clarke's brigantine.

Voted, That thofe of this body who belong to the town of Bofton, do return their thanks to their brethren who have come from the neighbouring towns, for their countenance and union with this body, in this exigence of our affairs.

Voted, That the thanks of this meeting be given to Jonathan Williams, Efq^{r,} for his good fervices as moderator.

Voted, That this meeting be diffolved, and it was accordingly diffolved.

LETTER ADDRESSED TO GEO. DUDLEY, Esq^{r,,}

Enclofing 3 news papers and an advertifement, in the name of the people, threatening vengeance on thofe who favored the tea fcheme.

Sir:

The ftate and condition of the Hon'ble Company's tea in America is as you will find in the enclofed papers.

Unlefs the Tea Act is repealed, no tea can be fold in America. Repeal the Act, and you may difpofe of all your teas. The Americans will not be flaves, neither are they to be trapped under the notion of cheap teas. Death is more defirable to them than flavery,— it is impoffible to make the Americans fwallow the tea. The miniftry may amufe the Company, by telling them their tea fhall be fold, and the Act preferved, but they are groffly miftaken. None of it is yet landed, neither fhall it be.

Your humble fervant,

ANGLO AMERICANUS.

Bofton, New England,
Decr 13^{th,} 1773.

The papers enclofed contain an account of the proceedings of the town of Bofton, on the 29th & 30th November, and of the refolves of fome of the neighboring towns. (The papers are in the mifcellany bundle.)

LETTER ADDRESSED TO GEO. DUDLEY, Esq^{r.,}

Enclofing a Bofton news paper of the 16th Dec^{r.,} 1773.

Bofton, New England, 17th Dec^{r.,} 1773.

Gentlemen:

Your tea is deftroyed, which was brought in three fhips, Cap^{ts.} Bruce, Hall and Coffin, and the brig with tea is caft away. If the tea is got on fhore, it will fhare the fame fate. Every poffible means has been ufed to fend it home fafe again to you, but the tea confignees would not fend it; then application was made to the commiffioners of the cuftoms to clear out the veffel, — they would not do it, then to the Governor to grant a pafs, which he refufed, and finally the people were obliged to deftroy it, *(fe defendendo,)* or elfe, by an unlawful unrighteous Act, impofing a duty this tea would have deftroyed them. This whole province, of fome hundred thoufand people, and the other provinces on the continent, are determined neither to ufe it, or fuffer it to be landed, nor pay the duty. Force can never make them, and if the Company can ever expect to fell any tea in America, they muft ufe all their intereft to get this Tea Act repealed, otherwife they will never fell one ounce.

There is the utmoft deteftation of tea; even fome of our country towns have collected all the tea they had by them, and burnt it in their public common, as fo much chains and flavery. Get the Tea Act repealed, and you'll fell all your tea, otherwife you muft keep all. The people will rifk life and fortune in this affair, — the very being of America depends on it. I am forry the Company are led into fuch a fcrape by the miniftry, to try the American's bravery, at the expence of their property. The artifice of the miniftry is to difpofe of your tea, and preferve the vile Tea Act; but they'll mifs their aim, — the Americans will not fwallow cheap tea, which has a poifon in the heart of it. They fee the hook thro' the bait. I am a well wifher to the Company, and alfo to America; but death to an American is more defirable than flavery.

I am, gentlemen, with all due refpect,
  Your honors moft obedient, humble fervant,
    ANGLO AMERICANUS.

AN ACCOUNT OF THE DESTRUCTION OF THE TEA AT BOSTON,

As contained in the Boston news paper of the 16th Dec.

Boston, Thurfday, Dec' 16th, 1773.

It being underftood that Mr. Rotch, owner of the fhip Dartmouth, rather lingered in his preparations to return her to London, with the Eaft India Company's tea on board, there was, on Monday laft P.M., a meeting of the committee of the feveral neighboring towns in Bofton, and Mr. Rotch was fent for and enquired of, whether he continued his refolution to comply with the injunctions of the body on Monday and Tuefday preceding. Mr. Rotch anfwered that in the interim he had taken the advice of the beft counfel, and found that in cafe he went on of his own motion to fend that fhip to fea in the condition fhe was then in, it muft inevitably ruin him, and therefore he muft beg them to confider what he had faid at that meeting to be the effect of compulfion, and unadvifed, and in confequence that he was not holden to abide by it, when he was now affured that he muft be utterly ruined in cafe he did. Mr. Rotch was then afked whether he would demand a clearance for his fhip in the cuftom houfe, and in cafe of a refufal enter a proteft, and then apply in like manner for a pafs, and order her out to fea? To all which he anfwered in the negative. The committee, doubtlefs informing their conftituents of what had paffed, a very full meeting of the body was again affembled at the Old South meeting-house, on

Tuefday afternoon, and Mr. Rotch being again prefent, was enquired of as before, and a motion was made and feconded that Mr. Rotch be enjoined forthwith to repair to the collectors and demand a clearance for his fhip, and ten gent." were appointed to accompany him, as witneffes of the demand. Mr. Rotch then proceeded with the committee to Mr. Harrifon's lodgings, and made the demand. Mr. Harrifon obferved he could not give an anfwer 'till he had confulted the comptroller, but would, at office hours next morning, give a decifive anfwer. On the return of Mr. Rotch and the committee to the body with this report, the meeting was adjourned to Thurfday morning, at ten o'clock.

Thurfday.

Having met on Thurfday morning at ten o'clock, they fent for Mr. Rotch, and afked him if he had been to the collector, and demanded a clearance. He faid he had; but the collector faid that he could not, confiftent with his duty, give him a clearance 'till all the dutiable articles were out of his fhip. They then demanded of him whether he had protefted againft the collector; he faid he had not. They ordered him, upon his peril, to give immediate orders to the captain, to get his fhip ready for fea to-day, enter a proteft immediately againft the cuftom houfe, and then proceed directly to the Governor, (who was at his feat at Milton, 7 miles off,) and demand a pafs for his fhip to go by the caftle. They then adjourned 'till three o'clock, P.M., to wait Mr. Rotch's return.

Having met according to adjournment, there was the fulleft meeting ever known. (It was reakoned that there were 2000 men from the country.) They waited very patiently 'till 5 o'clock.

When they found Mr. Rotch did not return, they began to be very uneafy, called for a diffolution of the meeting, and finally obtained a vote for it. But the more moderate part of the meeting, fearing what would be the confequences, begged that they would reconfider their vote, and wait 'till Mr. Rotch's return, for this reafon, that they ought to do everything in their power to fend the tea back, according to their refolves.

They obtained a vote to remain together one hour longer. In about three-quarters of an hour Mr. Rotch returned, his anfwer from the Governor was, that he could not give a pafs 'till the fhip was cleared by the cuftom houfe. The people immediately, as with one voice, called for a diffolution, which having obtained, they repaired to Griffin's wharf, where the tea veffels lay, proceeded to fix tackles and hoift the tea upon deck, cut the chefts to pieces, and threw the tea over the fide. There were two fhips and a brig, Capt[n]. Hall, Bruce and Coffin, each veffel having 114 chefts of tea on board. They began upon the two fhips firft, as they had nothing on board but the tea; then proceeded to the brig, which had hauled to the wharf but the day before, and had but a fmall part of her cargo out. The captain of the brig begged they would not begin with his veffel, as the tea was covered with goods belonging to different merchants in the town. They told him the tea they wanted, and the tea they would have; but if he would go into his cabin quietly, not one article of his goods fhould be hurt. They immediately proceeded to remove the goods, and then to difpofe of the tea.

Copley

Sam Phps Savage

(See page LVII.)

LETTERS AND DOCUMENTS. 339

Mr. Pownall[1] prefents his compliments to Mr. Wheler, and fends him, by Lord Dartmouth's directions, extract of a letter received yefterday from the Lieutenant-Governor of South Carolina. If the India Company have received any advices, Lord Dartmouth will be obliged to him for a communication thereof.

Whitehall, 29th Jan., 1774.

EXTRACT OF A LETTER FROM GOV. BULL,[2]

Dated Charles Town, 24 Decr. 1773, to the Earl of Dartmouth.

On the 2^d inft., Capt. Curling arrived here with 257 chefts of tea, fent by the Eaft India Company, with the fame in-

---

[1] John Pownall, many years Clerk of the Reports, Secretary of the Board of Trade (1754-68,) Deputy Secretary of State (1768-76,) and afterwards a Commissioner of the Board of Customs, a Magistrate and High Sheriff of Lincolnshire, died in London, July 17, 1795; aged seventy. His brother, Thomas, Governor of Massachusetts in 1757-60, afterwards, while a member of Parliament, opposed the American policy of the Government.

[2] William Bull, M. D., Lieutenant-Governor of South Carolina, from 1764 to 1776, was the son of William, who held the same office from 1738 to 1743, and who was the son of Stephen, one of the early settlers of South Carolina, and Surveyor-General of the Province. William studied medicine at the University of Leyden, and was the pupil of the celebrated Boerhaave. He settled in practice in his native Province; became a member of the Council in 1751, and in 1763 was Speaker of the Assembly. Faithful to the Crown, he accompanied the British troops to England, on their departure in 1782, and died in London, July 4, 1791; aged eighty-one.

ſtructions to agents appointed here as at Boſton, New York and Philadelphia. The ſpirit which had been raiſed in thoſe towns with great threats of violence to hinder the landing and diſpoſing of the tea there, was communicated to this Province by letters, gazettes, and merchants. Several meetings of the inhabitants of Charles Town were held, to conſider of meaſures to effect the like prohibitions here, but tho' the warmth of ſome were great, many were cool, and ſome differed in the reaſonableneſs and utility thereof. The gentlemen who were appointed agents for the Eaſt India Com^y were prevailed upon by threats and flattery to decline the truſt, and in imitation of the northern towns, declarations were made that it ſhould not be landed.

The tea was all this time kept on board the ſhip, the captain being apprehenſive of ſome violence on his attempting to land it, and there being no perſons empowered to take charge of it. When the period of 20 days after his arrival approached, at which time the collector of his Majeſty's cuſtoms, by his inſtructions, is required to ſeize goods liable to pay duty, to ſecure the payment thereof, tho' the merchants of the town had generally diſagreed to this meaſure of prohibiting the landing the tea, yet ſome warm, bold ſpirit, took the dangerous meaſure of ſending anonymous letters to Capt Curling and ſome of his friends, and the gentleman who owned the wharf where the ſhip lay, requiring Curling to carry his ſhip from the wharf to the middle of the river, threatening great damages on failure.

Theſe letters being communicated to me, I ſummoned his Majeſty's council, that I might do everything in my power to prevent any ſuch dangerous attempts to diſturb the public peace, and interrupt the feizure and landing and ftoring by the collector. I accordingly, by their advice, gave orders to the fheriff to be ready at the call of the collector, (but not to move without,) with all his officers, to fupport the collector, in landing it, and to feize and to bring to juftice any perfons who fhould dare to interrupt him in the execution of his duty. It being known that fome meafures were taken, tho' the extent thereof was carefully concealed, the collector, on the 22^{d,} feized, landed, and ftored the teas in ftores under the Exchange, without one perfon's appearing to oppofe him. The tea is to remain in ftore 'till the collector fhall receive further orders relative thereto.

Various were the opinions of men on the fubject; fome were for drinking no tea that paid duty, and were confident of a fupply of fuch; others were for putting every dutied article on the fame footing, as wine, &c.; but others confidered wine as a neceffary of life. It is my opinion that if the merchants who viewed this meafure of importing tea in a commercial rather than in a political light, had fhewn their difapprobation of the intended oppofition to land it, by action rather than by a refufal to fubfcribe to a propofed affociation, and a contempt of the public meetings on this occafion, and the agents of the Eaft India Company had not been fo hafty in their declining to accept their trufts, all might have gone on well, according to the plan of the Eaft India Company, and to our benefit in purchafing that article, now become one of the neceffaries of life, at a much cheaper rate than at prefent.

COPY OF A LETTER FROM Mr. JOHN MORRIS,

At Charles Town, South Carolina, to his Brother, at London.

Charles Town, 22ᵈ Decʳ⁻ 1773.

Dear Brother:

Capᵗ⁻ Curling arrived here the 2ᵈ inſt., with 257 cheſts of tea. There were many meetings of the merchants and planters, but by the reſult they came to no determination; the gentlemen that the tea was conſigned to refuſe receiving it. The tea ſtaid on board 20 days. We then gave the captain a permit to land it by ſunriſe. In the morning I went on board, and called the captain out of his bed, begged he would begin to get the tea out of his veſſel. I expected that he would not have been permitted to land it, but we immediately got ſix cheſts into the warehouſe, and the ſailors hard at work hoiſting out the reſt. We began about 7 o'clock, and had by 12 about half the tea in the warehouſe, and the reſt before the door. There was not the leaſt diſturbance; the gentlemen that came on the wharf behaved with their uſual complaiſance and good nature to me, and I believe the ſame to the reſt of the officers that were there. I thought it my duty to exert myſelf on this occaſion, which I did with great pleaſure, (as I was ſerving my old maſters,) as well as doing my duty as a revenue officer.

I am, &c., &c.,

Corbyn Morris, Efqʳ⁻   JOHN MORRIS.[1]
Cuſtom Houſe.

[1] John Morris, Comptroller of Customs at Charleston, S. C., was permitted, in November, 1775, on account of his impaired health, "to pass and repass to

LETTER FROM Capt. ELLIS,

Of the New York Eſtabliſhment, to the Chairman.

Cox & Mair's Office, 4th Feb^{y.}

Sir:

By the Engliſh papers I learn you are fully appriſed of the proceedings of the people of Philadelphia and Boſton, and the refolves of the New Yorkers. I have, notwithſtanding, ſent you the lateſt papers. The ſhip with the teas bound to Charles Town, is made the property of the cuſtoms, having neglected the uſual forms of office in that port. This intelligence I had by a ſhip from Carolina to New York, the 1ſt Jan^{y.,} and may be depended on. I left New York the 2^d ultimo; the ſhip bound to that port was not then arrived.

I have the honor to be, ſir,

Your very humble ſervant,

J. J. ELLIS,

18th Regt.

---

his Island," during the pleasure of the Provincial Congress, on condition of parole, to keep away from the King's ships. He went to England, and died there in 1778.

BOSTON.

Castle William, 7th Dec'r,, 1773.

QUESTIONS PROPOSED BY FRANCIS ROTCH,
AN OWNER, AND
JAMES HALL, MASTER OF THE SHIP DARTMOUTH,

Who has now the Tea on board, configned to Meffrs. Richard Clarke & Sons, Mr. Benjⁿ Faneuil, Meffrs. Tho· & Elifha Hutchinson, and Mr. Jofhua Winflow, with the Anfwers of the Confignees, except Mr. Winflow, who was abfent. Referred to by the Confignees in their Letter of the 7th Jan., 1774.

QUESTION 1ST.

By Capt. Hall and F. Rotch, to the gentlemen, confignees, in writing:

We are now ready to deliver the tea, and beg to know if you, gentlemen, are ready to receive it, and will produce the requifites ufual and neceffary to the landing or delivering the faid tea alongfide the fhip, either in your own perfons or by your agents?

ANSWER.

Gentlemen: We underftand that there was a large body of people affembled in Bofton on the 29th & 30th November, who voted that the tea fhipped by the Eaft India Company, and configned to us, fhould not be landed; that the duty fhould not be paid, and that the tea fhould be returned in the fame fhip that brought it out. It alfo appears by the printed proceedings of that affembly, that you confented it fhould go back in your fhip. We alfo underftand that there is continually on board your fhip a number of armed men, to prevent it being landed. We therefore judge it out of our power to receive it at prefent, but when it fhall appear to us to be practicable, we will give the neceffary orders refpecting it.

Question 2$^{D.}$

As your reply to our firft queftion, gent$^{n.,}$ appears to us not to the point, we muft and do demand a categorical anfwer whether you will or will not immediately, either by yourfelves or your order, or otherwife, qualify any other perfon or perfons to receive the teas configned to you now on board our fhip, as we are now entirely ready, and will, if in our power, deliver the faid teas immediately, if application is made?

Answer.

Gentlemen: It appears to us that the anfwer we have made to your firft queftion is a full reply to the fecond.

Question 3$^{D.}$

As you, gentlemen, by the tenor of your firft and fecond reply, refufe to give us a direct anfwer to our queftions, whether you will or will not receive the teas mentioned therein, we now demand our bill of lading given by Cap$^{t.}$ Hall, in confequence of his receiving thofe teas on board in London River, and the amount of the freight of the faid tea, fay ninety-one pounds feven fhillings and feven pence lawful money?

346   LETTERS AND DOCUMENTS.

ANSWER.

Gentlemen: We fhall not deliver up Captain Hall's bill of lading, nor pay the freight of the teas until we can receive them.

[Copy.]   FRANCIS ROTCH.
JAMES HALL.
THO^{s.} & ELISHA HUTCHINSON.
RICHARD CLARKE & SONS.
BENJⁿ FANEUIL, JUN^{r.}

[Copy.]   AT CASTLE WILLIAM, IN NEW ENGLAND,
11th Decr. 1773.

QUESTIONS PROPOSED BY JAMES BRUCE,

Mafter of the fhip Eleanor, burthen about 250 tons, now lying in the harbour of Bofton, in New England, with part of her cargo, from London, confifting of one hundred and fourteen chefts of tea, configned to Meffrs. Richard Clarke & Sons, Thos. & Elifha Hutchinfon, Benjⁿ Faneuil and Jofhua Winflow, of faid Bofton, Merchants.

QUESTION I^{ST.} BY CAP^N BRUCE, TO THE CONSIGNEES AFORESAID, IN BEHALF OF HIMSELF AND OWNERS.

Gentlemen: I am now ready to deliver the tea configned to you on board my fhip, and beg to know if you, gentlemen, are ready and willing to receive it, as I can produce the requifites ufual and neceffary for landing or delivering the faid teas alongfide the fhip, either by yourfelves, your agents or affigns; and as my cargo of lumber is ready for

LETTERS AND DOCUMENTS. 347

fhipping on difcharge of the faid tea, I demand an immediate and pofitive anfwer to my queftion.

ANSWER.

Sir: It appearing by the printed accounts of a number of people affembled, at Bofton, on the 29th and 30th Novr. that they voted the teas fhipped by the Eaft India Company fhould not be landed, but that they fhould be returned to England in the fame bottoms in which they came. And it further appearing that John Rowe, Efq^{r.} part owner of the fhip of which you are commander, was prefent at faid meeting, and did promife to ufe his utmoft endeavors that the teas brought in your veffel fhould be fent back, and was alfo chofen one of a com^{tee} by the faid meeting, and as you now tell us that you have received orders from certain perfons, called a com^{tee} of fafety, not to land any part of faid tea, and that a number of armed men have been and ftill are kept aboard or near your veffel. We reply, that for the reafons mentioned, we think it at prefent out of our power to receive the teas, but that as foon as it fhall appear practicable, we will give the neceffary orders for doing it.

2^D QUESTION.

As I have no control upon, nor influence with, the people in Bofton who may oppofe the landing of the teas, I cannot be chargeable with their conduct. My bufinefs is with you, gentlemen, and it is to you only I can and do make application for directions how to difpofe of the faid teas, and you will oblige me and my owners, and I defire you would let me know whether you will or will not receive or difpofe of the faid tea, either on fhore or otherwife?

Answer.

As we fee nothing in your fecond queftion effentially different from your firft, we muft refer you to our anfwer already given.

3ʳᴰ Question.

Will you, gentlemen, or either of you, deliver the bills of lading, which I figned for faid tea at London, and pay me the freight for bringing it to Bofton?

Answer.

Sir: We will not deliver the bills of lading, nor pay the freight of the teas, until we can receive them.

[Copy.]   Jas. Bruce.
               Richᴰ Clarke & Sons.
               Thoˢ & Elisha Hutchinson
     Witnefs: Benjᴺ Faneuil, Junʳ

Signed, Jɴᵒ Munro, Not. Pub.

PROTEST.

Capᵗ James Bruce, of the Eleanor, againft the Confignees, for refufing to receive the teas at Bofton, in New England, on the 11ᵗʰ day of December, 1773, and in the fourteenth year of His Majefty's reign.

Perfonally appeared before me, John Monro, Notary Public, by royal authority, duly admitted and fworn. James Bruce, mafter of the fhip Eleanor, burthen about two hundred and fifty tons, then lying at Griffin's wharf, with part of her cargo from London on board. amongſt which were eighty whole and thirty-four half cheſts of tea, conſigned to Meſſrs. Richard Clarke & Sons, Thomas & Eliſha Hutchinſon, Benjamin Faneuil, and Joſhua Winſlow, of ſaid Boſton, merchants. And the ſaid James Bruce, having requeſted me, the ſaid Notary Public, to attend him to Caſtle William, in the harbour of ſaid Boſton, we went on the ſaid day, and then and there, the annexed queſtions and anſwers were entered. Written queſtions were put by the ſaid James Bruce, and the reſpective anſwers were made in writing (alſo annexed) by the conſignees then preſent, and in my preſence, and in the preſence of each other, interchangeably ſubſcribed and delivered by the ſaid James Bruce and the ſaid Richard Clarke & Sons, Thomas and Eliſha Hutchinſon, and Benjamin Faneuil, and declared by them to be their ſentiments and determinations.

Wherefore, the ſaid James Bruce, on behalf of himſelf, and all others concerned, did, and I, the ſaid Notary Public at his requeſt, and on behalf as aforeſaid, do by theſe preſents, ſolemnly proteſt againſt the ſaid conſignees, and ſuch of them aforeſaid, for all and all manner of damages whatſoever, already ſuffered, and which may, can or ſhall be ſuffered, by their neglecting and refuſing to receive, demand and take poſſeſſion of the tea aforeſaid, agreeable to his requeſt, made and written, and annexed to theſe preſents.

Thus done, proteſted and given under my notarial ſeal of office, in preſence of Robert Garland Cranch and John Dyer.

In teſtimoniam veritas,

Signed, Signed, J$^{no.}$ MONRO,
JAS. BRUCE. (L.S.) Not. Pub., 11th Jan$^{y.}$ 1774.

LETTER FROM Mr. ROTCH TO THE CONSIGNEES,

Referred to in their Letter of the 8th of Jany 1774.

Boſton, 6th Jany 1774.

Gentlemen:

Annexed you have an account of the freight of 80 whole and 34 half cheſts of tea, ſhipped by the Hon'ble Eaſt India Company, on our ſhip Dartmouth, James Hall, maſter, from London, conſigned to you, with the damages we have ſuſtained by the ſaid tea being kept in our ſhip by your not giving the neceſſary orders or directions about it, or by your not qualifying yourſelves, or otherwiſe, for receiving the ſame.

The charge of demurrage of the ſhip, &c., may poſſibly at firſt ſight appear extravagant, but when you conſider the conſequences of a ſhip regularly eſtabliſhed in any trade, (which, in the preſent caſe will, I expect, eventually be of near two hundred guineas damage,) by the loſs of freight from London in the ſpring, when you conſider this, with the extra loſs on a periſhable commodity, as hers was of oil, the extra ſtowage of three-quarters of that cargo, and the difference of advance of the ſeaſon, I cannot but think you muſt be reconciled to the propriety of the charges I have made.

I encloſe you a copy of Capt. Cooke's and our cooper's requeſts, to ſupport the charges of demurrage of the ſloop Triton, and the wages and expences of thoſe coopers, and beg to know by the bearer (who will wait your anfwer) whether you will or will not pay the amount of this account, fay £289 19s. 6d. lawful money.

I am, very refpectfully,

Your affured friend,

FRANCIS ROTCH.

To RICHARD CLARKE & SONS,
THOS. & ELISHA HUTCHINSON,
BENJAMIN FANEUIL, Junr., and
JOSHUA WINSLOW.

Owners, Shippers, Confignees, or concerned in 80 whole and 34 half chefts of Teas, fhipped from London by the Hon'ble Eaft India Company, for Bofton, configned to Richard Clarke & Sons, Thomas & Elifha Hutchinfon, Benjⁿ Faneuil, Jun^{r.,} and Jofhua Winflow.

To the Owners of the *Dartmouth*, JAMES HALL, *Dr.*

1773.
To freight of 80 whole and 34 half chefts of
tea from London, ... £91 17 7
To demurrage of the fhip from 7 to 20 Dec^{r.,}
13 days.
Deduct 2 days for grav^g the fhip, 2 days, 11 at
£12, ... 132 0 0
To Capt. James Hall, and his mate's wages, 11
days, ... 3 18 3
To demurrage floop Triton, from 9 to 20 Dec^{r.,}
12 days, at 48s., ... 28 16 0

To the captain's wages, 6 days, . . 12 0
To the mate's and 4 hands' wages and victuals,
    12 days each, ... 7 9 8½
To Jas. Smith and 2 journeymen coopers from
    Dartmouth, their wages and expences from
    7th to 20th December, 13 days, at 6s., . 11 14 0
To cafh paid Samfon, S. Blowers,[1] and John
    Adams, Efqr's advice, ... 7 4 0
To wharfage the fhip and floop, 23 days, at
    6s. 8d. per week, ... 1 2 0
To cafh paid for Protefts, &c., £3 19s. 6d.
    fterling, ... 5 6 0
                                            ─────────
                                            £289 19 6½

Bofton, 31st December, 1773.

Errors excepted.

In behalf of myfelf and the owners of the fhip.

FRANCIS ROTCH.

---

[1] Sampson Salter Blowers, a distinguished lawyer and jurist, a native of Boston, and a graduate of Harvard College, (1763,) was, in 1778, proscribed and banished as a loyalist. In 1770, he was associated with John Adams and Josiah Quincy in behalf of the British soldiers who were on trial for their agency in the Boston Massacre. He settled in Halifax, N.S.; became successively Attorney-General and Speaker of the House; Chief Justice of the Supreme Court, and a member of the Council, retiring from public life in 1833. Judge Blowers was born March 22, 1742, and died in Halifax, N.S., October 25, 1842, being over one hundred years of age. The fact that he never wore an overcoat in his life, told us on good authority, does not satisfactorily account for his great longevity.

PROTEST.

Mr. Francis Rotch, Pardon Cook, and Wm. Hayden, againſt Conſignees and Tea, at Boſton, in New England, on the 10th day of December, in the year of our Lord 1773, and in the fourteenth year of His Majeſty's reign.

Perſonally appeared before me, John Monro, Notary Public by royal authority, duly admitted and ſworn, Pardon Cook, maſter, and Wm. Hayden, mate of the ſloop Triton, burthen about ſeventy-five tons, and Francis Rotch, one of the owners of the ſaid ſloop, and they, the ſaid Pardon, Willm and Francis, being by the people called Quakers, ſolemnly affirmed, and each of them for himſelf, doth affirm in manner following, that is to ſay, the ſaid Pardon and William affirm and ſay they ſailed from Dartmouth, in New England, with the ſaid veſſel, on the 28th day of laſt month, then loaded with ſpermaceti oil, and bound for ſaid Boſton, where they arrived on the 8th inſt., and made application to the ſaid Francis to have the ſaid cargo diſcharged on board the ſhip Dartmouth, as agreeable to their orders and directions. And the ſaid Francis Rotch affirms that he could not in perſon, nor by his ſervants, or any other, unload and reſhip the ſaid cargo of oil on board the ſhip aforeſaid by reaſon of her not being cleared of a certain quantity of teas ſhipped at London, and conſigned to Meſſrs. Richard Clarke & Sons, Thomas and Eliſha Hutchinſon, Benjn Faneuil and Joſhua Winſlow, of ſaid Boſton, merchants, who have all and each of them, except Joſhua Winſlow, neglected to demand and refuſed to accept the ſaid teas, by which the faid fhip is detained in the harbour of faid Bofton, and unfit to receive the faid oil as intended by the faid owner, mafter and mate; wherefore, the faid Francis Rotch, and the mafter aforefaid, did, on behalf of themfelves and all others concerned, and I, the faid Notary Public, at their requeft, and on behalf aforefaid, do by thefe prefents folemnly proteft againft the faid confignees, and each of them, and againft the faid tea, and againft all others concerned, for all and all manner of damages already fuffered, and to be fuffered, on account of the faid oils not being fhipped as aforefaid, contrary to the intention and ftrict meaning of the faid owner and mafter, &c.

Thus done, protefted, and given under my notarial feal of office, in prefence of Robert Garland Cranch and John Dyar.

In teftimoniam veritas,

J$^{no.}$ MONRO,

Not. Pub., 11 Jan., 1774.

FRANCIS ROTCH.
PARDON COOK.
WM. HAYDEN. (L.S.)

PROTEST.

Capt James Bruce, of the Eleanor, againft the Committee at Bofton, and others, who Prevented the Landing the Teas.

At Bofton, in New England, on the 11th day of Decem$^{r.,}$ in the year of Our Lord 1773, and in the 14th year of his Majefty's reign, perfonally appeared before me, John Monro,

Notary Public by royal authority, duly admitted and fworn, James Bruce, mafter of the fhip Eleanor, burthen about 250 tons, and he being fworn on the Holy Evangelifts of Almighty God, depofed and doth depofe and fay, that on the 1st day of this inftant Decemr., he arrived with the faid fhip at Bofton aforefaid, then loaded with fundry goods or merchandize from London, amongft which were 84 whole and 34 half chefts of tea, configned to Meffrs. Richard Clarke & Sons, Thos. and Elifha Hutchinfon, Benjamin Faneuil and Jofhua Winflow of Bofton, merchants, that on the 2d inft., the deponent was ordered to attend at 11 o'clock in the forenoon of the next day, on a committee of the people of the faid town, and he having attended accordingly, was then and there commanded by Mr. Samuel Adams and Jonathan Williams, Efqr., in prefence of, and affembled with, John Rowe, John Hancock, Wm. Phillips and John Pitts, Efqrs., and a great number of others, in Faneuil Hall, not to land any of the faid tea at his peril, but to proceed to Griffin's wharf, in faid Bofton, and there difcharge the reft of his cargo. And that the faid deponent was obliged to comply with the faid orders, and was and is nightly watched by 25 armed men on board the faid fhip, appointed, as he fuppofes and verily believes, to prevent the faid teas from being landed.

Wherefore, the faid James Bruce, on behalf of himfelf and all others concerned in the faid fhip or cargo, did, and I, the faid notary public, at his requeft, and on behalf as aforefaid, do by thefe prefents folemnly proteft againft the faid committee and each of them above mentioned, and againft all others voluntarily acting, watching, and proceeding by their directions, and all perfons whatfoever oppofing and forbidding the landing the tea aforefaid for all, and all manner of damage and damages fuffered and to be fuffered, by means of the commands, watchings, oppofition and prohibition aforefaid. Thus done, protefted, and given under my notarial feal, in the prefence of Rob[t.] Garland Cranch and John Dyar.

In teftimoniam veritas,

J[No.] MONRO;

JAMES BRUCE. (L.S.) Not. Pub., 11 Jan., 1774.

PROTEST OF CAP[T.] JAMES BRUCE,[1]

Of the Eleanor, againft the Deftroyers of the Tea.

At Bofton, in New England, on the 17th day of December, in the year of our Lord, 1773, and in the 14th year of his Majefty's reign, perfonally appeared before me, John Monro, Notary Public by royal authority, duly admitted and fworn, James Bruce, mafter, Ja[s.] Bruce, jun[r.,] mate, and John Tinney, boatfwain, of the fhip Eleanor, burthen about 250 tons, and the faid James Bruce, jun[r.,] and John Tinney, being fworn on the Holy Evangelifts of Almighty God, feverally depofed, and each of them doth depofe and fay, that on the evening of the 16th inft., they, thefe deponents, were on board the faid fhip, then lying at Griffin's wharf, at faid Bofton, and part of her cargo from London on board, amongft which

---

[1] Captain Bruce was a loyalist of Boston, and as such was proscribed and banished. A loyalist of the same name was living at Shelburne, N. S., about the year 1805. — *Sabine.*

were 80 whole chefts and 34 half chefts of tea, configned to Meffrs. Rich⁴· Clarke & Sons, Thoˢ· and Elifha Hutchinfon, Benjⁿ Faneuil, and Jofhua Winflow, of faid Bofton, merchants. That about the hours of 6 or 7 o'clock in the fame evening, about one thoufand unknown people came down the faid wharf, and a number of them came on board the faid fhip, fome being dreffed like Indians, and they having violently broke open the hatches, hoifted up the faid chefts of tea upon deck, and then and there ftove and threw the faid chefts with their contents overboard into the water, where the whole was loft and deftroyed. Wherefore, the faid James Bruce, mafter of the faid fhip, on behalf of himfelf and owners of the faid fhip, and all others concerned, did, and I, the faid notary public, at his requeft, and on behalf as aforefaid, do by thefe prefents folemnly proteft againft the faid unknown perfons or people, and againft all others whatfoever and however concerned, for all and all manner of damage or damages already fuffered, and which hereafter may, can, or fhall be fuffered by the violence and proceedings of the faid unknown people, and the deftruction of the tea as aforefaid.

Thus done, protefted, and given under my notarial feal of office, in prefence of Robert Garland Cranch and John Dyar.

In teftimoniam veritas,
(Signed,)
Jnᵒ· Monro,
Not. Pub., 11 Jan., 1774.

James Bruce.
James Bruce, Junʳ·'
John X̲ Tinney. (L.S.)
    ᵐᵃʳᵏ·

358 LETTERS AND DOCUMENTS.

Cap¹· Hezekiah Coffin,¹ Mafter Jethro Coffin, mate, and Mr. Wm. Hewkey, mariner, of the brig Beaver, and Mr. Francis Rotch, part owner, James Hall, mafter, and Alexʳ· Hodgdon, mate of the Dartmouth, made the like proteft, which are among the American papers.

LETTER FROM THE AGENTS AT NEW YORK, TO Capᵀ· LOCKYER,

Referred to in their Letter of the 27ᵗʰ Decʳ·¹ 1773.

New York, Decʳ 27, 1773.

Sir:

It is our intention that this letter fhould meet you below, at the Hook, that you may be apprifed of the danger of bringing your fhip into this port.

All the tea fhipped by the Hon'ble Eaft India Company to Bofton has been deftroyed on board the veffels that brought it. The fhip Polly, Cap¹· Ayres, arrived lately at Philadelphia with the tea deftined for that port, and was compelled to return with it without being fuffered to come into the harbour, and there are advices in town that Charles Town has made the fame determination with refpect to the tea arrived at South Carolina, and you may be affured the inhabitants of this city have adopted the fame fentiments, and are fully determined to carry them into execution.

---

¹ Captain Hezekiah Coffin, of Nantucket, married Abigail Colman, and died in 1779. It is said that he saved from the destruction of his cargo, tea enough to enable him to purchase a set of silver spoons.

We therefore think it is a duty we owe to the faid Company, as we can neither receive the tea or pay the duty, to apprize you of your danger, and to give you our opinion, that for the fafety of your cargo, your veffel, and your perfons, it will be moft prudent for you to return, as foon as you can be fupplied with fuch neceffaries as you may have occafion for on the voyage. Certain we are that you would fully concur with us in the propriety of this advice were you as well acquainted with the people's fentiments as we are, which you will learn from the enclofed papers. We fhall be glad to hear from you in anfwer hereto, and to render you any fervices we can in your critical fituation.

We are, your moft obd' ferv[ts.]

HENRY WHITE,
ABRAHAM LOTT & Co.
PIGOU & BOOTH.

To Cap[t.] Benj[n] Lockyer, of the fhip Nancy.

LETTER FROM CAP[T.] LOCKYER TO THE AGENTS, TENDERING THE CARGO,

With their Reply, referred to in their Letter of the 22[d.] April, 1774.

New York, April 20[th.] 1774.

Gentlemen:

Having confidered the circumftances mentioned in your letters, which I received on my arrival, I have left the ſhip and cargo at Sandy Hook, for their ſafety. Have now waited on you with a tender of the cargo of tea ſhipped by the Hon'ble Eaſt India Company, and conſigned to you. I am therefore ready to deliver the ſaid cargo according to the bill of lading. I am, &c.,

BENJAMIN LOCKYER.

Meſſrs. White, Lott & Booth.

New York, April 20, 1774.

Sir:

We have received your letter of this date, tendering to us the cargo of tea ſhipped on board the Nancy, under your command, by the Hon'ble Eaſt India Company, to our addreſs, in reply to which we have only to obſerve that we ſome time ago acquainted the Hon'ble Court of Directors how violently oppoſed the inhabitants in general were to the landing or vending the tea in this Colony, while ſubject to the American duty, and that any attempts in us, either to effect one or the other would not only be fruitleſs, but expoſe ſo conſiderable a property to inevitable deſtruction. Under theſe circumſtances it would be highly imprudent in us to take any ſteps to receive your cargo, and therefore we cannot take charge of the ſame, or any part thereof, under our cafe. We are, ſir,

Your moſt obed[t] ſerv[ts,]

HENRY WHITE.
ABR[M] LOTT & Co.
PIGOU & BOOTH.

Cap[t.] Benj[n] Lockyer.

PHILADELPHIA.

AN ACCOUNT OF THE PROCEEDINGS OF THE INHABITANTS OF PHILADELPHIA,

On the Meafure of the Company's Exporting Tea to that Place.

[Taken from a Philadelphia news paper.]

Monday' Dec' 27, 1773.

Upon the firft advice of this meafure a general diffatisfaction was expreffed, that at a time when we were ftruggling with this oppreffive act, and an agreement fubfifting not to import tea while fubject to the duty, our fellow fubjects in England fhould form a meafure fo directly tending to enforce the Act, and again embroil us with our parent ftate. When it was alfo confidered that the propofed mode of difpofing of the tea tended to a monopoly, ever odious in a free country, a univerfal difapprobation fhewed itfelf through the city. A public meeting of the inhabitants was held at the State Houfe, on the 18th October, at which great nnmbers attended, and the fenfe of the following refolves (which are entered in page 296, the people of Bofton having formed the fame refolutions).

In confequence of thefe refolutions, a committee waited upon the gentlemen in this city who had been appointed confignees of the expected cargo. They reprefented to them the deteftation and abhorrence in which this meafure was held by their fellow citizens, the danger and difficulties which muft attend the execution of fo odious a tafk, and expreffed the united defire of the city that they would renounce the commiffion, and engage not to intermeddle with the fhip or cargo in any fhape whatever. Some of the commiffioners refigned in a manner that gave general fatisfaction, others in fuch equivocal terms as defired further explanation. However, in a few days the refignation was complete. In this fituation things remained for a few days.

In the mean time the general fpirit and indignation rofe to fuch a height that it was thought proper to call another general meeting of the principal citizens to confider and refolve upon fuch further fteps as might give weight and fecure fuccefs to the unanimous oppofition now formed. Accordingly a meeting was held for the above purpofe, at which a great number of refpectable inhabitants attended, and it appeared to be the unanimous opinion that the entry of the fhip at the cuftom houfe, or the landing any part of her cargo would be attended with great danger and difficulty, and would directly tend to deftroy that peace and good order which ought to be preferved. An addition of twelve other gentlemen was then made to the former committee, and the general meeting adjourned 'till the arrival of the tea-fhip. Information being given of that, the price of tea was foon advanced, though this was owing to a general fcarcity of that article, yet all the poffeffors of tea, in order to give ftrength to the oppofition, readily agreed to reduce the price and fell what remained in their hands at a reafonable rate.

Nothing now remained but to keep up a proper correfpondence and connection with the other Colonies, and to take all prudent and proper precautions on the arrival of the tea-fhip.

It is not eafy to defcribe the anxiety and fufpense of the city in this interval; fundry reports of her arrival were received, which were premature, but on Saturday evening laſt an exprefs came up from Chefter to inform the town that the tea-fhip, commanded by Capᵗ Ayres, with her detefted cargo, was arrived there, having followed another fhip up the river fo far. The committee met early the next morning, and being apprized of the arrival of Mr. Gilbert Barkley, the other confignee, who came paffenger in the fhip, they immediately went in a body to requeſt his renunciation of the commiffion. Mr. Barkley politely attended the committee at the firſt requeſt, and being made acquainted with the fentiments of the city, and the danger to which the public liberties of America were expofed by this meafure, he, after expreffing the particular hardfhip of his fituation, alfo refigned the commiffion in a manner that affected every one prefent.

The committee then appointed three of their members to go to Chefter, and two others to Gloucefter Point, in order to have the earlieſt opportunity of meeting Capᵗ Ayres, and reprefenting to him the fenfe of the public refpecting his voyage and cargo. The gentlemen who had fet out for Chefter receiving intelligence that the veffel had weighed anchor about 12 o'clock, and proceeded to town, returned. About 2 o'clock fhe appeared in fight of Gloucefter Point, where a number of the inhabitants from the town had affembled, with the gentlemen from the committee, and as fhe paffed along fhe was hailed, and the captain requeſted not to proceed further, but to come on fhore. This the captain complied with, and was handed thro' a lane made by the people to the gentlemen appointed to confer with him.

They reprefented to him the general fentiment, together with the danger and difficulties that would attend his refufal to comply with the wifhes of the inhabitants, and finally defired him to proceed with them to town, where he would be more fully informed of the temper and refolution of the people. He was accordingly accompanied to town by a number of perfons, where he was foon convinced of the truth and propriety of the reprefentations that had been made to him, and agreed that, upon the defire of the inhabitants being publicly expreffed, he would conduct himfelf accordingly. Some fmall rudenefs being offered to the cap$^{t.}$ afterwards in the ftreet by fome boys, feveral gentlemen interpofed and fuppreffed it, before he received the leaft injury. Upon an hour's notice this morning, a public meeting was called, and the State Houfe not being fufficient to hold the numbers affembled, they adjourned into the fquare. This meeting is allowed by all to be the moft refpectable, both in number and rank of thofe who attended, it that has been known in this city. After a fhort introduction, the following refolutions were not only agreed to, but the public approbation teftified in the warmeft manner:

Refolved 1$^{st.}$ That the tea on board the fhip Polly, Cap$^{t.}$ Ayres, fhall not be landed.

2$^{d.}$ That Cap$^{t.}$ Ayres fhall neither enter nor report his veffel at the Cuftom Houfe.

3$^{d.}$ That Cap$^{t.}$ Ayres fhall carry back the tea immediately.

4$^{th.}$ That Cap$^{t.}$ Ayres fhall immediately fend a pilot on board his veffel, with orders to take charge of her, and proceed with her to Reedy Ifland, next high water.

5$^{th.}$ That he fhall be allowed to ftay in town 'till tomorrow, to provide neceffaries for his voyage.

6th. That he fhall then be obliged to leave the town and proceed to his veffel, and make the beft of his way out of our river and bay.

7th. That Capt. Heyfham, Capt. R. White, Mr. Benjamin Loxley and Mr. A. Donaldfon be a committee to fee thefe refolutions carried into execution.

The captain was then afked if he would conform himfelf to thefe refolutions. He anfwered that he would.

The affembly were then informed of the fpirit and refolution of New York, Charles Town, South Carolina, and the conduct of the people in Bofton, whereupon it was unanimoufly refolved:

8th. That this affembly highly approve of the conduct and fpirit of the people of New York, Charles Town and Bofton, and return their hearty thanks to the people at Bofton for their refolution in deftroying the tea rather than fuffer it to be landed.

The whole bufinefs was conducted with a decorum and order worthy the importance of the caufe. Capt. Ayres being prefent at this meeting, folemnly and publicly engaged that he would literally comply with the fenfe of the city, as expreffed in the above refolutions.

A proper fupply of neceffaries and frefh provifions being then procured in about 2 hours; the tea-fhip weighed anchor from Gloucefter Point, where fhe lay within fight of the town, and proceeded with her whole cargo on her return to the Eaft India Comy.

The public think the conduct of thofe gentlemen whofe goods are returned on board the tea-fhip, ought not to pafs unnoticed, as they have upon this occafion generoufly facrificed their private intereft to the public good.

Thus this important affair, in which there has been fo glorious an exertion of public virtue and fpirit, has been brought to a public iffue, by which the force of law, fo obftinately perfifted in, to the prejudice of the national commerce, for the fake of the principle on which it is founded, (a right of taxing the Americans without their confent,) has been effectually broken, and the foundation of American liberty more deeply laid than ever.

N. B. — It was computed by two different perfons, unknown to each other, that there were 8000 perfons affembled, befides many hundreds who were on their way, but did not reach the meeting in time, owing to the fhortnefs of the notice. Cap⁺ Ayres and Mr. Barkley, late one of the confignees, left Arch wharf on board a pilot boat (having been 46 hours in town,) to follow the fhip to Reedy Ifland. They were attended to the wharf by a concourfe of people, who wifhed them a good voyage.

FINIS.

ADDITIONS.

JOHN SPURR *(see p. 164).*

John Spurr was, after the Revolution, a prominent citizen of Charlton, Mass., and often represented the town in the State Legislature. He married the daughter of Rev. Elijah Dunbar, and left two sons; Elijah Dunbar Spurr, and Samuel Danforth Spurr. The widow of the latter, who is now living, is the mother of the first wife of Senator George F. Hoar.

THOMAS MELVILL.

Melvill's Tea Relic, as seen on page 131.

The publisher, in collecting illustrations for Tea Leaves, found one or more New England Societies claiming possession of some of this tea. Therefore it was necessary to look up the original Melvill stock of Bohea.

We show an illustration of it (full size), copied from a photograph (made by special request,) from a relative living in Illinois (since deceased), from whom we learn it has been handed down to the present generation, and has never been owned out of the family, and is now in possession of Mrs. Thomas Melvill's son, Galena, Illinois, to whom we are indebted for its use on this occasion.

A. O. C.

INDEX.

	PAGE
Samuel Adams,	21
Annapolis Tea-Ship Burned,	85
Biographical Notices of the Tea Party, and List of its Members,	92-171

Biographical Sketches;

Ancrum, Wm.	208	Johonnot, Gabriel	27
Appleton, Nathaniel	30	Kelly, Wm.	269
Blowers, S. S.	352	Knox, Thomas, Jr.,	49
Brattle, Wm.	311	Lloyd, Henry	227
Bruce, Capt.	356	Lott, Abraham	226
Bull, Wm.	339	Lovering, Joseph	49
Cheever, Ezekiel	46	Morris, John	342
Church, Dr. Benjamin	26	Pownall, John	330
Clarke, R.	210	Quincy, Josiah	61
Coffin, Capt.	358	Rotch, Francis	41
Cooper, Sir Grey	212	Rowe, John	63
Cooper, William	43	Royal, Isaac	311
Copley, John S.	329	Savage, Samuel Phillips	57
Crafts, Thomas	25	Scollay, John	37
Curtis, Obadiah	49	Tileston, Thomas	50
Danforth, Samuel	315	Wallace, Hugh and Alex.	233
Edes, Benjamin	25	Walpole, Thomas	204
Erving, John	226	Watson, Brook	203
Faneuil, Benj.	294	Wendell, Oliver	43
Hall, Capt. James	245	Wharton, Thomas	273
Hatch, Nathaniel	285	White, Henry	306
Hewes, Daniel	49	Williams, Jonathan	43
Hodgdon, Alex.	79	Williams, Thomas	230
Hutchinson, Thos. & Elisha	324	Winslow, Joshua	223

Ballads of the Tea Party,	172-176
Boston. Opposition to the Tea Act,	19-23, 260-66, 278, 303
Tea Party,	64-82, 89-94, 95-171
Destruction of the Tea,	58-94, 336-357
Proceedings of the Town,	279-303, 320-36
Proceedings of the Council,	309-20

INDEX.

	PAGE
Clarke R. & Sons, Attack on Warehouse of	28, 266, 284
Residence mobbed,	34
Letter to chairman East India Company,	279–91
East India Company,	11, 189
Franklin, Benjamin	185
Green Dragon Tavern,	66
Hutchinson, Thomas	20
Lamb, John	19
Letters and Documents,	189, 370

Letter from Mr. Wm. Palmer, enclosing Extracts of several Letters from Boston, &c., to show the state of the Tea Trade in America, and estimates of the advantages that will attend the Company's carrying on that trade to that place, ... 189

Memorial of Mr. Gilbert Barkley, recommending a Plan for carrying on the Tea Trade to America, and offering himself, and Mr. John Inglis, Merchant, of Philadelphia, as agents, ... 199

Letter from Mr. Brook Watson, to Daniel Wier, Esq., recommending Mr. John Butler, of Nova Scotia, and Messrs. Faneuil and Winslow, of Boston, as agents, ... 202

A Proposal of the Hon. Mr. Walpole's, for sending Tea to Philadelphia, 203

Plan of Mr. Palmer, for Exportation of Tea to America, . . 205

Letter from Messrs. Greenwood & Higginson, recommending Messrs. Andrew Lord, and William and George Ancrum, of South Carolina, as Agents, and offering their ship, the "London," Capt. Curling, to carry Tea to that place, ... 208

Letter from Mr Fred'k Pigou, Jun., Esq., recommending Pigou & Booth, of New York, and James & Drinker, of Philadelphia, as Agents, and offering vessels for those places, ... 208

Letter from Mr. Jonathan Clarke, offering Richard Clarke & Sons, of Boston, as Agents, ... 209

Letter from Grey Cooper, Esq., recommending Mr. Barkley as an Agent, ... 211

Letter from Messrs. Roberts & Co., recommending Messrs. Willing, Morris & Co., of Philadelphia, as Agents, . . . 212

Letter from Mr. Benjamin Harrison, offering himself as an Agent for Virginia, ... 213

Letter from Mr. George Browne, recommending Mr. Jonathan Brown, of Philadelphia, as an Agent, ... 214

Letter from Mr. Wm. Palmer, offering to advance the amount of 200 chests of Tea, on terms therein mentioned, . . . 215

INDEX. 371

	PAGE
Letter to several American Merchants to meet the Committee,	215
Letter from Mr. Gilbert Barkley, offering some further thoughts upon the Exportation,	216
Letter from Samuel Wharton, Esq., offering an Apologyy for not attending the Committee,	217
Some Thoughts upon the Company's sending out Teas to America,	218
Letter from Messrs. Watson & Rashleigh, reciting terms on which the Tea Agency may be conducted, and offering Security for their recommendation,	222
Letter from Mr. Jonathan Clarke, on the same,	224
Letter from Mr. Kelly, on the same, and recommending several persons of the different Colonies, as Agents,	225
Letter from Mr. Harrison, that Mr. Kelly will give his Proposals, .	227
Letter from Mr. John Blackburn, with an offer of Terms,	228
Letter to Samuel Wharton, Esq., to meet the Committee,	229
Request of Mr. Walter Mansell, for the Agency to South Carolina,	229
Letter from Messrs. Roberts & Co., offering Terms and Security for Willing, Morris & Co.,	231
Letter from Messrs. Pigou & Booth, offering Terms and Security for Messrs. James & Drinker,	231
Letter from Mr. John Nutt, recommending Mr. Roger Smith, of South Carolina, as an Agent,	233
Letter from Messrs. Bourdieu & Chollet, recommending several persons as Agents,	233
Letter from Messrs. Gale, Fearon & Co., recommending Mr. Daniel Stephenson, of Maryland, as an Agent,	234
Letter from Messrs. Davidson & Newman, declining any propositions on the present state of the Tea affair,	235
Letter to several American Merchants to meet the Committee,	235
Letter from Mr. Palmer, upon the Rate of Exchange from Boston,	236
Letter from Messrs. Bourdieu & Chollet, declining to offer any further proposals,	236
Letter to sundry American Merchants to meet the Committee,	237
Letter to sundry American Merchants, advising the quantities of Tea ordered to be shipped for the several Colonies, and requesting the firm of the houses they have recommended,	238
Letter from Messrs. Watson & Rashleigh, advising the firm of their recommendation,	238
Securities offered for Mr. Barkley and Mr. Mansell,	239
Letter from Mr. Pigou, with the firm of his recommendation,	239
Letters from Mr. Wharton, Mr. Browne, and Mr. Kelly,	240

INDEX.

	PAGE
Mr. Palmer's Opinion in what mode to ship Tea to America,	241
Letter from Mr. Clarke, with the firm of his house, and offering the "William" for freight,	243
Letters to Geo. Hayley, Esq., Thos. Lane, Esq., and Alexander Champion, Esq., to know if they have any constant traders to Boston or South Carolina, ready to sail,	244
Letter to Mr. Palmer, to point out what sorts of Tea are proper to be sent to Boston and South Carolina,	244
Mr. Palmer's Assortment of Teas for America,	245
Weight of Tea Exported to America,	245
Letters from several Persons concerning Vessels for Carrying the Tea to America,	245
Petition to the Lords of the Treasury, for Licence to Export Teas to America,	246
Licence from the Lords of the Treasury to Export Teas to America,	247
Letters from Sundry Gentlemen relating to Vessels to carry Tea to America,	251
Letter from Mr. Settle to Mr. Blackburn and Mr. Kelly, to come and Execute the Bond,	255
Letters from Mr. Blackburn and Mr. Kelly, in reply,	255
Sundry Freight Bills, for Tea Shipped,	256

So far concerns the outset of the Tea.

Note from Lord Dartmouth to the Chairman, to attend at Whitehall, on the subject of some Advices from America, respecting the Teas,	258
Letters to American Merchants to communicate what Advices they may have received,	258
Letters from American Merchants, in reply,	259
Letter from Mr. Jonathan Clarke to Mr. Wheler, advising his arrival at Boston,	260
Letter to Abram Dupuis, to communicate advice, referred in Mr. Clarke's Letter,	279
Messrs. Clarke & Son's Letter to Mr. Dupuis,	279
Mr. Faneuil's Letter to Mr. Watson, mentioned in Messrs. Clarke's,	292
Proceedings of the Inhabitants of the Town of Boston, on the 5th and 6th November, referred to in Messrs. Clarke's and Faneuil's Letters,	295
Note from the Secretary to Mr. Brook Watson, advising the Tea is ordered to Halifax, and desiring the names of the Consignees,	304
Security offered for Messrs. Butler & Cochran, consignees at Halifax,	305

INDEX. 373

PAGE

The Agents at New York's Petition to the Governor, referred to in their
 letter 1st December, ... 305
Petition of the Agents at Boston, and the Proceedings of the Governor
 and Council thereon, ... 309
Proceedings of the Town of Boston on the 29th and 30th November, . 320
Letter signed "Anglo Americanus," addressed to Geo. Dudley, Esq.,
 enclosing newspapers, ... 331
Letter signed "Anglo Americanus," addressed to Geo. Dudley, Esq.,
 advising the Tea's being destroyed, ... 332
Note from Mr. Pownall, to communicate Advices, and enclosing Letter
 from Lieut.-Gov. Bull, of Charles Town; also, Lieut.-Gov. Bull's
 Letter, ... 339
Letter from Mr. Jo. Morris, to Corbyn Morris, Esq., advising of the Tea's
 being seized at South Carolina, ... 342
Letter from Capt. Ellis, advising of the Tea's being seized at South
 Carolina, ... 343
Questions proposed to the Boston Consignees, respecting landing the
 Teas, ... 344
Protest of Capt. Bruce against said Consignees, for refusing to receive
 the Teas, ... 346
Letter from Mr. Rotch, to said Consignees, with an account of Charges
 and a Protest, ... 350
Protests of the several Captains against the Destroyers of the Tea, . 353
Letters from the Agents at New York, &c., to Capt. Lockyer, and one from
 him to them, ... 359
Proceedings of the Inhabitants of Philadelphia, on the measure of Ex-
 porting Tea to that place, ... 361

Liberty Tree, ... 24
Long Room (Whig) Club, ... 66
New York. Opposition to the Tea Act, . . 16–19, 269–271
 Arrival of Tea, ... 84–5
 Petition of the Consignees to the Governor, . . 305
 Letter from the Agents to Capt. Lockyer, . . 358–60
North-End Caucus, ... 23, 67
Philadelphia lends Opposition to Tea Act, . . . 17
 Tea sent back, ... 84
 Proposed Tea Depot in America, . . . 203
 Opposition to the Tea Act, . . . 272–277
 Resolves and Proceedings of October 18, . . 361–65
St. Andrew's Masonic Lodge of Boston, ... 66

INDEX.

	PAGE
Sons of Liberty,	18, 24, 26
South Carolina, Proceedings at	84-85, 339-43
Spurr, John,	164
Tea Act,	12
Introduced into New England,	14
Consignees,	23, 36, 51-53
Guard on Boston tea-ship,	45-50
State of Tea Trade in America,	191-98
Shipments to America,	256-7
Warren, Gen. Joseph	178
Additions,	367

ILLUSTRATIONS.

Tea Leaves, on cover,	
Destruction of the Tea in Boston Harbor,	Frontispiece.
Diagram Showing the Route from the Old South Church to Griffin's Wharf,	75
Melvill's Tea Relic,	131
Edward Proctor's Proclamation,	148
Lord North Forcing the Tea down the Throat of America,	155
Location of Tea Wharf,	173
Plan of Boston, 1775, and the Burning of Charlestown,	264

PORTRAITS.

Adams, Samuel	299	Melvill, Thomas, Hat on		180
Bradlee, Nathaniel	97	North, Lord		249
Franklin, Benjamin	185	Pitts, Lendall		142
Gage, Gov. Thomas	313	Purkitt, Henry		151
Hancock, John	288	Revere, Paul		157
Hutchinson, Gov. Thomas	308	Rotch, Francis		40
Hewes, George Robert Twelves	117	Rowe, John		62
Kennison, David	122	Savage, Samuel Phillips		338
Lovering, Thomas	182	Sprague, Samuel		164
Melvill, Thomas	133	Warren, Joseph		48

AUTOGRAPHS.

	PAGE		PAGE
Adams, Samuel	299	Melvill, Thomas	135
Bradlee, Nathaniel	97	Newell, Eliphelet	138
Bradlee, David	97	Purkitt, Henry	150
Bass, Henry	96	Prentice, Henry	146
Church, Benjamin	26	Pitts, Lendall,	145
Cheever, Ezekiel	46	Peck, Samuel	140
Chase, Thomas	102	Palmer, Joseph P.	139
Clarke, Benjamin	103	Proctor, Edward	149
Crane, John	108	Russell, John	159
Franklin, Benjamin	185	Revere, Paul	154
Faneuil, Benjamin, Jr.,	294	Rowe, John	63
Frothingham, Nathaniel	111	Rotch, Francis	41
Green, Nathaniel	114	Swan, James	168
Grant, Moses	113	Sprague, Samuel	164
Gore, Samuel	113	Sloper, Samuel	162
Hodgdon, Alexander	79	Shed, Joseph	161
Hancock, John	288	Sessions, Robert	160
Hutchinson, Thomas	308	Savage, Samuel Phillips	57
Inches, Henderson	27	Urann, Thomas	169
Kennison, David	122	Winslow, Joshua	223
Lovering, Joseph	182	Williams, Jonathan	43
Lincoln, Amos	125	Warren, Joseph	30
Lee, Joseph	124	Wyeth, Joseph	171
Molineux, William	137